Critical Acclaim for this book

'These are much-needed, eloquent and convincing voices of post-colonial women scholars and activists reclaiming their socio-political and spiritual spaces. How do Hindu, Christian, Muslim and Buddhist feminists in "the South," frequently threatened by fundamentalism in their home regions, propose to create sustainable models for the present and the future? This book shows how, in ways that are inventive, humorous, and critical of imitating "Western/Northern" solutions.'
Professor Jorunn Jacobsen Buckley, Department of Religion, Bowdoin College, Brunswick, USA

'This remarkable collection of essays should disturb the world of frozen knowledge and its ideas of what constitute sane dissent and a proper ideology of resistance. For the aim of these heretical essays is nothing less than the simultaneous defiance of mainstream religion, the standardised understanding of religious experience that academic respectability has popularised, and conventional research methods, emphasising clear-cut differences between the observer and the observed, faith and objectivity, the therapist and the faith healer. The familiar categories of the social knowledge industry blur, dissolve or recombine in strange, uncanny ways in these accounts of feminine spirituality, esoteric forms of resistance, and constructions of the inner life at the margins of the known world. This is unconventional scholarship at its most intriguing.'
Ashis Nandy, author of *Traditions, Tyranny and Utopias: Essays in the Politics of Awareness and The Savage Freud and Other Essays on Possible and Retrievable Selves*

'This volume is not another feminist critique of fundamentalism but takes us beyond religion into feminine spirituality from the point of view of various cultures – Muslim, Hindu, Christian and Buddhist. The book is a formidable step forward in crosscultural reflection on spirituality and feminism.'
Jan Nederveen Pieterse, Professor of Sociology, University of Illinois, Urbana-Champaign and author of *Development Theory: Deconstructions/Reconstructions*

Gendering the Spirit

Women, Religion
& the Post-Colonial Response

EDITED BY

Durre S. Ahmed

Zed Books

LONDON & NEW YORK

Gendering the Spirit was first published by Zed Books Ltd., 7 Cynthia Street, London N1 9JF, UK and Room 400, 175 Fifth Avenue, New York, NY 10010, USA in 2002.

Distributed in the United States exclusively by Palgrave, a division of St. Martin's Press, LLC, 175 Fifth Avenue, New York, NY 10010, USA.

Cover designed by Andrew Corbett
Typeset in 10/13 pt Bembo by Long House, Cumbria
Printed and bound in the United Kingdom
by Biddles Ltd, www.biddles.co.uk

A catalogue record for this book is available from the British Library
US cataloging-in-publication data is available from the Library of Congress

ISBN 1 84277 026 8 hb
ISBN 1 84277 027 6 pb

Contents

Part III · Perspectives on Violence

Notes on Contributors

Dr Durre S. Ahmed has Master's degrees in Psychology (Pb); Sociology (Columbia); Communication (Columbia) and a Doctorate in Communication and Education (Columbia). She is Director, Graduate Programme in Communication and Cultural Studies, National College of Arts, Lahore, where she is also Professor of Psychology and Communication and Chairperson, Department of Academics. She is the author of *Masculinity, Rationality and Religion: a Feminist Perspective* (Lahore: ASR, 1992).

Dr Madhu Khanna has a PhD (1986) in Hindu Shakta Tantra from Wolfson College, Oxford University. *Yantra: The Tantric Symbol of Cosmic Unity* and *The Tantric Way* (co-authored) were published by Thames and Hudson. The founder member of Tantra Foundation, New Delhi, at present she is an Assistant Professor at the Indira Gandhi National Centre for the Arts, New Delhi.

Sister Mary John Mananzan is National Chairperson of GABRIELA, a national federation of women's organizations in the Philippines, President of St Scholastica's College and Executive Director of the Institute of Women's Studies. She co-founded the Citizen's Alliance for Consumer Protection, of which she is Secretary-General. The General Assembly of Ecumenical Associations of Third World Theologians recently elected her as its Executive Secretary-Treasurer.

Dr Hema Goonatilake received her PhD from the School of Oriental and African Studies, University of London, in 1974. She was a faculty member at the University of Kelaniya, Sri Lanka, until 1989 when she joined the United Nations as a gender expert. She is currently the Country Representative of the Heinrich Böll Foundation in Cambodia.

Grace P. Odal teaches at the Department of Anthropology in the University of Manila, Philippines. Her research interests include Philippine folklore and mythology as well as indigenous approaches to knowledge and spirituality.

Acknowledgements

The chapters in this book were originally written as papers for the annual Women and Religion Symposium sponsored by the Heinrich Böll Foundation (HBF) between 1996 and 2000. The authors would like to thank Roshan Dhunjibhoy, Regional Representative of HBF for South and South East Asia, for facilitating a series of discussions which simultaneously opened up more questions and led to further articulation of issues and ideas. As the indefatigable moving spirit behind the Symposium, Roshan brought together scholars and activists from across the region for fruitful multi-level encounters. Other participants included Chatsumarn Kabilsingh, Ranjani de Silva, Sister Rosario, Jorunn Buckley and Saima Jasam.

The terms 'North' and 'South' are used in this book. These are far more conceptually and culturally complex than the terms imply. But given the relative nascency of its subject, this book nevertheless uses them for reasons of convenience. Thus, 'South' refers to its widest dictionary (Websters) meaning, as constituting 'developing nations, the Third World'.

I

Women and Religion

Alternative Perspectives

1

Introduction
The Last Frontier

DURRE S. AHMED

The subject of religion is increasingly – and frequently seriously – impinging on the lives of men and women in a manner few could have imagined in the closing decades of the twentieth century. Today it is a key factor in the analysis of numerous issues including questions of identity, culture, nationalism, human rights, ethnicity and globalization. From the anti-abortionists of the religious right in the US to the rise of Hindu nationalism, the Taliban, or the bloodshed in the Balkans, religion has become deeply and violently entangled with politics and culture. The Freudian 'illusion' and Marxist 'opiate' notwithstanding, across the board it seems that humans remain 'incurably' religious.[1] The fact is that religion has always been around as a social, cultural and political force. In the first half of the twentieth century, two nations – Israel and Pakistan – came into existence on the basis of religion and what we are witnessing today, particularly in the Middle East and South Asia, is in a sense the logical outcome of the (unresolved) attendant issues and questions contained in those moments of genesis.

The connections between religion, politics and culture are rendered even more complex in view of the broad spectrum of movements at work in what is a global religious revival. While there is a tendency to associate this revival primarily with fundamentalism, in actual fact there are numerous religious movements with wide-ranging agendas and the vast majority are not committed to violence. Spanning North and South,[2] these revivalist movements reflect different types of concerns related to the contexts from which they have emerged. In the South,

3

for example, it is frequently suggested that they are a reaction to corrupt ruling elites and widespread poverty, as well as an attempt to consolidate a sense of identity in the face of rapid change and modernization. Given their undeniable, frequently strident presence, sociologists have argued that 'it is time to recognize religious movements as social movements and religion as part of politics. Doing so creates the space that makes political solutions thinkable and, possibly, feasible.'[3]

It is only in the last few decades that academia's disconnection from a significant dimension of the life of the vast majority of humanity has begun to change. If religion is being given considerable attention today, this has as much to do with the nuisance it is becoming as with any remission in its long eclipse by twentieth-century global intellectual establishments. North and South, given the dominance of Freudian and Marxist ideology, it had become the norm to deride religion on the assumption that 'those who think cannot believe and those who believe cannot think'. As Berry and Wernick observe in *Shadow of Spirit: Postmodernism and Religion*,[4] in post-Enlightenment terms religion had come to be seen as 'philosophy's shadow', a sort of counterfeit compared to the genuine superiority of rationalist thought. It was only towards the end of the last century that the stranglehold of this position began to lose its grip in the North, a major factor being women's positive involvement with spirituality, especially in the New Age movement,[5] a shift of consciousness now clearly registered in the enlarged discourse(s) of feminist cultural studies.[6]

The current involvement of women with religion can be viewed as part of a *zeitgeist* which is characterized not only by the increasing interest in spirituality of both men and women, but also by the ubiquitous presence of a 'women's perspective' in contemporary affairs. Even in contexts where women are disempowered through poverty, custom or politics, the issues around them remain prominent. Acknowledged or not, the 'voice' and 'presence' of woman – as activist and cultural critic – are today undeniable.[7] Since the latter half of the twentieth century, a steady stream of feminist scholarship has questioned not only the construction of the idea of gender itself, but also its relationship to the production of knowledge such as history, psychology, the environment, and different areas in science such as biology and genetics. Taken as a whole these feminist contestations and re-viewings, along with the slow but steady empowerment of woman, are part of a rising constellation on the horizons of human consciousness and knowledge. Given that both women *and* religion form significant elements of the present *zeitgeist*, it was only a matter of time before their (women's) engagement with it became fully evident.

In a global revival regarding an ancient and complex subject, the significance of texts such as the present volume does not lie primarily in distinguishing itself from other expressions of feminist spirituality. Nor do the individual chapters lay claim to any definitive view of a religion. Given the relative nascency of the subject as a whole, the idea is to add to the globally emergent narratives of women and spirituality, and thus to bolster the range of alternatives to fundamentalism everywhere. It is therefore premature to talk of differences. If anything, there is the self-evident, urgent need to articulate, identify, understand and highlight the inherent commonalities of radical women's spirituality on a global basis.

Feminism, Academia and Spirituality in the North

By the 1990s an increasingly self-critical academic trend in the North had begun commenting on the 'unexpected emergence' and a 'recently revived interest in religion … that has surfaced within the new postmodernist … intelligentsia'.[8] As attempts are made to fill up what Sartre called the 'God-shaped hole in human consciousness', anthropologists now not only argue that the discipline should 'reconstitute' its attitudes towards the study of what it still tends to regard as 'faulty beliefs about supernatural realms' but go as far as to suggest that the moral underpinnings of religions should somehow be absorbed into the anthropological endeavour.[9] Well-known cultural critics such as Christopher Lasch have been scathingly critical of modernity and its psychological toll on the Western intellectual and have advocated a return to religion.[10] However, when it comes to women's spirituality, – as, for example, in the case of the widely popular New Age religions – the intellectual's return to religion is revealed as a macho and patriarchal affair, unequivocally dismissive of what are widespread forms of feminist spirituality. Lasch proposes a return to mainstream Judaeo-Christianity, forgetting that this was precisely what drove many women away in the first place.[11]

Nevertheless, women in the North have been steadily broadening the scope of their spiritual views and expressions within and outside academia. There is now a vast body of literature spanning New Age spirituality as well as critiques, reinterpretations and revisionings of Judaism and Christianity.[12] However, to the extent that questions of feminist spirituality were peripheral to the feminist movement and given the general denigration of religion *per se*, the issue of women and religion still remains on the margins of intellectual and theological discourse. In a sense, the situation is comparable to the 1960s and the earliest stages of the feminist movement.

This is not because of an absence of attempts by feminist theologians and scholars in different disciplines. For the most part, academia has had little to say about the work of women who have long been articulating alternative philosophies and analytic frameworks for religion and related scholarship. Naomi Goldenberg, Charlene Spretnak, Mary Daly, Marija Gimbutas, Carol Christ, Riane Eisler, to name just a few, are to womens' spirituality what the writings of Friedan, Steinem, Greer and Brownmiller were to the feminist movement in the 1960s. Similarly, the psychoanalytical critiques of patriarchy by Julia Kristeva and Luce Irigaray adumbrate a radical and controversial women's spirituality. These women, and many others, have produced impeccably researched and imaginatively argued studies, exposing the violent patriarchal biases of some of the most fundamental religious assumptions of their Judaeo-Christian heritage. Frequently, such socio-theological critiques are simultaneously critical of the academic attitude towards the study of religion, thereby exposing the parallel existence of entrenched intellectual prejudices against women's spirituality.

As Spretnak points out in *The Politics of Women's Spirituality*, one reason why the writings of Daly *et al.* were neglected was the relationship of Western academia with religion:

> A larger problem was the categorical dismissal of spiritual issues by academic Western philosophy ... given that situation, it would be an almost reckless act for a feminist philosopher to note in professional company that the feminist spirituality movement had rejected core assumptions of patriarchal philosophy early on and proceeded to develop alternatives. The chasm widened further when deconstructive postmodernism got a grip on academia, as that orientation holds spirituality, or any version of holistic perception, in the highest contempt among all 'social constructions'.[13]

The rooster factor

Insisting on taking just one 'position' regarding, for example, holism or the essentialism versus deconstruction debate,[14] only leads to polarization within feminism. All scholarship, feminist or otherwise, falls victim to what the Cambridge philosopher Jenny Teichman called the 'peacock' or 'rooster factor' in academia.[15] She showed that rivalry between purportedly incommensurable theories is often only an illusion based on *rivalry between men*, which has more to do with the masculinist tendency of competitive castration rather than knowledge *per se*.

Given that men and women are both different and similar, the logical extremes of deconstructionism – the currently popular analytic method – seem frightening, since they preclude common ideals which are prerequisites for any form of social activism. This being so, rather than accepting that one must choose one or the other, the issues around women and religion require one critically to utilize *both* perspectives, even while exposing the androcentric biases of mainstream religions and articulation of alternatives.

A recent study on the intersections between Anglo-American techno-science and feminist spirituality exemplifies these various currents which need to be negotiated when it comes to understanding feminist spirituality in the North. It aims, on the one hand, to 'transgress the paradox ... of postmodern cultural critique' which, even as it rejects the Enlightenment, also rejects spiritual thought. At the same time, it wants 'to steer clear' of essentialism, which the authors see as a major element of New Age and Western spiritual feminist thought, one that explains why 'major trends in feminism have committed a fair number of calories to keeping spiritual ecofeminists, goddess-worshippers and the like at a safe distance'. However, as the millennium turns it is evident that the situation is changing:

> it is no longer a prerogative of narrow circles of Parisian intellectuals, marginalized New Age scholars or feminist goddess-worshippers to theorize new religious insights. By contrast, spirituality and mysticism seem to impose themselves with increasing power on the post-Marxist agendas of secularized Western intellectuals....[16]

Women and Religion in the South

Most questions around women and spirituality in the South as yet remain embedded in seemingly more significant discourses on, for example, geopolitics, modernity, nationalism and ethnicity. They appear most frequently in the context of violence, or else within 'rooster-factor' theological debates, and so tend to depersonalize women's relationship with religion.

The brutal excesses of fanaticism in the South have both highlighted and obscured the complex and dynamic relationship between women and religion. On the one hand it is obvious that most conservative mainstreams advocate a repressive attitude to women. At the same time it is equally evident that, within and without fundamentalist movements, women are increasingly getting involved in issues of spirituality. By definition, those who opt for the conservative *status quo* mostly do not contest or question. Obviously, one is not referring to situations of (en)forced acceptance but to those women who have consciously and freely chosen to engage with the spiritual and religious sphere, including fundamentalism. But what concerns us more is the potentially wider range of women's responses to religion and the tendency of fundamentalism towards their denial and exclusion. Whereas there is now a range of information regarding the fundamentalisms of different religions, the spectrum of response to religion by women who regard themselves as religious is by no means exhausted.

For women in the South especially, there is an unstoppable momentum towards re-visioning this most primordial and enduring of human concerns, since it is they who bear the brunt of what is frequently a brutal vision of religion. While this is particularly so in certain Muslim societies the issue is equally problematic in terms of a psychological, social and physical repression that is imposed on women by all religious traditions. To insist on the validity of religion in these circumstances is an act of courage. It is not, however, a brute sort of courage that comes simply as a survival instinct of some pitiably trapped animal. On the contrary, it is courage gained through a creative engagement with religion in which faith and different types of sacred and secular knowledge reinforce each other. Rather than simply 'deconstructing' and reducing religion to social, economic, and historical elements, this approach embraces it in a manner that challenges the *status quo*.

Drawing from a wide range of historical, cultural, theological and imaginative discourses, such a position is sustained by both a critical analysis of the causes of religious oppression and a creative revisioning of its elements.

In many countries in the South, the nature of the issues is such that, sooner or later, accusations of heresy may lead to precarious situations in real life. In passing, it should be noted that here the term 'heresy' is used (and abused) more literally, and not in the 'poetic' sense that is implied by feminists such as Kristeva. While this book does locate itself in a more flexible and imaginative use of the term, the texts (and authors) remain rooted in the lived realities of what are frequently violent religious and political contexts. These are starkly different from those inhabited by European and American academics who, from the Southern perspective, do indeed live in ivory towers. In any case, in the South, heresy is frequently dangerous territory – but one that must be traversed if worn-out ways of thinking and being are to be outgrown.

Women and heresy

Heretics see themselves firmly as part of a religious tradition but are not considered so by the mainstream/malestream. As with the word 'religion', a great deal of the original meaning of 'heresy' has been obscured by the political and intellectual accretions of Christianity. It is forgotten that Christianity itself began as a 'heresy'. In its original pre-Christian usage the word meant: to choose, to take for oneself, the middle voice.[17] As such, heresy as a 'position' has always been around in any overly institutionalized domain with established power hierarchies. The seemingly rational world of science has had its heretics – frequently the harbingers of revolutionary change.

In the West especially, it is interesting to note that the image of the heretic in the collective imagination is vividly connected with women such as Joan of Arc and the witches of various periods. As a case study of a 'heretical' Islamic sect in this book suggests, the violence it evokes from mainstream orthodoxy can be related to the heretic's predisposition towards what is termed, in Jungian and certain feminist discourses, as the 'feminine'. From this perspective, religious fanaticism is frequently a hyper-masculine reading of religion. Any interpretive attempt to proportionalize patriarchy – that is, cut it down to size by highlighting the more 'feminine' dimensions of the Divine – invites violence as sanctioned by the verdict of heresy.

Male or female, religious or academic, it is important to remember that heretics are historically the cross-cultural pollinators of civilization. This owes as much to persecution and migration as it does to the inner dynamics of defending religious diversity. And, as Peter Wilson has pointed out, heresies are often 'the means for transfer of ideas and art form from one culture to another', acting as hidden modes of discourse between civilizations:

> Since the Moghul period, sufism and Vaishnavite Bakhti Yoga have influenced each other in Northern India. Islamic and Hindu art and spirituality produced a civilization of tolerance, creativity and beauty. The colonial period almost destroyed this world....[18]

However distant and marginal at this point in time, the questions raised globally by women about spirituality in general and their own in particular can have far-reaching implications. As Daniel Bell's review of the intellectual and cultural 'wars' in American academia indicates, questions of gender and interpretation are here to stay.[19] One can add that once these are combined with religion they may well become the catalyst for diluting if not averting the much-proclaimed impending 'clash of civilizations'. In short, women's heretical (re)engagement with religion holds the possibility of reclaiming a spiritual, even socio-political space, which can be inhabited with dignity by both men and women. The contents of this book represent another small step in that direction, bringing postcolonial women's voices into what in many ways has been, until now, a hidden conversation across civilizations.

Major Themes

The book is divided into three sections. Part I provides a broad-based approach to some basic assumptions about women and religion, both at the conceptual (in this instance psychological) level and as issues of women *vis-à-vis* specific religions (Christianity and Hinduism). Part II provides case histories of women past and present, illustrating how in fact they have always challenged the religious establishment, not so much by rejecting a religion as by demanding equal rights within it, frequently along unique and individualistic lines. They show how the independent yet spiritually committed woman has been around for a long time into the present, continuing to inspire many and provoke many more. As such, they illustrate and add to the diversity of models and possibilities inherent in women's spirituality. Part III discusses the themes of violence and resistance but not, however, in the usual way. Rather, the attempt is to reconceptualize and move towards resistance through a more nuanced understanding of the seeds of religious violence.

Spirituality and scholarship

Many of the chapters utilize anthropological, historical, theological and literary texts and studies which illustrate how women conceptualize their spirituality and relationship to religion. This conceptualizing is as applicable to the authors themselves as it is to the subjects they have documented and analysed. For example, Part II on relatively unknown 'hidden women' may be seen as documenting not only different models of female spirituality but also emergent and legitimate forms of scholarship *about* spirituality and religion.

The account of Madhobi Ma in India, and those of the Philippines, may well evoke scepticism. Perhaps it is time to face such matters squarely. Rather than offer apologetics and justifications, one must insist that these accounts be considered for what they are: records and descriptions of spiritually powerful women, by women who, in turn, see themselves as religious and simultaneously have strongly established their competence as scholars in different disciplines. Odal's training in anthropology is evident, Khanna is today the leading scholar of *tantra* and Mary John Mananzan is an internationally acknowledged theologian, activist, scholar and nun. While some of these accounts can be considered devotional they are equally 'objective' and remain firmly anchored in the norms of their disciplines.

The descriptions are important, first, for their rich detailing of the possibilities in the religious experience, enabling the reader to participate, as Khanna says, in 'a stolen moment from a vision of eternity'. Second, these accounts are no less important for their intellectual courage and integrity. The authors refuse to pretend to an intellectually (read politically) correct but humanly impossible criterion of modern scholarship, one which tries to separate the subject and object of study, and the observer from the observed. Rather than paying what is frequently a prejudicial and pseudo-academic lip service to the subject, there is a genuine respect for what is observed. These observations and analyses are filtered from *within* the experience being described via a language which, while indeed being devotional, also underscores the author's confidence in her training and analytic abilities.

Many of the studies in this book suggest that religion for women is not confined to theological hairsplitting but is actively lived in the world of day-to-day life – not just in spiritual practice, as a deeply private response to the cosmic, but also as it forms responses to a given social, political or academic universe. Most of the chapters in this book locate their subjects in contexts beyond the theological. Given the nature of the material, particularly in terms of the individual profiles, it is a disciplinary necessity: their present 'hidden' status notwithstanding, somehow the spirituality of these women was/is inextricably intertwined with their socio-political realities. The same may be said for some of the authors: to the extent that any intellectual position implies its politics, there is no separation between the personal and political.

Rather than focusing on the bizarre, unusual and dramatic, and seeing these as 'anecdotal' evidence of something that women 'fall for' as spiritual, one should therefore remember who the observers are, and the intellectual integrity and organic unity between the different conceptual levels of their accounts, including the personal/professional. One should also keep in mind Maffesoli's observation that 'in the tracks of Western iconoclasm, contemporary radical thought finds it difficult to integrate everything which belongs to the non-conscious, the non-rational or to the vast domain of non-verbal communication'.[20] More importantly, one should be looking at these descriptions in terms of powerful primary and secondary data which enable a glimpse of emergent patterns: of biography, events and attitudes that these women – both authors and subjects – bring to the way they express themselves as spiritual and wordly beings.

Religious history and women

Goonatilake's study of the history and teachings of Buddhism can be considered paradigmatic of the changing status of women and the institutionalization of religion. She reminds us that in the initial stages, when the founder was still alive, basically women had equal status.

Seeming restrictions and differences had more to do with the then current social norms than with anything doctrinal aimed at proving that women, seen as inherently inferior, were incapable of a high spiritual practice.

But with the death of the founder, the male-dominated establishment proceeded to denigrate, marginalize and impose all manner of restrictions on women. From outright changes in scripture to overt and covert misogynist interpretations, over the centuries male custodians of a Teacher's or Prophet's message attempted to make women's lives and spirituality conform to the demands of a patriarchy which was not necessarily synonymous with the teachings of the founder. The struggle by women to retain their religious independence is thus as old as the religions themselves. As Goonatilake shows, Vinaya Buddhist women had their own line of teachers; they were pioneer historiographers and travellers who were instrumental in the spread of early Buddhism. That such women have been obscured by revisionist religious history and layers of time does not mean that they did not exist as a steady undercurrent to a religion, right into the present.

Religious inclusivism

One of the main problems with fundamentalism is the tendency towards an exceedingly narrow vision which is not only intolerant of different views/interpretations within a religion but also of other religions. As the chapter on the Kashmiri mystic Lalla discusses, a great deal of modern scholarship on religion reflects narrow, exclusivist definitions of its concepts. Lalla's defiant – almost in-your-face – spirituality continues to confound Hindu and Muslim scholars, both of whom would claim her as exclusive to their tradition. The women in this book, as authors and subjects, have a much more inclusive approach, freely relating to traditions other than their own. As the chapters on Christianity, Hinduism and Islam indicate, there is a blurring and crossing of religious boundaries. But traditional analyses of religious history largely remain fettered to a narrow and sterile view of religion, dominated as they are either by male historians or by psychologically monochromatic, hyper-masculine 'definitions', research, and interpretations.[21]

Khanna's account of a present-day *tantric* guru can be considered paradigmatic of a certain type of women's spirituality. At its best, quite capable of absorbing more than one religion; finding a natural (hereti-cal) affinity with seemingly very different religious languages. These differences are not experienced as alien or a religious betrayal but rather as different streams flowing into a larger river, merging into a seamless whole. Madhobi Ma's lineage of teachers and gurus includes both Muslims and Hindus. In fact, her chief guru and preceptor was/is a Muslim. Madhobi Ma and the Kashmiri Lalla present a vivid contrast to the prevailing exclusivist, and hence macho, religious mood in India and Pakistan. In their own ways, these ancient and modern women bear witness to the dynamic and all-embracing *raison d'être* of both Hinduism and Islam.

Odal's and Mananzan's fascinating accounts of spiritually influential women in the Philippines present a different type of Catholic libera-tion theology. It is an engagement drawing legitimacy by reclaiming indigenous world views which, as both writers imply, do not so much jeopardize and 'profane' Catholicism in the Philippines as enrich and deepen it. Catholicism is not rejected but imaginatively reintegrated into precolonial traditions. However, this reintegration is simul-taneously accompanied by a critical evaluation of 'malestream' Catholicism. Mananzan, for example, give a no-holds-barred assess-ment of the way strains of official Catholicism continue to oppress women in the Philippines.

The best medicine

Another startling dimension to women's spirituality has to do with humour. The writings on the Philippines lend credence to a survey conducted in the 1990s which indicated that it is the most spiritual country in the world.[22] While Afghanistan may dispute this, it is unlikely that it would also be a serious contender for what will hope-fully be a future survey of humour and spirituality among nations. Odal's *Mutya*-Mother signals what can on the one hand be considered a distinct style of women's postcolonial response to religion, in this instance the encounter of Catholicism with indigenous Philippine culture. On the other hand, it is simultaneously paradigmatic of what seems to be an undercurrent in the spirituality of many women, giving it a distinctly trangressive, heretical flavour.[23]

There seems to be no social scientific literature on the seemingly unlikely connections between humour and spirituality or religion.

Researching the subject of humour (academically) itself becomes an exercise in self-inflicted depression. As with so much else, innumerable theories have come and gone without us being any the wiser about it. According to the experts' review in *The Oxford Companion to the Mind*, part of the problem lies in the (self-evident) fact that 'humour loses much of its splendour, infectiousness and power under laboratory scrutiny'. One of the few references to gender and humour cites research which suggests that women find jokes funnier when heard by the left ear, with the implication that this ear routes to the right hemisphere of the brain, which processes information more holistically than the left hemisphere.[24]

Leaving aside such sad 'social scientific' attempts at dissecting this quintessentially human behaviour/response, certain more philosophically inclined explanations have prevailed, perhaps because they are based on more intuitively accurate perceptions. Freud's connection between fear and its resolution through humour is well known, and common sense observations suggest that humour is useful in relieving psychological strain and stress. But the arts, especially literature, perhaps provide far more accurate depictions about human behaviour than scientific studies, especially when it comes to gender.

Walter Ong has made some astute observations of the 'Don Quixote Syndrome', the 'masculine preoccupation with bravado and dominance, often pointless and poignant'.[25] In the world of humour, males seem to function from a position of disadvantage because, according to Ong, the syndrome suggests that 'masculinity has something futile to it'.[26] This theme is reflected in observations on the differences between the comedian and comedienne, who typically operate from a consciousness that is bodily – *psycho-anatomically* – different.[27] Until recently, there were very few female clowns. Perhaps because many comic figures directly suggest the 'behaviour and accoutrements of the limp phallus – total ineffectiveness. The phallus can be mocked as the womb cannot be.' As Ong points out, unlike Charlie Chaplin, female comic figures tend not to be hapless victims:

> They often talk about themselves as victims, calling attention to the chaos around them, but they are seldom as much at the mercy of chaos as is the Chaplinesque male …. Quite the contrary, they are often subtly in charge, amused at themselves in their plight, advertising feminine viability even

amid utter chaos, unflappable, nurturing mothers, centers of stability in a world of infantile (often regressive adult–male) turbulence.[28]

The psychosexual aesthetics of comic masculine icons such as Don Quixote and Chaplin suggest that masculine/feminine need not necessarily always be seen in terms of hierarchy/power/oppression. Personalities such as the *Mutya*-Mother, or even Lalla's cryptic attitude regarding her nudity, are a refreshing contrast to the often extreme and uncompromising attitudes in feminism regarding (no) difference and gender. In consonance with the observations of Ong and others on female humour, these women – in their own ways, including their spiritual somersaults of attire, name and ritual – provide comic relief in a domain which is today overwhelmingly (and frequently literally) taken in a deadly serious manner. They use humour not only to heal their surroundings of a rigid and suffocating religiosity, but also to highlight what is perhaps an inherent strength of their gender in these matters. Given the strong metaphorical connections between spirituality and sexuality, particularly in different types of mysticism, a detailed study of humour and gender in this context may yield significant insights regarding differences in male and female spirituality.

The trickster

Those who are unable to appreciate the profound and necessary links between humour and religion are perhaps excessively dominated by academic Western notions of religion and its attendant behavioural norms. As Odal's analysis (Chapter 6) explains, the *Mutya* is the Philippine counterpart of 'the trickster', an archetypal figure which appears throughout religions and cultures. Jung devoted considerable attention to this mythological motif, relating it to the transformative potential in our psyches – in the figure, for example, of Hermes-Mercury, representing communication, the messenger between divine and human, between conscious and unconscious. Like its namesake, the element mercury, this figure cannot be pinned down, having a slippery, elusive, quicksilver quality – hence 'the trickster'. Hermes' relationship with healing is still evident in the winged staff insignia of the medical profession. Odal's work is anthropology at its best, skilfully weaving an analysis drawn from folklore, myth, linguistics and politics with wider connections between these in the Philippines and South Asia. Her *Mutya*-Mother comes across as authentic, a woman of enormous spiritual capacity, a healer who knows that laughter is good spiritual medicine.

The meaning and significance of the archetype of the trickster has been all but lost to the modern study (and practice) of religion. *The Encyclopedia of Cultural Anthropology* states that, in studying the religion of Native Americans, 'Western anthropologists found it incongruous that joking and humorous activities occurred simultaneously with rituals and ceremonies and often parodied and mocked them.'[29] Even though our observers could not shake off their all too serious Judaeo-Christian assumptions about the incompatibility of humour and religion, credit is due to them for at least recognizing their combined functions. These include the symbolic significance of different humorous–spiritual activities and the function of social critique which 'permits criticism without being overly aggressive'.

Pundits and pundamentalists

The sombre writings of Schopenhauer, Kant and Spencer have variously suggested that laughter is the expression of our recognizing an incongruity. This idea has been operationalized by developmental psychologists in the study of young children and ways in which learning occurs. For example, Rothbart has observed in children as young as four months that when the perception of an unexpected (incongruous) event leads to laughter, it may also lead to curiosity, fear, problem solving or concept learning.[30] In short, humour has the potential for learning/growth/development. However, the incongruous event must be safe or playful and a degree of resolution of the incongruity must be feasible.

Humour happens when our usual way of thinking and perceiving is challenged. At its best, it is neither abrasive nor unkind, but a playful presenting of *possibilities* such as, for example, the ambiguities of meaning in the pun. Thus, when playfully confronted by spiritual incongruity, we are rendered (potentially) vulnerable, made 'open' to possibilities and meanings *other* than established ones. Without aggressively forcing one to abandon existing belief, a good joke may provide us with a choice; we may identify with and learn from the possibilities it implies. Freedom and choice are meaningful only if there is more than one thing/concept to choose from, and in this context humour becomes a transgressive, liberative and transformative force. If we are urged to be like children in approaching the Divine, then women such as *Mutya*-Mother and Lalla can be considered sophisticated educators of the way. They take what can be considered an 'irreverent' and 'perverse' delight in carnivalizing established religious norms and terms, not to mention the liberties they take with the visual accoutrements of high-serious religion. But these women are actually devout spiritual 'pundamentalists', opening us up to multiple meanings and possibilities inherent in the human–divine relationship. Punsters *par excellence,* they are the antithesis to grim (and boring) one-dimensional certainty, in short, to all types of fanaticism.

Hysterics, heretics and healers

Many of the studies in this book describe the phenomenon of trance. While this is not the place for a technical exposition, one element of these descriptions concerns the recurrence of taking on different forms/faces. These 'switches', as perceived by the observers, can once again be related to the trickster archetype. But apart from the obviously powerful impact it has on the viewer, such (e)merging can also be related to a heretical consciousness. The heretic recognizes that boundaries are permeable, that the other/s is/are within. Women such as Lalla, Suprema and *Mutya*-Mother cross these inner and outer boundaries, creatively mingling seemingly different religions. They suggest that heretical consciousness is hybrid, refusing to adhere to some pristine ideal of 'pure' dogma.

Heresy, then, is a position of rebellion against external centralized authority, chosen consciously and representing the 'middle voice' which, like freedom, is possible only when there is consciousness of more than one voice. As evident in the history of all religions, it is a continuous and radical 'tradition', a permanent revolution expressed frequently in mystical or non-dogmatic language.[31] In its subversion of dogma, heresy indeed 'weakens' what are frequently ossified strains in a tradition. But in its embrace of diversity it not only doubly reinforces itself, but revivifies – even through controversy – the traditions of which it partakes. By virtue of hybridity, heretical consciousness is frequently creative consciousness.

It can be argued that if such a consciousness has to do with permeable boundaries, inner and outer, then how does one distinguish between hysterics and heretics? In fact, the typical modern response to trance phenomena relies on the psychological label of 'hysteria'. As Peter Wilson's observations on the art and culture of the Indian sub-continent and of other areas and periods suggest, heresies played a major role in the emergence of a high degree of aesthetics, tolerance and creativity. It is perhaps more fruitful, Wilson concludes, to ask what heresy *does*, not what it *is*.[32] Hysteria, whether individual or at the mass level, is rarely aesthetic and creative, and is more akin to a civilizational convulsion. Similarly, unlike the hysteric, the heretic is frequently a healer of individuals, not only through laughter but also through the ideas and art forms that emerge from a collective consciousness inspired by it.

Decolonizing the Imagination

Pieterse and Parekh state that 'Decolonization is a process of emancipation through mirroring, a mix of defiance and mimesis'. Commenting on various forms of postcolonial cultural politics (but not religion) the authors observe that:

> keynotes of the postcolonial sensibility are reflexivity and play. Reflexivity also in the sense of self-questioning ... decolonization and internal decolonization have been so preoccupied with animosities and enemy forces that little room remained for questioning one's own position. Play, because the postcolonial world is more fluid ... boundaries, to those who have experienced crossing them, become a matter of play rather than an obsession .... The element of play opens possibilities for innovation....[33]

These observations strike a responsive chord with the themes outlined earlier on the nature of women's scholarship and spirituality, heresy, humour and healing; many of the subjects and authors are at the cutting edge of postcolonial sensibility. Underlying the themes is a cognitive mirror that may offer some reflections, particularly for the Southern intelligentsia which finds itself increasingly besieged by different brands of fundamentalism.

Religion and the Southern intelligentsia

To the extent that Western civilization has had an indelible impact on the world, the relationship of the Southern intellectual with religion can be viewed as ironic, even poignant. Whereas in the North, the intellectual's earlier attitude to religion can be justified as part of a historical process in which modernity and secularism overwhelmed and marginalized religion, in the South the situation has been largely the reverse. That is, while modernity certainly has had an impact, for the vast majority of non-Western cultures it was not religion but secularism, espoused mostly by the intelligentsia, that was marginal.

Even as Southern intellectuals assert themselves through the postcolonial project, they must also turn inward to a deeper, more personal level. They must not only defiantly engage the North with an alternative view of history that is, more often than not, either self-celebratory or a victimized West-bashing, but also face their hubris: they must critically assess the core reasons for the short shrift and denial given to religion by intellectuals inhabiting overwhelmingly visible and obviously religious contexts. The insights such a self-analysis would provide will be uncomfortable to say the least, since they may have little to do with colonialism and, to put it bluntly, rather more to do with a failure of cognition – which in turn is related to the rather mundane human need to follow fashion, in this case the intellectual kind. These reasons, of course, run counter to the self-image of a 'thinking' person. Nevertheless, they need to be confronted and examined, if only in order to be liberated by irony and the capacity to laugh at oneself as one 'sees through' the intellectual persona and the need to be always taken seriously.

Mythos and logos

The (in)ability of 'seeing through' is related to the realm of the imagination and Karen Armstrong's analysis of fundamentalism in Judaism, Christianity and Islam provides a framework for understanding its relationship with religion.[34] Armstrong distinguishes two ways of thinking, *mythos* and *logos*, both of which are essential to humans and serve as complements to each other in the desire for knowledge and truth. *Mythos* has to do with meaning, with 'making sense' of the complex, often emotional experience that is life. The strange stories of mythology – and every society has them – were not meant to be taken literally. They were imaginary, psychological; metaphors for situations and experiences which are simultaneously ubiquitous to humanity and have a powerful impact on the individual. For example, birth and death, love and its loss or betrayal, are myth themes which engage us at a differ-ent level than, say, the molecular structure of water. How we construct the meaning of *mythos* has a profound impact upon our behaviour.

Equally important, *logos* concerns the rational, pragmatic and scien-tific, and enables us to function in the practical world. In the pre-modern world these two domains were kept separate but valued equally. According to Armstrong, in the last two centuries, the sense of *mythos* was steadily lost in the West; today it is regarded by many as false superstition. Those who regard scientific rationalism as the only truth try to turn *mythos* into *logos*. Religious fundamentalists make the same mistake the other way round.

The problem is one-dimensionality, an insistent attempt to demon-strate the superiority of one aspect over the other. Whether one chooses to opt for a technoscientific view of the future or retreat into the past, one thing is certain: the human need for a meaningful exis-tence remains a reality. At the same time, regardless of the fundamen-talist vision, it is equally certain that, particularly for those who have experienced even a rudimentary modernity and even more so for many women, there is no going back to a literal past. 'Western civiliza-tion', as Armstrong says,

> has changed the world. Nothing – including religion – can ever be the same. All over the globe … people are finding that … the old forms of faith no longer work for them…. They cannot provide the enlightenment and consolation that human beings seem to need. As a result men and women are trying to find out new ways of being religious … attempting to build insights into the past.[35].

In short, given the legacy of modernity, religion has to be approached imaginatively.

The use of the word 'imagination' here does not refer to flights of fancy but to a complex epistemological framework best exemplified in the writings of, among others, Gilbert Durand, Carl Jung, Mircea Eliade and Paul Ricoeur. Whether in Ricouer's notion of 'a poetics of experience' and the dynamic centrality of metaphor, or in Eliade's view that the soul-stifling aspects of modernity can only be countered through awakening the imagination which is innately predisposed to perceive the sacred/symbolic, these writers conceptualize the imagi-nation as providing analytic frameworks for understanding and articulating religion and religious experience. As a whole, this body of work signals:

> a remarkable change in attitude on the part of Western religious and philo-
> sophical tradition toward the place and role of imagination. Such a change
> reflects the transition in contemporary scholarship from an exclusive
> emphasis on logical, propositional, or dogmatic formulation as the sole
> criteria of truth. There is increasing acknowledgement of an existential and
> experiential notion of truth that refers to a sense of ontological self-
> awareness and responsibility, which permeates all that we are and do. In
> this process, imagination has an integral role to play ....[36]

Hindsight, insight and decolonization

To the extent that many Southern intellectuals were philosophically swept away by *logos* at the expense of *mythos*, it is the realm of the imagination that has to be critically reclaimed and decolonized. As Pieterse and Parekh point out in *The Decolonization of the Imagination*, the underlying issues have to do with 'the relationship between power and culture, domination and the imaginary ... in the context of imperialism and colonialism, different lines of inquiry converge on the theme of the imagination'.[37] This interest in the imaginary is different from the iconoclasm of earlier rationalists and positivists since 'it posits instead the imaginary as constitutive of community and society'. As a metaphor, colonialism has come to be seen as a political, economic and cultural condition which exists globally, and it has been argued that one can speak of 'any number of metaphorical "colonisations" having to do with region, class, race and gender'.[38] One can add religion to this sort of colonization drawing, as it does, its strength from *mythos*, which is fed directly from the depths of the human imagination.

By and large, not having the resources of their counterparts in the North which enable the latter endlessly to pursue theoretical somer-saults on tightropes set up, to begin with, by themselves, those located in the South cannot afford such luxuries, particularly since they are increasingly under threat from different types of religious extremism. However, given the globally emergent religious *zeitgeist*, there is also a tendency among some no longer to feel defensive about returning to religion. More often than not, the result is in the form of a somersault into an ultra-orthodox view of religion. Bypassing the necessity of insight into their own initial anti-religion stance and the imagination required to laugh at one's human failings, the analysis is usually tilted towards simple West/modernity bashing. Decades of analytic training are set aside in favour of an uncritical acceptance of what is frequently a narrow and ultra-conservative, masculinist expression of religion, with faith becoming an overwhelming substitute for knowledge.

The idea of a 'chasm' between faith and knowledge, which can only be 'leaped' across, is part of the intellectual heritage of Western civiliza- tion and the credal contingencies which are central to fundamentalist Christianity; it is not necessarily endemic to all religious traditions.[39] The Southern intellectual's reliance on faith to the exclusion of reason, not to mention the conceptual and investigative resources of modern knowledge as applied to his/her religion, at best is frequently a mental- analytical cop-out; at worst, it borders on fundamentalism. In both instances it betrays a still colonized imagination *vis-à-vis* religion.

Finally, as certain scholars have long argued, 'religion' itself can be considered a cultural construction reflecting various agendas.[40] Recent research in postcolonial studies reinforces this view.[41] The following description of the construction of 'Hinduism' may well be applicable to other religions:

> Hinduism is a European homogenization of quite diverse religious systems ... a fabrication or distortion of those practices not otherwise classifiable or recognizable as Buddhist, Muslim, Christian, Sikh, or Jain. The designation, the initial context for which was the colonization of India, has in turn been appropriated by the indigenous population to whom it was first applied as a category by which they themselves now describe themselves to Westerners.[42]

According to Cooey, this type of 'sin of commission' has scholarly counterparts of 'omission' in, for example, the marginalizing of women's practices and roles compared to those of men, reflecting not so much the values of the communities being studied as the androcentric assumptions of the male and female scholars. Urging a high level of academic self-critique in these matters, she also points out the 'schol- arly bias toward textual and elite manifestations of traditions as opposed to their oral, visual, and popular counterparts'.[43]

Back to the future

It is this cognitively complicated nexus of *mythos* and *logos*, of one's personal and collective religious, cultural and intellectual history, the

world of fact and the world of meaning, which the Southern intellectual must (re)negotiate if his/her re-engagement with religion is going
to be different, socio-politically less sanguinary and more salutary
than that of the fundamentalist. Compared with those in the North
the task here is more difficult yet also easier. The difficulties have to
do with the genuine physical threat posed by many fundamentalists.
Yet, even as meaning and interpretation are being hijacked by them,
unlike in the West, here religion is widespread and *mythos* still very
much alive, not only at the most diffused levels of culture, but also in
relatively well-preserved text, ritual and orthopraxies. Beyond the
fundamentalist fringe, and in spite of rational secularism, Buddhism,
Hinduism, Islam, Taoism, even Christianity are widespread, palpably
living traditions in the South. As such, the *mythos* of each remains
accessible to all and there is relatively a lesser need to actively create
new religions in the mould, for example, of many of the New Age
religions in the West.

If by now all the 'non-Western' religions are in varying degrees
globally present, so are their critiques and revisionings, by both men
and women.[44] At the same time, all the major religions are being
realigned contextually to the extent that today one can speak, for
example, of American Buddhism or European Islam. As a whole, these
movements function to destabilize the fundamentalist impetus towards
making a monolith of a religion, revealing that historically and into the
present there have been numerous Islams, Buddhisms, Christianities,
etc. Dynamic dissent is integral to the religious impulse and is exemplified in prophetology. Most prophets did not so much 'invent' new
religions as strongly disagree with certain elements of existing ones.

Additionally, all religions are historically replete with figures –
men and women – whose ideas were considered 'radical' and drew
different responses from the common people and the ruling establishment. Historically, the diversity engendered by splits between official
and popular versions, along with numerous other cultural forces,
have ensured that no religion has ever become a monolith and hence
retained its vitality. The postmodern recognition of the significance
of diversity has had theological precursors who argued that diversity
between and within religious beliefs reflects the infinite and creative
dimension of the Divine; each is valuable, highlighting different facets
of a nevertheless essential Unity.[45]

Since historically all religions have had a radical 'malestream', at one level the questions have less to do with gender and more with diversity of spiritual styles. Many women, past and present, have relied on the ideas of males to deepen their own spiritual understanding. Nevertheless, such solidarity and reclaiming of the past must take into account factors such as the role of patriarchy, not to mention the present widely experienced oppression by women through different religions. The present situation requires a sort of triple vision: reclaiming the radical past (male and female) and revisioning it in contemporary contexts, particularly feminism(s). Finally, this vision must include a comparative perspective which, even as it highlights diversity, must simultaneously focus on identifying the unifying aspects of women's spirituality.

The politics of interpretation and meaning

Reclaiming the *mythos* of a religion goes beyond blind adherence to ritual towards imaginative engagement with the intellectual issues of meaning and interpretation. And it is here that *logos* can play its part. This is not the *logos* of either scientific rationalism or fundamentalism, which would have us engage in (dis)proving the number of angels that can dance on the head of a pin, but *logos* in its widest sense of the application of the vast resources in knowledge (both ancient and current) accumulated by modernity, including the full range of historical, psychological, linguistic and cultural insights. All these need to be interfaced with religion in order to construct architectures of meaning, – a task which, of necessity, includes an active engagement with the politics of interpretation. As Jung (who was also accused of heresy) said, 'religion can only be replaced by religion'.[46] This is no doubt a daunting task and the burden of knowledge is a heavy one. (Hence, perhaps, the adage 'ignorance is bliss'.) But Christ, one must recall, carried his own cross. Similarly, 'believing' intellectuals, North or South, can no longer take refuge exclusively in faith but must carry their own burden which includes the experience and knowledge resources of (post)modernity – and the knowledge, now, that there are many different knowledges about religion.

The logical place to start is, of course, with one's own tradition but, given the globalization of information today, there is no excuse not to have a multi-levelled understanding of others as well. Beyond an awareness and understanding of this multiplicity, the struggle over meaning and interpretation must include (re)search to elicit those per-spectives which do not denigrate or marginalize women and women's spirituality. All these dynamics have to be considered and examined if the Southern intelligentsia, particularly, is to avoid repeating its past hubris and in that way respond effectively to the fundamentalists. In this context, Delores William's outline of a Christian 'Womanist Theology' is equally applicable to all religions and to both men and women searching for religious alternatives to fundamentalism: 'It must include a multi-dialogical and didactic intent along with a commitment both to reason *and* to the validity of female imagery and metaphorical language in the construction of theological statements.'[47]

The Final Frontier

This text presents a spectrum of issues linked to women and religion, particularly as they appear in South and South East Asia. At one level it is a book about defiance of the academic and religious mainstream. At another, it is about what Odal (Chapter 6) calls the underground world of non-institutionalized religions, 'the underside of things that exist on the margins and peripheries of society and yet touch the most vital and elemental aspects of life'. Here, women as healers, goddesses, nuns, unrecognized and hidden saints, gurus and hybrid heretics all come together to show how there continues to be a particular devotional subculture which, even as it defies orthodoxy, offers profound religious alternatives to it. Mostly shunned or 'discredited' by the intellectual and religious establishments, it has flourished for millennia, sustaining and nourishing countless individuals. Finally, the book can be seen to reflect the newly emerging spirituality of women in South and South East Asia as it is being shaped by the subjectivities and experiences of women facing a range of political and social injustice. As one of the authors has noted elsewhere,

> Women's emerging spirituality is therefore not just a vertical relationship with God .... It is risk rather than security ... joyful rather than austere ... expansive rather than limiting. It celebrates more than it fasts .... It is vibrant, liberating, and colourful.[48]

• • •

One may ask, 'So what?' To the extent that such defiance and heresy have always been around, all religions nevertheless continue in varying degrees to discriminate against women. What difference will such writings by and about women make?

In the short run, perhaps, such texts may indeed make no difference, but then very few ideas – including religious ones – have had instant and long-lasting impact. Nevertheless, there is a difference between the past as it has been steadily punctuated by radical forms of women's spirituality and as it is being manifested today. The difference has to do with literacy, with reading and writing, and the inevitable transformation of consciousness – in analysis, comprehension, knowledge, cognition and communication – that is engendered through literacy. Never before in history have so many women been empowered through 'the word', enabling them to articulate their ideas and share these with vast numbers of other women and men. Literacy and language is crucial to consciousness and communication. Given the explosion in technology today, vast numbers of females have at their disposal a variety of media through which they can express, analyse and above all communicate and share with each other the most radical of conceptions. Granted, there are also many who still do not have access to either literacy or the new information technologies. But neither did the West become literate overnight once Gutenberg invented the printing press.

Thus, the crucial difference between women (and men) heretics of the past and present has to do with communication. 'Information', as Bateson said, 'is a difference which makes a difference.'[49] This sort of difference-as-impact is already evident in numerous disciplines, many of which are themselves heralding their own postmodern demise, as in 'the end' of philosophy, history and art. Much of this reviewing has occurred as a consequence not only of postcolonial voices but also of information technologies which have opened up diverse opinions on any given subject, making its arena of discussion global rather than just local. The problems posed by globalization should not obscure the debt owed to it by feminism. The potential for what may happen to our understanding of religion in these circumstances is similarly far-reaching.[50] The subject of women and religion thus remains post-coloniality's final frontier.

Whereas in the past the idea of heresy was largely limited to definition/accusation/punishment within theology, today in countries such as India and (particularly) Pakistan heresy is on the way to becoming a norm. As competing brands of religious fanaticism bid for greater political power and redefine religion along increasingly rigid, exclusivist and bigoted lines, conceptions of heresy/blasphemy/ apostasy are converging steadily to encompass men and women from all levels of civil society. (In the process many are being forced to study and re-examine religion.) Ordinary people belonging to different Islamic and non-Islamic communities are persecuted, and it does not end there. Writers, social workers, actors, musicians, artists, scientists, human rights activists, environmentalists and journalists are being attacked and threatened by religious fanatics for being 'subversive' and 'irreligious'.

But even as the scope of what constitutes heresy expands, past restrictions are less applicable: in spite of persecution and violence against increasing numbers, there is no longer the old constraint (other than fear) to conduct these conversations in whispers. Once a hidden mode of discourse between a small number of participants, limited further by contingencies of time and space, heretical dialogue is already becoming – thanks to communication technologies – a polylogue among different groups, cultures and religions. With time, no longer veiled and silenced by literalism and history, the difference between past and future may well be the contemporary woman's (re)engagement with religion.

Notes and References

1 J. Barnhardt, 'The Incurably Religious Animal', in Emile Sahliyeh (ed.), *Religious Resurgence and Politics in the Contemporary World*, SUNY series in Religion, Culture and Society (Albany: State University of New York Press, 1991).

2 While recognizing that the term 'fundamentalism' is propagandist and misleading, one is also in agreement with Karen Armstrong that 'like it or not, the word "fundamentalism" is here to stay … the term is not perfect but it is a useful label for movements that despite their differences, bear a strong family resemblance'. *The Battle for God* (New York: Knopf, 2000), p. x. For the most comprehensive study on the subject see the Fundamentalism Project's Martin E. Marty and R. Scott Appleby (eds.), *Fundamentalisms Observed* (1991), *Fundamentalisms and Society* (1993), *Fundamentalisms and the State* (1993), *Accounting for Fundamentalism* (1994) and *Fundamentalisms Comprehended* (1995) (Chicago: University of Chicago Press).

3 J. Nederveen Pieterse, 'Fundamentalism Discourses: Enemy Images', *Women Against Fundamentalism*, 1, 5 (1994).

4 P. Berry and A. Wernick (eds.), *Shadow of Spirit: Postmodernism and Religion* (London and New York: Routledge, 1992).

5 A decade ago *Time* magazine published an extensive essay by the conservative commentator Henry Grunwald on religion and the year 2000. The following extracts provide a general picture of the New Age movement. Assessing the various liberalizing reforms in mainstream Judaism and Chrisitanity, Grunwald notes: 'But none of these reforms are arresting the sharp decline of the mainstream churches ... denominations outside the mainstream are doing well, including Fundamentalists .... Equally significant is the flood of substitute religions. The most prominent of these is the so-called New Age movement – a vast, amorphous hodgepodge of spiritualism, faith healing, reincarnation, meditation, yoga, macrobiotic diets, mystical environmentalism and anything that helps transform the self. Its followers sound as if they were born again, but without Christ .... A motto often used by them is borrowed from Joseph Campbell: "Follow your bliss". The New Age bliss has grown to extraordinary proportions, with magazines, books, records, mass merchandizing.... The New Age phenomenon points to a void that our society has left in people's lives. They don't need Sartre to find existence meaningless .... The irrepressible religious impulse – the revenge of the sacred, as it has been called – is perhaps even more clearly displayed outside our own country. Note the spread of Islamic Fundamentalism, the strength of Hinduism, both often accompanied by violence. Throughout the Third World ... in Eastern Europe and the former Soviet Union... religion is once again a major force.' The Internet is an excellent resource for understanding the New Age movement. The following is just one example: 'The New Age movement means different things to different people ... all New Age topics have one basic underlying theme. That theme is personal spiritual development. Every day there are thousands upon thousands of people around the world who are waking up to the knowledge, understanding and realization of who they really are, where they came from, and why they are here. This collective transformation of individuals can be described as the New Age movement. As a whole, the New Age movement is dynamic, rapidly-growing, and gaining momentum. A key component of the New Age which many people prescribe to is the belief that our planet and its population are literally moving into a New Age. This New Age is one of awakened consciousness where people give up their limited third-dimensional survival mode of existence and awaken to a higher, more enlightened world. The New Age is strongly related to some of the concepts defined in the branch of philosophy commonly referred to as metaphysics. Popular metaphysical topics often include discussion and analysis of subjects beyond the physical third dimension. Some examples of metaphysical topics include: free energy, out of body experiences, UFOs, psychic phenomena, alternative healing, and other topics that our conventional sciences find difficult to explain. One reason that there are so many different tools to assist the New Ager is that different people find differ-

ent values within each tool. For many, the Tarot works well. Others like crystals. Others meditate or channel. It matters little how one achieves higher understanding and wisdom. What is most important is that an effort is being made to transcend our limitations and seek out a higher good ('New Age FAQ/What is the New Age'. Andrew Lutts. http://www.salemctr.com/ newage/context1.html). Also, http://websyte.com/alan/newage.htm

6 See, for example, Mette Bryld and Nina Lykke, *Cosmodolphins: Feminist Cultural Studies of Technology, Animals and the Sacred* (London: Zed Books, 2000).

7 To use the singular 'woman' to denote a diversity of women is to invite criticism and the label of essentialism. While this is not the place to get entangled in these debates, it must also be said that the linguistic underpinnings of such issues, along with the dominance of English in academic discourse, remains to be examined in detail in order to separate the substantive from the trivial. In Finnish and Urdu, for example, 'woman' can be used as both singular *and* plural without necessarily evoking stereotypes or loss of nuance.

8 Berry and Wernick, *Shadow of Spirit*, pp. 3, 57.

9 Michael Lambek, 'The Anthropology of Religion and the Quarrel Between Poetry and Philosophy', *Current Anthropology*, 41, 3 (2000).

10 Christopher Lasch, 'The Soul of Man under Secularism', *New Oxford Review* (Berkeley: 1991); *The Culture of Narcissism* (New York: Warner Books, 1979); *The True and Only Heaven: Progress and its Critics* (New York: Norton, 1992); 'The Fragility of Liberalism', *Salmagundi* (Fall 1991).

11 Christopher Lasch, 'The New Age Movement: No Effort, No Truth, No Solutions', *New Oxford Review* (April 1991). See also his 'New Age Nonsense' in *The Wilson Quarterly* (Summer 1991).

12 For example: Rosemary Reuther, *Religion and Sexism: Images of Women in Jewish and Christian Traditions* (New York: Simon and Schuster, 1974); Carol Christ and Judith Plaskow, *Womanspirit Rising: a Feminist Reader in Religion* (San Francisco: Harper and Row 1979); Charlene Spretnak (ed.), *The Politics of Women's Spirituality* (New York: Doubleday Anchor, 1982, 1994); Mary Daly, *Gyn/Ecology: the Metaethics of Radical Feminism* (Boston: Beacon Press, 1987); Riane Eisler, *The Chalice and the Blade: Our History, Our Future* (San Francisco: Harper Collins, 1987, 1988); Naomi Goldenberg, *Changing of the Gods* (Boston: Beacon Press, 1979). The writings of French feminists such as Julia Kristeva and Luce Irigaray are also critically significant.

13 Charlene Spretnak (ed.), *The Politics of Women's Spirituality* (New York: Doubleday Anchor, 1994), p. xviii.

14 The problematics of feminism and women's spirituality are particularly evident when one considers the debates around 'essence' versus 'diversity'. The former position assumes that there is something essentially different between men and women, while the latter posits that gender is in fact a social construction. At one level the postmodern turn has demonstrated convincingly how knowledge is embedded in local contexts. Deconstruction of dominant historical, anthropological and literary knowledge reveals a power base and shows how domi-

nant knowledge becomes dominating knowledge, in the process destroying vital diversity. On the other hand there is the self-evident fact that relations between men and women seem to have something in common all over the world. No society is free from violence of some sort against women, particularly in situations of conflict. Similarly, the postmodern social constructionist view of gender is unable to account fully for the fundamental biological functioning of the (male or female) body and its relationship to human behaviour. Interestingly enough, while the postmodern perspective gained strength through feminist and postcolonial scholars, the essentialist view has also had its strongest proponents among women. See, for example, Judith Butler, *Bodies That Matter* (London/New York: Routledge, 1993); Marilyn Fry, 'The Necessity of Difference: Constructing a Positive Category of Women', *Signs*, 21 (1996): 990–1010; Diana Fuss, *Essentially Speaking: Feminism, Nature and Difference* (New York: Routledge. 1990); J. C. Simth and Carla J. Ferstman, *The Castration of Oedipus: Feminism, Psychoanalysis, and the Will to Power* (New York: New York University Press, 1996); Elizabeth Spelman, *Inessential Woman* (Boston: Beacon Press, 1998). Also, Durre Ahmed, 'Essence and Diversity in Gender Research', Feminist Research Centre Monograph, Aalborg University. 1995. For an excellent feminist summary of this debate *vis-à-vis* religion, see Paula Cooey, *Religious Imagination and the Body: a Feminist Analysis* (New York: Oxford University Press, 1994).

15 Jenny Teichman, review of Macintyre's 'Three Versions of Moral Enquiry', *The New York Times Book Review*, 6 August 1990. Also her 'Don't be Cruel or Unreasonable', review of Richard Rorty's 'Contingency, Irony and Solidarity', *New York Times Book Review,* 23 April 1989.

16 Bryld and Lykke, *Cosmodolphins*, pp. 36–8.

17 *The Compact Oxford Dictionary* (Oxford: Clarendon, 1991).

18 Peter Wilson, *Scandal: Essays in Islamic Heresy* (New York: Automedia Press, 1988), p. 13.

19 Daniel Bell; 'The Cultural Wars: American Intellectual Life, 1965–1992', *The Wilson Quarterly* (Summer 1992).

20 M. Maffesoli, 'The Imaginary and the Sacred in Durkheim's Sociology', *Current Sociology*, 41, 2 (1993): 59–68 (1993).

21 '[S]cholars of religion have also constituted what counts as religious by way of omission … witness, for example, the extent to which women's practices and roles were, and often still are, overlooked or subordinated in status to men's, even in egalitarian populations, thereby reflecting the androcentric assumptions of the male and female scholars rather than the values of the communities studied.' Paula Cooey, *Religious Imagination and the Body: a Feminist Analysis* (New York: Oxford University Press, 1984), p. 123.

22 Scrafin Talisayan, 'Patotoo: Concepts of Validity among Some Indigenous Filipino Spiritual Groups', in Teresita Obusan QC (ed.), *PAMAMARAAN: Indigenous Knowledge and Evolving Research Paradigms* (Manila: Mamamathala Inc., 1994), as cited in Odal's 'The Study of a "Mutya" Figure'.

23 For more studies on this theme of humour and women's spirituality see *The*

Hidden Woman (Lahore: HBF, 1999), HBF series on Women and Religion, Vol. II.

24 R. Gregory (ed.), *The Oxford Companion to the Mind* (New York: Oxford University Press, 1990), pp. 320–3.

25 Walter Ong, *Fighting for Life: Contest, Sexuality and Consciousness* (Ithaca: Cornell University Press, 1981), p. 63.

26 *Ibid.*, p. 99.

27 M. Grotjahn, *Beyond Laughter* (New York: McGraw Hill, 1957), cited in Ong's *Fighting for Life*, p. 103.

28 Ong, *Fighting for Life*, p. 67.

29 D. Levinson and M. Ember (eds.), *The Encyclopaedia of Cultural Anthropology* (New York: Henry Holt, 1996), Vol. II, pp. 618–21.

30 M. Rothbart; 'Incongruity, Humour, Play and Self-regulation of Arousal in Young Children', in Chapman and Foot (eds.), *Humour and Laughter: Theory, Research and Applications* (Chichester, 1976).

31 See Wilson, *Scandal*.

32 One can only agree with Wilson's answer to the question of what heresy *is*: basically, who cares!

33 J. Nederveen Pieterse and Bhikhu Parekh (eds.), 'Shifting Imaginaries: Decolonization, Internal Decolonization, Postcoloniality', in *The Decolonization of the Imagination* (London: Zed Books, 1995), p. 11.

34 Karen Armstrong, *The Battle for God* (New York: Knopf, 2000). Armstrong's framework is based on Johannes Sloek, *Devotional Language*, translated Henrik Mossin (Berlin and New York: 1996).

35 Armstrong, *The Battle for God*, pp. xii–xiii.

36 Morny Joy, 'Images and Imagination', in *Encyclopaedia of Religion* (New York: Macmillan, 1987), Vols VII and VIII. Similarly, Gilbert Durand has discussed the work of writers such as Corbin and the idea of the 'creative imagination': 'We should not be surprised therefore to find that, over the last half century, developments … resulting from Freudian psychoanalysis and Jungian depth psychology have converged with a new orientation of the old history of religion discipline. Thus, with Mircea Eliade, Henry Corbin, and Georges Dumezil – to cite only a few authors – reflections on the phenomenon of religion have broken away from etiological reductions within purely historical, social … contexts to enter the territory of a more anthropological field – one centered on the properly religious function of the creative imagination.' (Gilbert Durand, 'The Imaginal', in *Encyclopaedia of Religion*). While they are not strictly historians of religion or theologians, Luce Irigaray and Julia Kristeva can also be considered as part of this shift.

37 Pieterse and Parekh, *The Decolonization*, pp. 4–5.

38 Ella Shohat and Robert Stam, 'The Cinema after Babel: Language, Difference, Power', in *Screen*, 26, 3–4 (1985): 35–58, cited in Pieterse and Parekh, *The Decolonization*.

39 See Hossein Nasr, *Knowledge and the Sacred* (Edinburgh: Edinburgh University

Press, 1981). The absence of a chasm between faith and knowledge in other religions is why, for example, there is really no equivalent to the creation/evolution debate. It is a non-issue. Similarly, the question of abortion. But as with abortion and Islam, it is perhaps a matter of time before the creation vs evolution 'problem' is imported and the theological debates begin. Until the Cairo conference on population, abortion had never been an issue in Islam.

40 See, for example, Wilfred Cantwell Smith, *Faith and Belief* (Princeton: Princeton University Press, 1979); Jonathan Z. Smith, *Map Is Not Territory* (Leiden: Leiden University Press, 1978); also, Paula Cooey, *Religious Imagination and the Body: A Feminist Analysis* (New York: Oxford University Press, 1994).

41 Gerald J. Larson, 'Discourse about "Religion" in Colonial and Postcolonial India', paper presented to the Critical Theory Group at the National American Academy of Religion Meeting, Kansas City, 24 November 1992, cited in Cooey, *Religious Imagination*, p. 123.

42 Cooey's summation of Larson's research ('Discourse') in *Religious Imagination*, pp. 122–3.

43 Cooey, *ibid.*

44 In Islam, for example, the work of Fatima Mernissi is well known, providing alternative readings to established historic-theological issues and narratives: *Women and Islam: an Historical and Theological Enquiry* (Oxford: Blackwell, 1991); *Hidden from History: Forgotten Queens of Islam* (New York: Polity Press, 1993). See also Farid Esack, *Quran, Liberation and Pluralism* (Oxford: Oneworld, Publishers, 1997). Sachiko Murata's work on gender arrangements in Islam addresses contemporary concerns through classical texts. In the best tradition of comparative studies, it simultaneously demonstrates the parallels between Taoism and Islam: *The Tao of Islam: a Source Book of Gender Rlationships in Islam* (Albany: State University of New York Press, 1992). Similarly, across the Muslim world, women scholars are bringing radical perspectives to the Quran: *For Ourselves: Women Reading the Quran* (WLUML, 1997). In a more imaginative vein, the Iranian writer Shahnur Parsipur evokes an alternative view of female spirituality in the Islamic universe through fiction. Suroosh Irfani: 'The Tree of Paradise and the Meaning of Night: an Odyssey of Consciousness', *Islamic Culture* (July 1996). In a different context, a feminist analysis of the modern Muslim Pakistani intellectual's approach to religion suggests that the liberal is a mirror image of the religious fanatic – soulmates particularly in their narrow view of both women and religion. Durre Ahmed, *Masculinity, Rationality and Religion: a Feminist Perspective* (Lahore: ASR, 1992, 2001).

45 This is a basic idea of, for example, the Andalusian sufi Ibn al Arabi. See William Chittick, *The Sufi Path of Knowledge: Ibn al Arabi's Metaphysics of Imagination* (Albany: State University of New York, 1989).

46 William McGuire (ed.), *The Freud/Jung Letters*, translated Ralph Mannheim and R. F. C. Hull (Princeton: Princeton University Press, 1974), pp. 293–4.

47 Delores William, 'Womanist Theology: Black Women's Voices', in Ursula King (ed.), *Feminist Theology from the Third World: a Reader* (New York: Orbis Books, 1994), p. 83.

48 Mary John Mananzan; 'Theological Perspectives of a Religious Woman Today – Four Trends of the Emerging Spirituality', in Ursula King (ed.), *Feminist Theology*, p. 347.

49 Gregory Bateson, *Mind and Nature* (New York: Dutton, 1994), p. 99.

50 The future is already prefigured in some salient statistics about the Internet: as *Asiaweek* reported, 'If current trends hold, women will make up the majority of the online community in 1999, according to International Data Corp., a US market research firm. During 1997, about 43% of Net surfers were female' (15 January 1999). Similarly, an informal search of the Internet revealed more than eight hundred sites on women and religion. Thousands of other sites related to every conceivable religion, old and new, are listed in Mark Keller, *God and the Internet* (Chicago: IDG Books, 1996).

2

The Goddess–Woman Equation in Śākta Tantras

MADHU KHANNA

It is generally agreed that while women have been kind to religion, religion has not been favourable to them.[1] Feminist critiques of classical Hinduism unequivocally assert that Hinduism betrayed women.[2] The study of the early scriptures, the Vedas, amply proves that women could not become priestesses, run religious institutions, or have direct access to spiritual liberation. These criticisms are often framed in the context of the great divide that exists between the exalted image of the divine feminine and her inferior status on the social plane.

The great epics contain numerous instances of exemplary role models for women, sanctioned by the dominant Brahmanical tradition. Some of the most powerful idealizations and images are illustrated in the characterization of two epic heroines, Śitā and Pāravatī. Śitā in the *Rāmāyana* embodies the ideal Hindu wife who forsakes all the luxuries of life to live with her husband, Rāma, in exile for fourteen years. Abducted by Rāvaṇa, she is held captive in a grove where she spends her days worshipping and waiting for Rāma to rescue her. Finally, when rescued, she is made to undergo *agni-parikṣā*, an ordeal by fire to prove her fidelity. Unable to bear any more, she entreats mother earth to take her back into her womb. The earth cracks and swallows Śitā into her womb. The ideal woman is selfless and has no desire of her own. She is only a passive instrument of others. The other epic heroine is goddess Pāravatī, whose only aim in life was to have Śiva as her husband. To achieve this end, she performs fierce austerities for sixty thousand years. Next, she desires sons and lives happily with her husband, spending a life of devotion and self-sacrifice. The suffering heroines of the Hindu epics are celebrated for their wifely self-effacing virtues. Traditionally, young girls are taught to emulate the exemplary traits of these two heroines. The portrayals of Sītā and Pāravatī are supported by the 'Theology of Subordination' of the feminine, which expounds the notion of male superiority over the female. This view, when reflected on the social cosmos, amounts to the sovereign authority of men, as fathers and husbands, over women. Alongside the role-model legends there is a vast body of literature dealing with *strīdharma*, or the normative *dharma*, that outline the conduct and postures of good and evil to be followed by Hindu women, reinforced in the *dharmaśāstra*[3] and *smṛti*[4] literature. The *Manusmṛti*, or Laws of Manu, for example, compiled from the second century AD, expound the Brahmanic attitudes on caste, theology and law. The Laws of Manu laid the foundation of their social, legal and moral code and introduced several innovations that concerned women. The code eulogized the eternal nature of *dhārmic* marriage and introduced a husband-deifying ideology according to which the spouse must be worshipped as a god by a faithful wife. *Manusmṛti* was also instrumental in abolishing female property rights and prohibiting widow remarriage. Daughters were disqualified from performing *śrāddha* rituals in favour of their fathers. Marital restrictions placed on women decreased their authority considerably and introduced an era of sexual double standards that perpetuated the 'Theology of Subordination' and weakened the autonomy of women.

The bulk of myths linked to Sītā and Pāravatī give us but one paradigm of the goddess–women equation in the continuum of history. Another viewpoint on the ideal Feminine and its corresponding images of women comes from the Śākta Tantras. Outside the pale of mainstream Hinduism, for example in some forms of Tantra, several traditions attempted to create a distinct 'world of their own', setting aside the patriarchal ethos of Brahmanical religion. It must be stressed here that in the Hindu context there is no such category as an absolute *dharma*.[5] Even the views of the dominant tradition, which appear as absolute, are displaced or transformed by an endless series of expropriations and reappropriations of meaning. It is in the context of this very flexible interpretation of gender *dharma* that we frame our discourse. Moreover, given the diverse and culturally pluralistic environment of India, different interpretations can be applied to interpret images of women. If we follow a diachronic analysis we find that texts emerging from different textual milieus present a significant departure from the dominant tradition, and that certain key images of the feminine get recast within their own ontology of the feminine. Alongside these sources, there is a significant body of material, the *Śāktācara* or rules of conduct followed by the Śāktas.[6] The *ācāras* have a much broader frame of reference, as they exemplify the reverential attitude towards women.

References abound on the Śākta attitudes towards women, sexuality, the body and the senses, and the religious roles women are authorized to play. Unfortunately, much of the debate on women in Tantra has centred around their role in sexo-yogic rituals.[7] It is generally held that women are mere passive co-partners, who are 'used' as instruments by men to promote their religious ends. According to this extreme view, at best the woman is a passive receiver; at worst, she is an object of male fantasy. This generic view has gone unquestioned. Within these two shifting self-images there is room for speculation. Few attempts have been made to identify areas within Śākta Tantra which have a positive value for women. The social and ritual roles of women need to be explored in the context of the larger issues of *Śāktācara*. These sources merit consideration, as they illuminate a very different conceptual framework within which the woman is reframed. These pro-women *ācāras* may decentre hierarchies and tilt, if not shift, the balance within the tenuous relationship that exists between *dharma* and gender.

This chapter, then, locates itself in the Śākta Tantras, and addresses the relationship between the idealized image of the feminine, the great goddess of the Śāktas, conceived to be the primal energy of the cosmos, and the secular woman on the human plane. Tantra introduces ways by which meanings and representations of women are approached to promote their autonomy. These ideas challenge the very nature of phallocentric discourse which has permeated the *smārtized* systems of representations that submit women to patriarchal models and images. The chapter explores the attempt of the Tantras to promote a positive and constructive alternative to the 'sexist' image of feminine representation. The chapter is divided into two parts. The first section summarizes the 'reconstruction' of the feminine principle in the Śākta world view; the second traces the form in which the goddess—woman equation is expressed.

The Goddess in Śākta Tantras

The goddess flowering took place in the context of the heterodox movement within Hinduism called Tantra. Tantra embodied a critical and controversial attitude towards women, their sexuality, their relationship with their bodies and senses, social classes and the traditional notion of purity and impurity. The emergence of Śākta Tantrism was characterized by several distinct features. It gave rise to a scriptural corpus dealing exclusively with the goddess cult. The textual sources codified and 'rewrote' goddess theology and descriptions of her nature, her cosmic functions and her relation to the male deity. Goddess theology introduced a female pantheon and cosmology. These inventions transfigured the image of goddess icons. To mark their superiority over male gods, the Tantric goddesses are often depicted either seated, standing or in copulation with their male consorts. By AD 600 and after, the goddess emerges as a rival to the male deities and acquires a distinctive position in her independent cult. With the resurgence of the Tantras (AD 900–1600) she sweeps to a victory that both 'feminizes' and energizes Hinduism.

While there are an innumerable number of goddess personifications, as an illustration I shall refer to two models of the autonomy of the feminine principle. The first, traced to the text of the *Devīmahatmaya*, illustrates the autonomous figure of goddess Durgā. The narrative accommodates the all-embracing image of the goddess in a mythic context. In the myth, she is independent, 'husbandless' and without a male partner. Unlike the epic heroines, her autonomy does not stem from her consorthood. The other image relates to the Pratyabhijñā-based Trika tradition of the goddess Tripurasundarī, whose autonomy is rooted in the androgynous category of the cosmos based on the fundamental inseparability of the dyad of the male (Śiva/Prakāśa) and the female (Śakti/Vimarśā) principles. Though distinct, these two principles form an uninterrupted unity throughout creation.

According to Coburn,

> the *Devī-mahatmaya* must be judged the classic text of Hindu goddess worship, and one of the major religious documents produced in the sub-continent. Its conception of the Devī as singular and unique Śakti makes it intelligible to most monastic Tantric traditions.[8]

The text is sprinkled with Tantric elements throughout. The most celebrated account of the goddess is recounted in a myth which centres around the conflict between the gods and demons. It describes in detail the defeat of Mahisha, a demon who had earned a boon that he would remain invincible to all beings save a woman. Mahisha became so powerful that he defeated the gods and drove them out of their celestial paradise. Angry and powerless, the gods emitted a flood of energy. A radiant substance spewed forth like streams of flames, which combined into a cloud that grew larger and larger until it congealed into the body of a woman. The divine woman, with parts formed by the gods, was given weapons and a lion as a vehicle. She was created to contain the Śakti of the cosmos and so had an edge over the gods, the power to delude and defeat the demons. The Śākta imprint of the text is obvious from the myth of the origin of the goddess. The gods empower her with their potency and entrust the most difficult task of restoring the balance of the cosmos to a woman.

The compilers of the text have adapted the narrative to accommodate the all-pervasive feminine principle in a mythic context. Through the narrative, the text reverses the role of, and violates the model ascribed to Hindu women[9]. Quite contrary to the model set out for women, who are submissive and subordinate to males, Durgā holds forth on her own and needs no one to support or empower her. She is not portrayed in a domestic context. Nor is her charm and body exploited to win a husband. As a battle queen, she is shown playing a role traditionally ascribed to men and assumes an independent and autonomous status. In one episode, the demon Mahisha, seeking a lover, sends his emissary to Durgā. He tries to remind her of her unprotected status.[10] Rather than being suppressed by his patronizing proposal, Durgā challenges him and tells him that she will marry one who will defeat her in battle. Throughout the encounter she remains unperturbed and looks right through the 'male' game.

The legend describes in great detail the fierce battle that ensues. Durgā defeats the demons one by one. When the encounter with her adversary reaches its climax, she splits herself into her most terrible form, armed with a sword as Kālī. She also creates innumerable sister helpers who assist her in battle. On the battlefield, emaciated, widemouthed with red lolling tongues, they devour the army of demons. She, laughing terribly, 'flung the elephants into her mouth, crunched horses and chariots with her teeth, crushing others with her feet; and lick[ed] the blood from the battlefield' until the demon army was destroyed.[11]

In the closing scene the gods acclaim her as the highest principle of the cosmos, as 'the power of creation; preservation and destruction, the ground of Being'. The goddess herself explains that her function is to 'intervene' like an *avatāra*, or incarnation, and restore the balance of the cosmos. In the *Devīmahatmaya*, Durgā's cosmic role is recast through her myth. Although all the goddesses of the Hindu pantheon embody the *śaktis* of the male god, rarely do they manifest their power so openly and powerfully. They are partial *śaktis*. In contrast, Durgā's characterization contains the full blossoming of the *śaktis* concept in its 'totality'.

The other figure of great significance who claims an exclusive status in the Śākta Tantras is the goddess Tripurasundarī. Widely known as Lalitā, Kāmeśvarī, Rājrājeśvarī, Śrīvidyā (after her esoteric fifteen-syllable mantra) or simply Tripurā, she is one of the most sublime personifications of the goddess. The philosophical tradition of Tripura-sundarī is traced to the Pratyabhijñā-based Trika school of the Kashmirian Āgamas. The sophisticated ontology of the Śaivādvaitvāda of Kashmir is absorbed in the feminine theology of the Tripurā cult. The theology of the goddess defines her cosmic role and function and her relation to Śiva, her consort, and the objective world. These sources represent one of the most sophisticated models of Śākta Tantra. In the world view of this tradition, the universe is composed of the union of two principles. They are called Param-Śiva and Vimaraśa-Śakti. Śiva, identified as pure consciousness, is the all-inclusive transcendent essence. Śakti or primal energy, his vibrant, creative power, is personified as the great goddess, his consort. Śiva, the male principle, is the static or inert principle and Śakti is the dynamic aspect of creation. She is the energetic principle that sustains creation. Śakti is the creative power of the cosmos and prime mover of creation. Without her, nothing can stir or be imbued with life. The potent energy of the goddess is the source of empowerment of her male consort: 'Śiva devoid of energy is unable to accomplish anything but he is empowered ... when he is united with his Śakti.'[12]

In her descent for manifestation, there are three principal stages of transformation of Śakti, In the first stage, she is one with Śiva in a blissful union (*sāmarasya*). In the next stage, veiling herself with her own māyā-Śakti, the goddess emanates her threefold energies of Will (*icchā*), Knowledge (*jñāna*) and Action (*kriyā*). The trinity of energies then emanate into the differentiated cosmos. Thus, the essence and character of the goddess is expressed in her triple nature, her name. All-pervasive and all-inclusive, she presides over all the categories of the cosmos, eulogized as a triad. This triad is the basis of the *śrīcakra* symbolism and her nature. Her triadic nature has been interpreted by Bhāskararāya:

> there are three gods, three vedas, three fires, three energies, three notes, three worlds, three abodes, three lotuses, three categories of Brahman and three letters of mantra. Whatever in this world in threefold, as the three objects of human desire, O goddess, your name [Tri-purā] is in accordance with all these.[13]

The two principles, Śiva and Śakti, are the ultimate cause of creation and are distinguished in all composite things, but are one in essence. Thus all the polarities of life – such as body and mind/soul, subject and object, truth and falsehood, inertia and activity, light and darkness, male and female, purity and impurity – can be subsumed under these two principles. The most fundamental teaching of this school is that the entire universe is composed of these two opposite but complementary male and female principles. From the minute atom to the galaxy, everything has an androgynous kernel and is an amalgam of the two. This theology is mapped out symbolically in the most significant aniconic symbol of the goddess, the *śrīcakra*. The *śrīcakra* is composed of nine interlacing triangles: five *śakti* triangles with their apex downwards and four *śiva* triangles with their apex upwards. These nine triangles are superimposed on one another to form the cosmic field of creation. They are encircled by two rings of lotus petals and a square, centred around a *bindu*. The *bindu* at the centre symbolizes the state of unity of Śiva-Śakti. The circuits encircling the invisible *bindu* mark out the evolutionary stages of manifold creation. The *śrīcakra* is the goddess in the fullness of creation and embodies the two dynamic flows of the cosmos, emanation and involution, explained in her theology.

Each goddess of her respective cult is the source of an array of female personifications who are considered to be parts of her emanations.[14] They emerge from her body as sparks emanate from fire. These goddesses personify different aspects of the principal goddess and preside over different orders of manifestation. They facilitate different cosmic functions. Tripurasundarī, for example, has 110 emanations who preside over the *śrīcakra* to symbolize the subtle and gross levels of the cosmos. Her most intimate emanations are the sixteen Nityāśaktis. Kālī manifests in ten forms as Mahāvidyās, Tārā, Bhuvanesvari, etcetera. The fifty letters of the Sanskrit phonemes, known as Mātrikās, also have their female personifications.

One of the most distinctive features of the Śākta goddess is that she is no longer idealized as merely a wife of the male god, but is conceived of as his creator. She is the transforming power of creation and in that cosmic role appropriates the powers and attributes of the holy trinity who are visualized as no more than her mounts.[15] Several sources reiterate that the power and strength of the holy trinity comes from the goddess alone. In her presence, the might of the male deities is humbled.

> The rumour goes that Brahmā is the creator, Viṣṇu
> Is the Preserver, and Maheśvara is the Destroyer!
> Is this true? O goddess, through Thy force,
> That we create, preserve and destroy.[16]

This is the standard imagery that celebrates the goddess's autonomy over the holy trinity. From a purely Śākta perspective, the goddess not only contains the functions of the trinity but also eclipses the supremacy of the quiescient Śiva and the trinity. She is a complete representation of all the attributes of Śiva. Thus:

> O Energy of Śiva, obeisance offered to thy feet will of itself be homage to the three gods, who are born of thy three qualities.[17]

In the Śākta Tantras, the goddess reclaims her supremacy by combining multiple traits in her characterization. The comely husband-obeying figure of an earlier period is replaced by powerful autonomous personifications. The goddess combines the dynamic polarity of contrasting traits: benign and terrifying, erotic and demure, motherly and virginal, saintly and heroic, ferociously powerful yet calm and silent.

> At the time of giving birth she is a mother,
> At the time of worship, she is a divinity,
> At the time of union, she is a consort,
> And at the time of death, she is Kālikā herself.[18]

The goddess is 'recreated' to accommodate contrasting traits and is conceived of as an apocalyptic fusion of benign (*saumya*) and terrifying (*raudra*) qualities. These two traits are well represented in the mythology of Durgā. Durgā is propitiated as a protector and preserver of the cosmos when she assumes a peace-loving, benign form as a mother of the universe, bestowing beneficence, compassion and mercy. Her auspicious form grants boon and fortune. In this role she embodies the perfection of human qualities. While this is the most sublime of her personifications, she also veils another identity of guarding and protecting the cosmos from anti-divine forces. She is approached by the gods at an hour of cosmic crisis when the demons are intent upon disturbing the stability of the world. In her destructive role as a demon slayer and a battle queen, her benign features are transfigured into fierce ones. In the legend of the *Devīmahatmaya*, when the confrontation with the demon army reaches its furious climax, the goddess creates her terrible epithet in Kālā and assumes a new visage. The golden-complexioned, three-eyed goddess is instantly transformed into a dreadful and ferocious goddess, Kālā, whose complexion is black as ink. In contrast to the radiant and comely Durgā, Kālā is emaciated, with deep sunken red eyes and a lean, lolling tongue. She stands in the battlefield as an ultimate image of fury and a condensation of the power of annihilation. As an apocalyptic fusion of dynamic polarities, the goddess embodies the fullness of complementary categories of the cosmos, of life/creation and of death/destruction. The terrifying forms of the goddess are portrayed very vividly in her myths, but this portrayal can be understood and expressed in pure abstract and philosophical terms. Some goddesses, like the goddess Tripurasundarī, assume a creative and destructive role, but the destructive role is not overtly immanent in a 'terrifying' manifestation, but is latent in her cosmic function.

Beyond these extreme, all-embracing embodiments, the goddess has been portrayed as an omniscient and omnipotent deity transcending limitations of space and time (*deśakālānvacchinna*), as having no parts (*niṣkala*) and no qualities (*nirguṇa*). In this highest state (*parā/ādyā*) she is looked upon as a non-gendered deity, transcending the distinctions of empiric existence. Devī herself explains her sublime nature in the *Devīgītā*:

Wise men think of me in terms of *cit*, *saṃvit*, *parabranman*, etc. My original form is beyond inference, beyond end, beyond illustration and even beyond the concepts of life and death. I am identical with my energy called *māyā* which is neither *sat* [existent, real], neither *asat* [non-existent, unreal], nor a combination of both; it is beyond all these which exists until the final end. This *māyā* which is my inherent perpetual energy is like the heat of the fire, rays of the sun and light of the moon.... This *māyā* of mine is variously called *tapas*, *tamas*, *jaḍa*, *jñāna*, *pradhāna*, *prakṛti*, *śakti*, *aja*, etc. The Śaivas call it *vimarśa* while those well-versed in the Vedas call it *avidyā*.[19]

In summary, then, we may say that in the Śākta Tantras the epiphany is never a single creation but contains a total, all-inclusive vision of the whole. In this 'total' vision there is no room for fragmentation, and her association with her physical counterpart, the real woman on earth, is conceived to be *actual*. The philosophical position taken up by the Tantras dictates that women are extensions of the divine feminine.

Goddess–Woman Equation

One of the most interesting features of Śākta Tantra is that women share a continuity of being with the goddess. All women – irrespective of their caste, creed, age, status or personal accomplishments – are regarded as the physical incarnations of *Śakti*, the divine cosmic energy, the great goddess. All women at birth are the bearers of an intrinsic *Śakti*. This Śaktihood is not extrinsic to their female experience as something to be acquired from outside of selfhood, but a spark which inhered naturally as a part of being at birth. For this reason, respectful sayings and tributes are paid to women exalting their Śaktihood and their inseparable connection with the divine counterpart in the goddess. Thus, the woman–goddess equation is echoed throughout the Śakta texts:

Every woman in this world is, indeed, my (human) form.[20]

All women are Thee, and all men are Myself, O beloved. Merely by knowing this, the devotee attains spiritual powers.[21]

Every woman is born into the family (*kula*) of the great mother.[22]

Śākta Tantra does not make any gender evaluations in that they do not consider that women are subordinate to men. They claim that at birth all women, of the all cultures, naturally assume the power and divinity of cosmic energy and they are to be looked upon as the goddess's physical counterpart on earth. There is an inseparable bond that unites the physical women with the cosmic as they both reflect one another. It is for this reason that so many praise hymns exalt the nature and attributes of women. Thus we read in the *Śaktisaṃgama Tantra*:

> Woman is the creator of universe,
> The universe is her form:
> Woman is the foundation of the world,
> She is the true form of the body,
> Whatever form she takes...
> Is the superior form.
> In woman is the form of all things,
> Of all that lives and moves in the world.
> There is no jewel rarer than woman,
> There is not, nor has been, nor will be;
> There is no kingdom, no wealth,
> To be compared with a woman;
> There is not, nor has been, nor will be
> Any holy place like unto a woman.
> There is not, nor has been nor will be
> Any holy Yoga to compare with woman,
> No mystical formula nor asceticism to match a woman.
> There is not, nor has been, nor will be
> Any riches more valuable than her.[23]

The uniqueness of Tantra lay in the elaborate praise exalting women, praise that is far from empty of content. A genuine and sincere attempt is made in the Tantras to develop a code of ethics and rules of conduct which are entirely in favour of women. These pro-women codes are described in chapters on *kuladharma*, the rules for Śākta Tantrikas who follow the *Kula-path*, and passages exclusively dealing with the norms of ethics for goddess worshippers *(sāktācara)*. The true Śākta devotee has to honour all women and look upon them with great reverence. Some examples from the sources will show the sensitivity and respect accorded to women:

> Whenever he observes a group of women, the devotee should bow down with respect.[24]

> If by mere chance the gaze of the devotee falls on a woman, he should imagine in his contemplation that he is performing her worship.[25]

> Woman are not to be censured or angered.[26]

The *Tripurārṇava Tantra* says, 'Even outside the sacred circle, all women are born of thy parts' because it is the great goddess alone who, having assumed the form of the physical women, created this world.[27]

Tantra also attempted to take a strict stand against wife beating and sexual abuse of women. Thus the *Kulārṇava Tantra* states that 'one should not beat a woman even with a flower, even if she is guilty of a hundred misdeeds, one should not mind the faults of women, and should make known only their good points'.[28] Men are thus advised 'to desist from hating or hurting women, rather they should honour them in special ways'.[29] 'Men should not be angry at women, even if they (prove to be) wicked.'[30] Extreme sensitivity is shown to the women who are socially vulnerable. Even widows, low-caste women and prostitutes are worthy of respect.[31] The *Parānanda Tantra* says, 'A young courtesan is Brahma.'[32]

In Śakta circles all women, be they young maidens or mature women, are addressed as 'Mā' or 'Devī'. This title protects them from being looked upon in sexual terms. As it is rightly pointed out, 'To call a woman "mother" is a classic way for an Indian male to deflect a woman's hint at marriage or a courtesan's proposition.'[33] What is noteworthy in these texts is that here, perhaps for the first time in Hindu religious history, an attempt is made to actualize the divinity of women in the social sphere, and thus introduce an ethos of equality and reverence for them. In this respect Tantra stands apart from other orthodox traditions in India, for here one finds more than a mere triumph of the divine feminine; further, we get a liberal and definitive conceptual framework which can accommodate pro-women codes as a part of its system.

Body and Senses

The Śakta Tantras value the body and the senses highly. The woman's body and her five senses are made into loci of purity, a view which is radically different from the orthodox perceptions, where a woman's body is safe/pure either when pregnant or when it becomes barren with age and is too old to procreate. Both a woman's body and senses, on one hand, and her latent or manifest spiritual energy on the other, are equated with consciousness (*cit*). All the physical processes – such as her breath, her physical acts and postures, her gestures, her biological processes such as the menstrual cycle and her bodily substances – are considered to be sacred and a manifestation of the goddess. Thus, hair and menstrual flow, traditionally conceived to be impure, unclean and polluting, are said to be pure, clean and energy-bestowing.

To do justice to the Tantric view of the sacrality of the female body, it is necessary to contextualize it in relation to their concept of the divinity of the body. The human body is conceived of as a miniature cosmos. Behind the corporeal frame there exists an 'etheric' double which manifests in subtle form as pulsations of cosmic energy, techni-cally referred to as the *kuṇḍalinī-Śākti*. This Śākta resides in the divine body (*sūkṣma-śarira*), which symbolically mirrors all the elements and astral planes of the outer universe. Whatever forces govern the outer cosmos govern also the inner planes of the body cosmos. It is held in the Tantras that we do not experience our consciousness as external to our body. The subtle aspects of consciousness of the unity of creation, manifests in, and through, the subtle channels of the body cosmos. Tantra has evolved a very elaborate symbolic code of the *cakras*, energy vortices and subtle channels, together with a yoga to unfold the mys-teries of creation. Together with this, the Śākta Tantras also absorbed the traditional knowledge system on the biological basis of the bio-rhythms that govern a woman's body.

From very early times, it was accepted that the rays of the full moon act as a regulating device on the pineal gland, causing ovulation at full moon and menstruation at the new moon in the dark fortnight of the month. The recognition that there is empathy between woman's men-strual cycle and the moon phases became a regulating device for the understanding of female sexuality and what modern feminists would call 'lunaception', a form of natural birth control. Menstrual cycles, governed by the moon, also guided the rhythms of daily survival, to determine the right time for the planting of seeds. Perhaps using these views as a basis – that moon phases are intimately connected to certain parts of the female body – the deity Kāma is understood to travel over the woman's body throughout the entire moon cycle. Consequently, each phase of the moon is equated with certain energy zones of the woman's body in its waxing and waning phases. The energy points marked zones for contemplation during the sexo-yogic ritual of union.[34] It must be understood that Tantra accords a place of value to the body and the senses in the service of spiritual liberation, not as a form of sacrifice but as yoga, which refines the senses into the sublime experience of cosmic unity. Rather than degrading the female body, it celebrates the sacredness of a woman's body and her senses in several forms of non-procreative yogic rituals performed for spiritual liberation.

Cultural attitudes towards the female body and reproductive system are shaped by the attitude towards female sexuality. Although a woman is valued for her fertile powers, the attitude towards menstruating women remained oppressive. In orthodox Brahmanical tradition, a woman is unclean (*aśauca*), defiled and impure (*apavitra*) during menstruation. The idea of menstrual pollution is linked to the symbolic codes of Brahmanical religion. The origin of the polluting act is traced to a myth of god Indra's slaying of the demon Vṛtra (*Rig Veda*, Ch. 1, verse 32). Vṛtra is a vicious demon of drought, a withholder of the waters of heaven, wielding immense power over lightning, mist, hail and thunder. He is figured as a shoulderless serpent, a dragon-like monster whose abode is in the rivers, in the clouds and celestial waters, or in the bowels of the earth. He is a symbol of danger and loss. Indra wages a war against him with his thunderbolt and slays him. By this act Indra, the supreme victor, releases the waters of plentitude which symbolically denote wealth, prosperity, cows and progeny. The texts of the *Dharma Śāstra* reframe a fragment from this myth to describe the reason for a woman's menstrual flow. In the later version of the myth, Indra is punished for the crime of killing Vṛtra, who has assumed the status of a learned Brahman. Aware of the heinous crime, Indra runs helter skelter for protection and asks the womenfolk to take upon themselves the third part of his guilt of Brahmanicide. The women agree to do so in favour of a boon for progeny. The guilt of Brahmanicide appears every month as menstrual flow.[35]

What is to be noted is that while menstruation removes the stain of sin inflicted by Vṛtra on Indra, it is also punishment which serves the purpose of keeping women subservient to the mechanics of patriarchal control. In a manipulative male move, Indra, to free himself of the load of guilt, conveniently transfers it to the passive gender, who remain in eternal bondge to it. It is not surprising, therefore, that the pollution of women during menstruation became a major theme of discourse.[36] A woman during menstruation is compared to a fallen women who is sinful and corrupt:

> On the very day on which a lady's menstrual course beings, she assumes the character of a Chandalini. On the second day [of the menstrual course] she is entitled a sinful woman. On the third day her character amounts to that of a corrupted woman, and on the fourth day she becomes like an anchorite woman. On that day [i.e., the fourth] she gets pure when she has performed her ablutions.[37]

Prescriptions and rules on the modes of the behaviour outlined in the Brahmanical sources reflect severe male control of purely feminine functions:

> [During that period] she shall not apply collyrium to her eyes, nor anoint [her body], nor bathe in water; she shall sleep on the ground; she shall not sleep in the daytime, not touch the fire, not make a rope, nor clean her teeth, nor eat meat, nor look at the planets, nor smile, nor busy herself with [household affairs], nor run; she shall drink out of a large vessel, or out of her joined hands, or out of a copper vessel.[38]

The dread of impurity and temporary untouchability attributed to women, and the overwhelming number of menstrual taboos imposed on them, go to show that the first three days of menstruation were looked upon as dangerous and threatening to women's sexuality. The blood is a potent substance of procreation and source of human life. The involuntary loss of blood 'in excess' poses a danger when a woman's procreative potency expressed through sexuality is capable of being violated by negative forces that may prevent connection. Taboos and restriction were a means to harness and control, at least symbolically, a woman's sexual potency, which should be chanelled only into procreation.

Although, by and large, menstruation taboos are applicable to all Hindu women, there are stray instances where these rules are relaxed in favour of Vaiṣṇava *bhakti*: the liberal ideal of emotional *bhakti* towards Viṣṇu is intended to immunize the woman devotee against the possible consequences of evil haunting her at the time of menstruation.[39] In contrast, in the context of Śākta theology, menstruation was not only normalized, it was given spiritual significance. The theology justified the laws of bodily and menstrual purity by reframing their meaning, to remove gender stigma. Taking a cue from Mary Douglas, who argues that the body may be conceived as a 'symbol' and 'mirror' upon which are inscribed the categories that define the universe, we may see pollution as the zone that violates those boundaries. Protecting one from the lines of demarcation of those boundaries protects one from chaos or meaninglessness. The Śāktas theorize that the boundaries crossed by us are those imposed by our relative understanding of polarities such as good and evil. The boundaries set by society on purity/pollution or good/evil are dissolved through pure awareness of unity. Pure awareness of the unity of creation can change the impure substances and agents into the pure. In direct contrast, the energy-bestowing bodily fluids, such as menstrual blood, are considered to be pure substances since they are a natural extension of the innumerable flows of the cosmos:

> The menustration of women
> Emanates from her body,
> How can it be impure?
> It is a substance through which (the Devotee)
> Attains the supreme state.[40]

> Faeces, urine, menstruation, nails and
> Bones – all these are,
> O beloved, considered to be pure by
> The Master of mantras.[41]

The Śākta Tantras reframe and relocate the menstrual impurity of women in a cosmic context. They view it as a natural flow of the body which is the microcosmic counterpart of the macrocosm. The biological rhythms of the body are a natural extension of a larger cosmic rhythm. The female body is sacred. The life-bestowing power of the goddess is equated with the life-giving power of the blood. This conceptual equivalence is beautifully illustrated in the icon of the goddess Chinnamastā, the goddess holding her decapitated head in her hand while two streams of blood flow into the mouths of her two attendants to nourish them. The reframing of the female body in a larger context in terms of micro–macro correspondences, and its re-endowment with the goddess's sacredness, diminish the psychological guilt, fear and shame attached to menstruation. The Śākta celebrates the sacredness the body exudes. The body is the repository of fluids which are the physical representation of a deity, worthy of offering to the gods. Tantra considers the time of menstruation to be suitable for performing the ritual of union, for it is at this time that a woman's real sexual energy is at its peak.[42] The menstrual blood consists of ova energy containing properties with a large amount of estrogen substance. It has been scientifically validated that, in its idle state in the body, it is the purest form of blood.[43]

Whereas the Brahmanical ideology links menstruation to sin, guilt, punishment and fear, and, by extension, regards a woman's body, senses and sexuality as dangerous and threatening, the Śākta Tantras challenge the orthodox conception and invert the orthodox values to their advantage. The larger-than-life attitude towards the beneficence and sacrality of the female body and its functions thus neutralizes the gender stigma attached to menstruation.

Śakti-pūjā

The affirmation of the women–goddess equation is actualized in ritual worship, where women of all ages and social classes receive worship as goddesses. There are innumerable occasions where the physical woman is adored as a goddess. One of the three most important forms is *kumarī-pūjā*, where young virgins or 'chaste', premenstrual girls receive worship. The young girl is represented as a powerful mother goddess. The *kumarī-pūjā* usually takes place on certain auspicious days dedicated to the goddess. The young girl is made to sit on a special pedestal (*pīṭha*) like the image and offered either five or sixteen ritual offerings. After the worship, she gets up and blesses the devotee who has performed the ceremony. Generally, unmarried girls of a Hindu household also go through this worship for a period of nine days during the autumn *navarātra* festival. For those nine days they are looked upon as incarnations of the weapon-wielding goddess Durgā. After the festival they are again ordinary mortals.

In the second major form of worship, the *suvāsinī-pūjā*, married and unmarried women are worshipped by their husbands or Śākta devotees as living incarnations of Tripurasundarī or Lalitā. They receive worship, either individually or collectively, on certain auspicious occasions. After the image of the goddess has been honoured, her power is visualized as being symbolically transferred to the woman, who is designated as a *suvāsinī*. The woman incarnated then receives ceremonial worship and is empowered. It is obligatory on the part of the worshipper to honour her with gifts and ornaments pleasing to her inclination and personality. After the worship, she symbolically conceives herself to be empowered by the goddess and then, in that mental state, blesses the worshipper. The short spell of her goddesshood invests her life with sacred meaning.

The third form of *śakti-pūjā*, practised exclusively by the Left-Hand Tantrikas, takes the form of the sexo-yogic ritual of union, observed only by an extreme Kaula sect. In the Kaula rite of the five Ms (*pañcamakāra*) offerings of wine, meat, fish, parched grain and ritualized sex are made to the goddess. In this ritual, the physical woman is looked upon as the human incarnation of the goddess on the earthly plane. A very elaborate code of ritual practices has been built into this secret rite. The main focus of the ritual is to use the senses and the body as an instrument of liberation. The rite consists of the arousal and sublimation of the latent sexual energy by uniting the twin ideal of the enjoyer and renouncer in a *bhogātmakam-yoga*, a form of yoga, unique to Tantra, centred on the relish of the sublime senses.

The above *pūjās* can be performed on girls and women of any caste group. As a matter of fact, the tradition of women worship in Śākta celebration or in the secret circles was an attempt to break the impervious boundaries set by caste-ridden hierarchies. Thus, women from widely separated classes, including low-caste virgins or women from the lowest rung of the social ladder, were included in the worship. These rituals attempt to cleave through the rigid norms of social identity.

It is accepted in Śākta circles that the goddess power uses her human vehicle for insightful communication before and during the ritual. The holy communication may not exist in the form of a blessing. It may appear in a dream, or in code language (*sāmketika-bhāṣā*). The women who undergo the ritual are said to express the pure 'truth', and, it is held, they assume an alternative identity during the worship.

Guruship and Transmission of Traditional Knowledge

Women have the authority to become priestesses and gurus, initiate disciples, run their own respective *āśramas* and hold positions of power in the religious sphere. The texts claim that females are the purest source of transmission of sacred revelation. Knowledge of the Tantras must be passed on through *yoginīmukha* or the 'lips of the self-realized female *yoginis*' and spiritually accomplished women. The Āgamas and the Tantras are often cast in the form of a dialogue where the goddess Pāravatī or Bhairavī assumes the form of a guru or teacher as the source of revelation.

It is evident from the list of the masters of several sects, and from an impressive range of textual sources, that many men received their first inspirations and subsequent initiations from female ascetics or *yoginīs*, self-realized female ascetics. It is held that a doctrine, to be valid as revelation, must be revealed by a *yoginī*. The author of *Mahārthamañjarī* has traced how the text was revealed to him in a dream by a *yoginī* who is an invisible transmitter of traditional knowledge and authority. Such *yoginīs* generally appear in a disembodied form, in a dream or in a state of semi-trance.[44] The text of the *Kaulajñāna Nirṇaya* speaks of the *yoginī Kaula* sect. This text embodies a tradition transmitted orally by a line of female ascetics who were accomplished (*siddha*) in *Kaula-Sādhanā*. This tradition has its origin in Assam in north-east India and was popular there. It was transmitted by women who were also designated as *yoginīs* (*Kāmarūpe idam śāstram yoginīnām grihe grihe, Kaulajñāna-Nirṇaya*, Ch. 22, verse 10). We also know that the first recipients of the Tantric wisdom in the Krama sect of Kashmir were the Tantric ascetics who also received the knowledge from the 'lips of the *yoginīs*' (*Yoginīvaktra sambhūta*).[45]

Female saints are not uncommon. One reads of the semi-divine legendary heroine Lopāmudrā, who is credited with starting her own lineage and is known to have transmitted her knowledge to her husband, sage Agastya. The divine lineage of female saints also finds its physical counterpart in earthly women. Thus we come across the name of Muktakeśinī, a highly accomplished seeress of the Hādimata *sampradāya* of the cult of goddess Tripurasundarī in the eleventh century, who was regarded as a living guru of this tradition. There are several references in the Tantras where it is stated that women have the authority to impart initiation (*dīkṣā*). Initiation by a woman is considered to be more efficacious than one given by a man.[46] Initiation by one's mother is the best.[47] This authority is the privilege only of women, not men:

> No rules apply to women, since all women are regarded as gurus, merely by receiving the principle mantra, she assumes the form of a guru. A woman-guru may initiate (others) by reading out the mantra from an authoritative text. Men have no authority to do this, only women are permitted to do so, because they are identical with the supreme deity.[48]

Few examples of this tradition have survived in our day. At the beginning of the twentieth century, Sri Ramakrishna Paramhansa had received initiation from a female Tantric[49] and passed on his spiritual prowess to his wife, Sharada Devi, who is universally regarded as a divine embodiment.[50] In my exploration, I have also come across a Tantric *yoginī* of a very high calibre. Her Holiness Madhobi Ma had five male gurus, who in turn passed their spiritual mantle to her, a woman disciple. She belongs to the Śākta tradition and initiates disciples, men and women of all castes, through *śaktipāt*. She is regarded as a living human icon of goddesses Kālī and Tārā. Her prowess spreads through many disciplines. She is both a guru, a healer, a ritualist, and a divine spiritual personality who has mastered the disciplines of Tantra.[51] This is a dramatic shift in a culture where women, by and large, are not empowered to play such roles.

Tantra gives prominence to the female principle and recognizes the ritual role of women at each state of *sādhanī*. Men and women share the same metaphysical, performative and social space. Several elements of Śākta *dharma* aid women to take to this path. The tradition does not discriminate between caste or gender, as far as the quest of spiritual *sādhanī* is concerned. Both house dwellers, married with children, and unmarried *yoginīs* or female ascetics have access to Tantric practice. The precepts of Śākta Tantra are applicable to men and women alike. In some cases, there are fewer restrictions for women than men.

Conclusion

We have given a broad overview of the feminine principle and a number of pro-women precepts found in the localized *dhārmic* codes of the Śāktas. What is noteworthy is that these stipulations appear in male-authored texts and were therefore legitimized by men. We also looked at how a woman shares unity of being with the goddess in a variety of ritual contexts – as an object of adoration in *śakti-pūjā*, as a guru and as a transmitter of esoteric knowledge. Some radical attitudes of the Śāktas on the body and the senses, and the normative prescriptions on purity and impurity, not only subvert and undercut certain dominant Brahmanical values, but go to show that the Śākta tradition is relatively open and free, and speaks directly about women's experience. The liberal attitude towards women has been conferred by the nature of Tantric ritual, which, by definition, is not 'diamorphic' or divided along gender lines. The male–female complementarity which lies at the heart of the Tantric philosophy continues to assert itself on all levels of the Śākta universe from the philosophical to the ritualistic. The pro-women precepts safeguard women's religious roles. This is perhaps one of the rare instances of a gender-inclusive mode of *dharma* in Indian religious history.

In contrast to the orthodox view, the vision of the Tantric goddess is supported by the theology of male–female equivalence. Here the male and female are coeval and the goddess's autonomy is taken for granted as a necessary condition for her survival. This archetype significantly alters our perception of male–female relationships and our view of ourselves in several dimension: physical/erotic, intellectual, social and cosmic. The goddess traditions in India – the first of which portrays the goddess as the wife of the masculine deity, while the other represents her as the energetic counterpart of the male consort – invite us to a more complete understanding of our personhood and also reveal to us what feminine nature is all about.

I make no exclusive claim that the Śākta women were/are not under the influence of the patriarchial structures of Brahmanical ortho-doxy. What I have explored in the foregoing discussion is that Śākta attitudes towards women appear to be relatively more consistent and in harmony with the lofty abstractions of the image of the feminine prin-ciple as both divine and mortal, transcendent and immanent, ideal and real, simultaneously. It is fair to say that, despite the constraints imposed by the orthodoxy on women, those who took this path fear-lessly and with devotion claimed their rightful positions as teachers, saints, mystics and accomplished *yoginīs*.

Notes and References

1 Note the oft-quoted remark made by the German Indologist Moriz Winter-
  nitz: 'Women have always been the best friends of religion, but religion has
  generally not been a friend of women', quoted by Annemarie Schimmel in her
  Preface to *The Tao of Islam* by Sachiko Murata (Albany: State University of
  New York Press, 1992). See M. Winternitz, *Die Frau in den indischen Religioness,
  Teuk I, Due Frau in Brahmanismus* (Leipzig: 1920).

2 See S. Kakkar, 'Feminine Identity in India', in R. Ghadially (ed.), *Women in
  Indian Society* (New Delhi: 1988), pp. 44–68; S. Wadley, 'Women and the
  Hindu Tradition', in *ibid.*, pp. 23–43; Sukumari Bhattacharjee, 'Motherhood in
  Ancient India', *Economic and Political Weekly* (Samaeekstra Foundation publica-
  tion), 25, 42–3 (20–27 October 1990): 50–7; Uma Chakravarti, 'Con-
  ceptualising Brahmanical Patriarchy in Early India: Gender, Caste Class and
  State', *Economic and Political Weekly* (3 April 1993): 579–85; Uma Chakravarti
  and Kum Kum Roy, 'In Search of Our Past: a Review of the Limitation and
  Possibilities of the Historigraphy of Women in Early India', *Economic and
  Political Weekly* (30 April 1988): 2–10.

3 On the *dharma* of women, see P. V. Kane, *History of Dharma Śāstra* (Poona:
  Bhandarkar Oriental Research Institute, second edition 1973–90, first edition
  1930–62); J. Leslie, *The Perfect Wife: the Orthodox Hindu Women according to the
  Strīdharmapaddhati of Trayambakayajvan* (Delhi: Oxford University South Asian
  Series, 1989).

4 For women's position in ancient India, see notes 2 and 3.

5 Derrett's remarks on the nature of *dharma* are worthy of note: 'The theoretical
  standards of the unseen world are not expected to be reproduced in the "seen"
  world uniformly.' See J. Duncan M. Derrett. *Dharmaśāstra and Juridical Literature*,
  in the series, *A History of Indian Literature*, Jan Gonda (ed.) (Weisbaden: Otto
  Harrassowitz, 1973), p. 13. There are distinct schools of *Dharma Śāstra* supported
  by the religious customs of particular areas. Different schools of *Dharma Śāstra*
  emerged, assimilating local beliefs and customs. The local *dharma* digests are
  treated with authority in that particular region where they were compiled.
  Thus, 'The *Vyavāharamayukha* is regarded as authoritative in South India;
  Vivādaratnākara in Mithila; *Dāyabhāga* in Bengal and Kāmārupa.' Cited in N.
  Sharma, *The Kamarupa School of Dharma Śāstra* (Calcutta: Punthi Pustak, 1994),
  p. 44.

6 These are to be distinguished from the forms of worship which have been recognized in the Tantras, such as *Vedācara, Vāiṣṇavācāra, Śaivācāra, Dakṣiṇācara,
  Vāmācara, Siddhāntacāra, Kāulācara*, etc. *Kulāraṇava Tantra*, eds. Arthur Avalon
  and Taranatha Vidyarnava (London: *Tantrika Texts 5*, Luzac and Co., 1917),
  Ch. 2: verses 6–8.

7 For a recent study of the sexo-yogic rituals practised by the Bauls of Bengal, see
  June McDaniel, 'The Embodiment of God among the Bauls of Bengal', *Journal
  of Feminist Studies in Religion*, 8, 2 (Fall 1992): 27–36. For a popular appraisal of
  the theme, see A. Mookerjee and M. Khanna, *The Tantric Way* (London:

Thames and Hudson, 1977) pp. 165ff.; Lyn Gatewood, *Devi and the Spouse Goddess. Women, Sexuality, and Marriage in India* (New Delhi: Manohar Publications, 1985), pp. 162–71.

8 Thomas Coburn: *Devi Mahatmaya. The Crystallization of the Goddess Tradition* (New Delhi: Motilal Banarasidass, 1984), p. 6.

9 David Kinsley: *Hindu Goddesses, Vision of the Divine Feminine in the Hindu Religious Tradition* (New Delhi: Motilal Banarasidass, 1986), p. 99.

10 *Devīmahatmaya (Durgāsaptaśatī)* (Gorakhpur: Gita Press, n.d), Ch. 5: verses 120ff.

11 *Ibid.*, Ch. 7: verses 10–14.

12 *Nityaṣoḍaśīkārṇava*, ed. V. V. Dwivedi (Varanasi: Yoga-tantra-granthamālā, Vol. 1, Varanaseya Sanskrit Vishvavidyalaya, 1968), Ch. 4: verse 6.

13 *Saubhāgyabhāskara*, Ch. 2: p. 254. For a detailed analysis of the nature and concept of the goddess Tripurasundarī, see Madhu Khanna, 'Concept and Liturgy of the Śrīcakra based on the Śivānanda's Trilogy', unpublished PhD thesis, Oxford University, 1986, Part II.

14 *Devībhāgavata Purāna*, ed. N. Singh (Delhi: Nag Publishers, 1986), Part 9: verses 137–42.

15 *Kālikā Purāṇa*, ed. Viswanarayana Sastri (Varanasi: Bhartiya Vidya Prakashana, 1972) Book I, Ch. 4: verses 55–61.

16 *Devībhāgavata Purāna*, Book 3, Ch. 4: verse 40.

17 *Saundaryalaharā* (The Ocean of Beauty) translated by Pandit S. Subramanya Sastri and T. R. Srinivasa Ayyangar (Madras: Theosophical Publishing House, 1972), verse 25.

18 *Mahārthamañjarā Parimal*, ed. Vraja Vallabha Dwivedi (Varanasi: Yoga-tantra-granthamālā, 5, Varanaseya Sanskrit Vishvavidyalaya, 1972), p.104.

19 *Devībhāgavata Purāna*, Part 7, Ch. 32, verses 2–10.

20 *Devīmahatmaya (Durgāsaptaśatī)*, Ch. 6: verse 2.

21 *Niruttara Tantra*, ed. Ramkrishna Shukla (Prayag: Kalyana Mandir Prakashana, 1979), Ch. 6: verse [4].

22 *Kulārnava Tantra*, Ch. 11: verse 64.

23 *Śaktisamgama Tantra*, ed. Benyatosha Bhattacharya (Baroda: Gaekwad Oriental Series 61, 1978), Part 2, Ch. 13: verses 43–9.

24 *Tripurārnava Tantra*, ed. S. P. Upadhyāya (Varanasi: Yogatantra Granthwade, 12, Sampuruananda Sanskrit Vishva Visvavidyalaya, 1992), Ch. 14: verse 80a.

25 *Kālī Tantra*, in *Kālī Tantra Shastra*, ed. Rajesh Dixit (Agra: Dīpa Publication, 1995, reprint), Ch. 8.

26 *Parānanda Sūtra*, ed. Ramadutta Shukla (Prayag: Kalyana Mandir, 1977), verses 16–17.

27 *Tripurārnava Tantra*, Ch. 14: verse 86; *Niruttara Tantra*, Ch. 2: verse 12a.

28 *Kulārnava Tantra*, Vol. 5, Ch. 7: verses 97–8.

29 *Kaulāvalī Nirṇaya* by Jnānāndanātha, ed. Arthur Avalon (Calcutta: Tantrika Texts 14, Sanskrit Text Depositors, 1907), Ch. 16: verse 33.

30 *Tantrarāja Tantra* by Subhagānanda, eds. Arthur Avalon and Lakshmana Shastri (London: Tantrika Texts 8, Luzac and Co., 1919), Ch. 5: verse 80.

31 *Kaulāvalī Nirṇaya*, Ch. 21: verse 96.

32 *Parānanda Tantra*, ed. Ramadutta Shukla (Prayag: Kalyan Mandir, 1977), verses 16–17. Stephanie Jamison, *Sacrificed Wife, Sacrifier's Wife. Women Ritual and Hospitality in Ancient India* (New York: Oxford University Press, 1996), pp. 12–15, has given us a fine sampling of, 'maxims … [that] define areas of anxiety about women – their fickleness or constancy, their "untruth" or fidelity, their weakness or power, their stupidity or intelligence'. The Tantric maxims stand apart from the ones cited by Jamison.

33 McDaniel, 'The Embodiment of God', p. 36.

34 The points on the female body which are energized on auspicious days of the bright and dark halves of the month are shown in an eighteenth-century painting from Rajasthan: see Mookerjee and Khanna, *The Tantric Way*, p. 178.

35 For it has been declared in the Veda, 'When Indra had slain (Vṛtra) the Threeheaded son of Tvashtri, he was seized by Sin and he considered himself to be tainted with exceedingly great guilt. All beings cried out against him (saying to him), "O Thou slayer of a learned Brahmana! O thou slayer of a learned Brahmana!" "Take upon yourselves the third part of this my guilt (caused by) the murder of a learned Brahman." They answered, "What shall we have (for doing thy wish)?" He replied, "Choose a Boon". They said, "Let us obtain offspring (if our husbands approach us) during the proper season, at pleasure let us dwell (with our husbands) until (our children) are born." He answered, "So be it." (Then) they took upon themselves (the third part of his guilt). That guilt of Brahmana murder appears every month as the menstrual flow.' *Vasiṣṭha Dharma Śāstra*, translated by G. Buhler (Delhi: Sacred Books of the East, Motilal Banarasidass, 1984, reprint), Ch. 5, section 7.

36 'Sānkhyāna–Gṛhyasūtra', in the *Grihya-Sutras, Rules of Vedic Domestic Ceremonies*, translated by Hermann Oldenberg (Delhi: Motilal Banarasidass, 1981, reprint), Ch. 11, Section 12: verse 10; Ch. 4, Section 7: verse 47; Ch.4, Section 11: verse 6; Ch. 6, Section 1: verse 3; 'Parāsara-smṛti', in *The Smṛti Sandarbha*, Vol. 2 (Delhi: Nag Publishers, 1988), Chapter 7, verses 13–19; 'Visnusmṛti', in *ibid.*, Vol. 1, Ch. 20, p. 447; 'Gautamasmṛti' in *ibid.*, Vol. 4, Ch. 18; Manuscript Ch. 3: verse 239: Manuscript Ch. 4: verses 40–2.

37 *Rati Śāstram or The Hindu System of Sexuality*, translated by Abinash Chandra Ghose (Delhi: Nag Publishers, 1977). pp. 50–1.

38 *Vasiṣṭha Dharma Śāstra*, Ch. 5: verse 6.

39 See, for instance, the *Varāha Purāna*, translated by Anibhushan Bhattacharya (Varanasi: Kashi Raj Trust, 1981), Ch. 142: verses 7–11.

40 *Jñānarṇava Tantra*, ed. Ganapataraya Yadavaraya Natu (Poona: Ananda Ashram Sanskrit Granthamala 69, 1977) Ch. 22: verse 31.

41 *Ibid.*, Ch. 22: verses 26–7.

42 Philip Rawson, *The Art of Tantra* (London: Thames and Hudson, 1978), p. 88.

43 Rosemary Dudley, 'She Who Bleeds Does Not Die', in *The Great Goddesses, Heresies: a Feminist Publications on Art and Politics*, 5 (1982): 112–16.

44 *Mahārthamañjarī*, p. 191; cf. *Śivasūtra, The Yoga of Supreme Identity*, translated by

Jaidev Singh (Delhi: Motilal Banarasidass, 1979), p. 4.

45 *Mālinīvijayavārtikā*, Ch. 2: verse 3, cited by Vanjivan Rastogi in *The Krama Tantricism of Kashmir*, Vol. 1 (Delhi: Motilal Banarasidass, 1979), p. 45. See also *Kaulajñāna Nirnaya*, ed. P. C. Bagchi (Calcutta: Glacutta Sanskrit Series No. 3, 1934), Ch. 22: verse 10.

46 Brahmanandagiri, *Sāktānanda Tārānginī* (Ram Kumar Rai, ed.) (Varanasi: Tantragranthamālā. No.17, Pracya Prakashana, 1993), Ch. 2: verse 31a.

47 *Ibid.*, 2.31.b. Also S. P. Upadhyāya (ed.), *Tripurārnava Tantra*, Ch. 1: verses 20a–21.

48 S. P. Upadhyāya (ed.), *Tripurārnava Tantra*, Ch. 1: verses 196–7.

49 See Ghanananda Swami, 'Some Holy Women Figuring in the Life of Ramakrishna', Chapter 14, in *Some Women Saints, East and West.* (Hollywood: Vedanta Press, 1979), pp. 122–35.

50 *Ibid.*, pp. 94–121.

51 See Madhu Khanna, 'Nectar Mother', Chapter 8 in this text. Also, *Voices of Transcendence: My Encounter with Madhobi Ma, a Contemporary Tantric Saint*, HBF Series on 'Women and Religion', Vol. II, *The Hidden Women* (Lahore: HBF, 1998).

3

Women in the Catholic Church

SR MARY JOHN MANANZAN OSB

I

History and Background

I deliberately use 'women religious' instead of 'religious women' because I intend to focus on women who choose the religious state of life. There can be religious women even though they do not enter the religious state. While I provide a general historical background, I will primarily discuss the Philippine experience when speaking of the contemporary situation of women religious.

Women in the Catholic Church

The Catholic Church is rooted in a patriarchal Hebrew–Christian tradition. Although Jesus himself broke through the patriarchal norms of Hebrew society in his relation to women by inviting them to participate in his mission, his followers, it seems, did not learn from him. The early Church, in order to survive as a marginalized community in patriarchal Roman society, had to 'repatriarchalize' itself. As Elizabeth Fiorenza puts it, this was a part of the 'apologetic development of cultural adaptation that was necessary because the early Christian missionary movement, like the Jesus movement in Palestine, was a counter-cultural conflict movement that underlined the patriarchal structure of the Graeco-Roman politeia'.[1] This led to the exclusion of women from church offices: women had to conform to the stereotypical roles of patriarchal culture. It was no longer a woman's call to discipleship that wrought her salvation, but her prescribed role as wife and mother.

This development continued with the Fathers and later on the Doctors of the Church, who were the official interpreters of scripture and tradition. The following is an example of the misogynistic writings of the Father of the Churches.

> Women, you ought to dress yourselves in mourning and rags, representing yourself as penitents bathed in tears, redeeming thus the fault of having ruined the human race. You are the door of hell; you corrupt him whom the devil dare not approach, you finally are the cause why Jesus Christ had to die.[2]

The Bible is often used to justify the discrimination and subordination of woman, especially the Creation story where it is emphasized that she was taken from the rib of Adam and is therefore a derived being. She is supposed to be created only for the sake of Adam because 'it is not good for man to be alone'. And so women feel that they themselves are not significant, but rather that their importance lies in their relationship of service to men. A woman is also accused of being the cause of Adam's sin and therefore a lot of guilt has been implanted in women.

The marriage theology in the Catholic Church is oppressive to the woman, since she is exhorted to be submissive to her husband 'in all things'. The injunction in the marriage rite which admonishes the woman to be 'obedient to her husband' and to the man 'to love his wife' shows the unequal status of woman in the so-called partnership. On her shoulders rests the success or failure of the marriage. Church laws control her reproductive rights, giving very limited possibilities of fertility control.

Church teachings put up as the ideal a submissive, meek and long-suffering woman. These are characteristics of a victim's consciousness. Since women are conditioned to have a victim's consciousness it is no wonder that they are continuously victimized. The overemphasis on virginity has made Catholic women, especially, feel like trash when they lose it, whether with or without their consent. Many prostitutes interviewed cite loss of virginity, in incest or rape, as the precipitating factor in their entering the trade, along with economic need as the basic reason. They think that since loss of virginity has made them 'worthless' and 'fit for the garbage' they might as well earn money from their bodies.

The clergy is exclusively male and the decision-making power rests with it; the main decisions in the Catholic Church are made exclusively by men. In the liturgy women are not given any major roles, even if the Church is 80 per cent full of women. The language is often sexist, calling on the 'brothers' to pray for the 'salvation of all men'.

Undeniably, the Catholic Church is one of the most patriarchal and hierarchical institutions in society today. It is in this context that I would like to discuss the status, role and development of Catholic women religious.

Women religious in Church History

Religious communities have always been considered as prophetic bodies in the Church. Women religious communities are doubly so since women religious live a life that is a deviation from the normal lives of women, who are brought up primarily to be wives and mothers.

Preceding any formal development of male religious were the virgins who were formally recognized by the Church as early as 100 CE.[3] They lived in their own homes and came together only for communal prayers and charitable services. During the age of the Desert Fathers, there were also Desert Mothers, though they are seldom mentioned in mainstream Church history. They were holy women who were sought after for the good advice they dispensed through parables.

In the West, the first evidence for the existence of female communities is the treatise of St Augustine, Bishop of Hippo, addressed to the Virgins of the city. These women were consecrated according to the rubrics of the local Church. Later on in the sixth century, a more universal formula was composed.

From the seventh to the tenth centuries, there were mushrooming communities of women governed by abbesses, who frequently assumed powers usually reserved for bishops, abbots and ordained clergy, such as hearing the confessions of their nuns. It is also remarkable that in double monasteries of monks and nuns, the abbess was usually the main authority for both communities. She exercised both religious and secular powers. She was responsible for the feudal obligations of vassals and for the administration of the lands which gave sustenance to the communities. She took charge of collecting tithes and chose the members of the village clergy.[4]

In a feudal society, the monasteries of women were the rare venues for the education of women. Abbesses taught their nuns to read and write Latin, equipping them to assume ecclesiastical and political responsibilities. Diarmuid O' Murchu gives examples of these powerful women.

> In the mid-seventh century, Salaberga of Laon in France founded seven Churches and took responsibility for 300 nuns. Her contemporary St Fura founded a joint community at Brie in the north of France, ruled as abbess, and assumed priestly and Episcopal power, hearing confessions and excommunicating members. In the twelfth century, at the Spanish Abbey of Las Huelgas, the nuns appointed their own confessors. As late as 1230, the Abbess Dona Sanchia Garcia blessed the novices like a priest and presided at chapter meetings for the twelve other monasteries under her authority.
>
> Of all these abbesses, perhaps the best known is Hildegard of Bingen (1098–1179) whose scientific treatises impressed both popes and emperors. She was also a doctor, pharmacist, playwright, poet, painter and musician.[5]

But, as early as the twelfth century, attempts were made to halt the power of women religious. Subsequent communities were founded with priests to act as chaplains, administrators and confessors to the nuns. In 1140, the Decretum legislated that only men could be ordained and this restricted ecclesiastical learning exclusively to them. In 1298, the Papal Bull Periculoso of Pope Boniface VIII ordained enclosure for nuns and was fully endorsed at the Council of Trent in 1563. According to this ruling, nuns could not leave their cloisters or receive visitors.

Because of this, alternative religious communities sprang up, such as the Beguines, in France, Belgium and West Germany, who tried to live religious lives without the restrictions. Some other alternative groups were later on declared to be heretical by the Church.

Despite their confinement, during the outbreak of the Black Plague the nuns extended outstanding service and hospitality to the afflicted. This inspired the foundation of later religious communities that were more active in nature, the earliest of which was the Ursuline congregation founded by Angela Mend (1474–1540). The Ursulines devoted themselves to the service of the poor, sick and elderly. Finally, papal approval for conventual but not monastic religious communities of women was granted and many other congregations sprang up such as the Daughters of Charity, the Sisters of Mary Ward and the Sisters of

Mary Mackillop. Later on, there were attempts to once again enclose these sisters. This, in turn, only led to the establishment of lay institutes such as the Teresiana the Grail.

Contemporary classification of religious communities of women includes contemplative congregations, active and missionary congregations, and lay institutes. They are either of papal right – that is, directly under Rome – or diocesan, meaning directly under the Bishop of the diocese who is their founder.

Life of women religious in pre-Vatican times

In order to show the radical change that women religious have undergone in the last 25 years, it is necessary to describe their way of life before the Second Vatican Council.

Even in congregations of active missionary sisters, the confinement was enforced. In other words, the living quarters of the sisters were off-limits to outsiders, nor could the sisters leave their enclosures except for necessary visits such as those to the doctor. They could not visit their relatives, not even dying parents. Relatives could, however, visit them once a month.

Within the community, real personal relationships were discouraged. The members never talked about their former lives; they did not even know each other's family names. Since silence was observed at all times except for necessary conversations and during times of recreation, there really was no time for sharing. There was unquestioning obedience of the rules and superiors. There was also a weekly Culpa which entailed accusing oneself of transgressions of rules in the presence of the community.

One's apostolate was confined to the work of the institution. There was no participation in public affairs and certainly not in the social and political spheres of life. Political activity was confined to voting during elections. Interest in national and world affairs was for the purpose of providing intentions to be prayed for.

The breakthrough: Second Vatican Council

In 1962, Pope John XXIII convened the Second Vatican Council which lasted until 8 December 1965. This ushered the Catholic Church into the modern world. After this event the Church was never the same again, but the group that experienced the most fundamental changes in their lives after Vatican II were the women religious. In a paper on *Emerging Spirituality of Religious Women*, I described this impact of the Council:

> Vatican II was a glorious explosion in our lives. It ushered in fresh air, an openness that gave wings to our heavy cross-bearing spiritual struggle. I do not believe the impact of Vatican II on religious women can ever be overemphasized. It also triggered a crisis that shook religious institutions and saw the exodus of men and women from the religious life. Precisely this crisis brought about more personalistic, less legalistic, more communal, less individualistic, more horizontal than merely vertical trends in the spirituality of the religious. We became human not the genderless neutral beings we appeared to be in pre-Vatican II days. It was because of this renewed humanity that we acquired a sensitivity to the sufferings of our people once we became aware of them.[6]

II

Fundamental Changes in the Life of Women Religious

Allow me to be autobiographical in describing this topic. I believe that my experience is typical of those of other religious women.

As a result of the emphasis put on the personal and professional development of women religious by Vatican II, I was sent by my congregation to study philosophy and theology in Germany and Rome. I became exposed to progressive German theology and acquired a wider horizon in my way of thinking.

After my studies in 1973, 1 came home to a country that had just come under martial law. I taught in a Jesuit University where I joined a group called the Interfaith Theology Circle that aimed at evolving a 'Filipino Theology'. We were criticized for doing intellectual gymnastics because our activities were confined to the academe. After a period of defensiveness, we realized that it was futile to develop such a theology without getting involved in the struggle of the people, who, by this time, had formed the National Liberation Movement.

This was what made me respond to the invitation from a telephone brigade among sisters in 1975. This brigade was calling for volunteers to come to the rescue of 600 striking workers in a wine factory, La Tondena. Such a thing was unheard-of in pre-Vatican days. This was my first experience of military violence. We were helpless when the military carted off the six hundred workers into detention camps. At the end of the biblical reflection that we held in order to understand our experience, we resolved to form a group called 'Friends of the Workers', pledging our help and support to the workers' struggle.

The La Tondena strike inspired about a hundred more in a period of three months and we went from one factory to the next, gaining valuable learning experiences from the people, and developing an insight into the root causes of their problems. While helping the workers we also became involved in the problems of slum dwellers, since they lived in squatter areas. We joined human barricades to stop demolitions of these communities. We formed composite groups that spearheaded rallies and marches and were recruited into negotiating teams to face the military in mass actions. Inevitably, we became involved in campaigns to draw attention to the fate of political detainees who were arrested in marches, rallies and pickets, or snatched from their houses in midnight raids.

I became chairperson of the Task Force for the Orientation of Church Personnel of the Association of Major Religious Superiors. My team and I designed modules for conscience-raising seminars which we gave to religious teachers, priests and church workers all over the country.

As Dean of College of a school for women, I worked out with other members of my faculty a reorientation of the school towards educating for social transformation. We revised our curriculum, methodology and pedagogical approaches, making sure that the students and faculty were exposed to the poor communities and were thus able to achieve an understanding of the injustice and oppression happening in the country.

In 1978, when a series of oil price hikes were decided upon without consulting the people, I helped form the Citizen's Alliance for Consumer Protection and became (as I still am) its Secretary-General. As such, I now found myself giving speeches to thousands of people in rallies, taking part in debates and talk shows on television, and generally using the media to present the people's position on various related issues.

In the late 1970s and early 1980s we spearheaded the establishment of the women's movement in the Philippines. I helped set up three women's organizations and in 1985 was elected National Chairperson of GABRIELA, a country-wide network of women's groups that linked together 200 organizations with about 50,000 individual members.

A number of women religious and women theologians joined the Ecumenical Association of Third World Theologians. I am at present the International Coordinator of the Women's Commission of this organization and our main task is the development of feminist theology from the perspective of Third World women. We understand our task to be the deconstruction of the oppressive factors in the Church and the rethinking and reconstruction of religious concepts, structures and practices to make them liberating forces for women.

Conclusion: Women Religious Today

My experience highlights the broader process of development among women religious in the Philippines. The first change typically is the opportunity for personal and professional growth. I can truly say that in the Philippines the women religious are conspicuously well-educated and professionally trained. They have enjoyed excellent opportunities for psycho-spiritual training and this has helped greatly in the development of their personal maturity. The second strand of development was in the awakening of a social consciousness that made women religious prominent in leading organizations for social transformation. In a recent survey, 80 per cent of the women religious respondents believed that women religious should be involved in politics – and by this they meant taking part in making decisions that affect the community.[7] The third route of development lies in the field of gender awareness. Many religious congregations of women have become sensitive to the gender issue and are putting their resources into raising women's gender awareness and helping female victims of violence.

This does not mean there is no room for improvement. The state of diocesan congregations of religious women is still deplorable. The women religious in these congregations are considered as handmaids

of the diocese serving not only the people but also acting as domestic help in seminaries and houses of bishops or priests. They don't
have the relative autonomy of the congregations under papal right.
And even these are finally still dependent on the Sacred Congregation of Religious Rome for the approval of their constitutions.
Women religious are considered lay people and therefore do not
participate in the major decision making done by the clergy for the
whole Church.

At this point, I would like to cite cases that did not occur in the
Philippines but could possibly occur. One is the case of the women
religious of the United States who signed the advertisement in the *New
York Times* saying that there are differences of opinion regarding the
issue of abortion in the Catholic Church. The signatorees were pres-
sured by the Vatican to retract their statement and those who refused
were forced to leave the convent after some very humiliating incidents.

Another case is that of Ivone Gebara of Brazil who had been disci-
plined by the Vatican for her 'theological errors'. She is now in Leuven
on a forced sabbatical, being obliged to take up theological courses that
are supposed to correct her erroneous opinions. Another is the case of
diocesan nuns in an African diocese where the priests sought sexual
services from them because 'they are afraid of AIDS'.

It is clear that the situation of women religious varies in different
countries and even in different dioceses. Whatever the women religious have gained in personal and professional maturity and in emanci-
pating themselves to the extent of involving themselves and becoming
active in the social transformation of their society, is due to their own
efforts and struggles, in spite of the patriarchy and the hierarchy that
still prevails in the Catholic Church.

Notes and References

1 Elizabeth Fiorenza; 'You Are Not to Be Called Father: Early History in a
   Feminist Perspective', in *Cross Currents,* 29, 3 (1979): 316.
2 Tertullian, quoted in Ander-Egg Ezechiel, *La Mujer Irumpe En La Historia*
   (Madrid: Marsiega, 1980), pp. 123–4.
3 Diarmuid O' Murchu, *Reframing Religious Life*, Missionaries of the Sacred Heart
   (Middlegreen: St. Paul's, 1995), pp. 187.
4 *Ibid.*
5 *Ibid.* p. 89.

6 Sr Mary John Mananzan, 'Emerging Spirituality Among Religious Women', in *Prophets For The Third Millennium* (Manila: Claretian Publications, 1990), pp. 138–9.

7 Institute of Women's Studies, *Women Religious Now: Impact of the Second Vatican Council on Women Religious of the Philippines* (Manila: Institute of Women's Studies, 1993), pp. 77.

4

Women, Psychology and Religion

DURRE S. AHMED

> What is required is a monotheism of reason and heart, a polytheism of imagination and art. – Hegel

While it is all very well to discuss women and, for example, Judaism, Islam or Buddhism, the *assumptions* that we bring to the issues are such that they preclude any genuine recasting of extant and widely held ideas about religion *per se*, as well as about women. It can be argued that the problem is not that religions are biased against women, but, rather, that the problem for women, and perhaps also for men, is a particular conceptual perspective about religion and gender.

This perspective is that of the Western intellectual tradition's 'dead white male', the legacy of Freud and Marx. It is an intellectual heritage which, regardless of where we come from and whatever our faith, has become part of a group of certain unquestioned assumptions. To the extent that modernization and development have touched every corner of the globe, many people have interiorized certain questionable ideas about life, nature, human psychology and religion. These assumptions are best illustrated in the historical development of Western psychology. Given that the roots of psychology are in religion, a critical (re)viewing of the former can assist in a more nuanced approach to the latter.

The word *psyche* means 'soul' and is derived from Greek mythology, referring to a human female of great beauty. As the etymology of 'psychology' suggests, it is a *logos* of the soul and, to this extent, its concerns are as much religious as they are mundane. The religious experience, after all, occurs in the psyche. However, given the dominance of Freud's ideas during the last century, the spiritual dimensions of the psyche have been either ignored or marginalized into the realm of 'pathology'.

Relying extensively on the work of Carl Jung and post-Jungians such as James Hillman, this chapter will discuss how some of our most fundamental assumptions about both women and religion remain distorted, preventing a more realistic understanding of religion generally, and particularly of women's spirituality. The choice of these contrasting perspectives (Freud/Jung) can be criticized for being *passé*, since it seems logical to assume that clinical psychology/psychiatry, like so many other disciplines, must have 'progressed' from their earliest days. While this may be correct in terms of methods available in what can be called the therapy supermarket today, the Freud/Jung differences continue as distinct epistemological premises underlying the vast majority of therapies. They form a tale of two cities, one or other of which almost all psychologists/psychiatrists eventually inhabit.

More importantly, it is at the popular level that Freud's ideas remain powerfully present. The spate of surveys and summaries marking the end of the twentieth century inevitably listed him as among the most influential thinkers of this age, his ideas equated with universal, 'common sense'.[1] Notions such as 'id', 'ego', 'superego' and 'unconscious' are part of the conceptual repertoire of a great many educated persons. On the other hand, Jungian concepts such as 'archetype', 'enantrodromia' or 'anima' cannot claim a similar widespread currency. Finally, even if, theoretically speaking, Freudian ideals of mental health (and religion) have been challenged and discredited in the North, no such claims can be made for psychiatry and clinical psychology in the South, where Freudian notions of personality continue to form a major part of medical and professional training and practice.[2] Even in America, as Steinem has shown, Freud's ideas live on, firmly established in training programmes at universities and medical schools.[3]

The (Post)-Jungian View

The Freudian view of personality, our sense of consciousness and self-awareness, relies extensively on the notion of the 'ego'. The principals and goals of ego consciousness are will-power and reason. Putting it simply, a mentally healthy individual should have a well-developed capacity for rationality, and the ability to exercise will-power over that which may not be amenable to logic and reason. The unconscious, then, is something to be tamed and civilized according to these criteria. Accordingly, religion is an 'infantile neurosis', something that humans invent and cling to out of childish fears. Given the scope of rationality and will-power, it was only a matter of time before religion would be outgrown. As such, it was an 'illusion without a future'. Although Jung agreed with Freud about the existence of the unconscious, his attitude towards the psyche was radically different. Based on many years of psychiatric practice and drawing on a vast knowledge of comparative culture, Jung's model of human consciousness relied less upon theoretical assumptions about what we *should* be like (none of Freud's personality concepts have a biological base), and more on the structure of the psyche *as it exists in human experience.*

The essence of this structure is one of diversity, in which what we term consciousness is numerous mosaics flowing through different levels of awareness. Our everyday life confirms the existence of this flow which is less like a unidirectional river and more of a recursive movement. For example, at any given moment, (pre)occupations, of guilt, loss and love may constantly intrude – fleetingly or forcefully – into whatever may be occupying our attention externally.

This reality of diverse ideas and emotions, according to Jung, is a mirror image of what can be called the earliest model of the psyche, which is mythology, and which is also the earliest expression of religion. The modern mind regards mythology as a quaint subject, evidence of a lost age when people did not have the benefit of science and had to resort to superstitions and stories of the exploits of gods and goddesses. However, when one studies comparative mythology, as Jung did (and it is important to know that every known civilization/society has its store of myths), a different picture emerges. Beneath the seeming confusion of improbable events, there are clear-cut themes, and these recur with variations across cultures throughout history. A study of these themes reveals not only the nature of the gods of the ancients, but also of human nature. These myth themes Jung named archetypes. Granted, today the original idiom of myth is devoid of meaning, not least because of literal over-use. But this language can lead to newer and sometimes more radical perspectives than provided by most contemporary theories of human behaviour. Apart from Jung, it includes, among others, the work of David Miller, Henry Corbin, Ernst Cassirer, Mircea Eliade, Heinrich Zimmer, Gilbert Durand, James Hillman and Joseph Campbell. This analytic approach, then, is not located in ideas of brain physiology, but in what has been called a 'poetic basis of mind'.[4]

One can note in passing that Freud, too, was deeply influenced by the power of mythology, as, for example, in his ideas of the Oedipus complex. Also, it is important to keep in mind that, while he was never given the Nobel prize for medicine, he did receive the Goethe award for literature. As he says about himself:

> A man of letters by instinct, though a doctor by necessity, I conceived the idea of changing over a branch of medicine – psychiatry – into literature. Though I have the appearance of a scientist I was and am a poet and novelist. Psychoanalysis is no more than an interpretation of a literary vocation in terms of psychology and psychopathology.[5]

Archetypal Theory

The concept of the archetype was first elaborated by Jung and, despite the fact that it is difficult to define precisely, the word has been absorbed into general usage. James Hillman further developed this idea and considers archetypes as axiomatic first principles, similar to models which are found in other fields, like 'matter', 'energy', 'health', 'society' and 'art'. These ideas hold worlds together and yet can never be pointed to, accounted for, or even adequately circumscribed. 'They are the deepest patterns of psychic functioning governing the perspectives we have of ourselves and the world, as axiomatic self-evident images to which psychic life and our theories about it ever return.'[6]

From the Jungian perspective, archetypes are symbolic representations of typical human experiences, but experienced in such a way that they have a profound, even cosmic significance for the individual. All of us, at one time or another, have experienced such situations, which, on one hand, can be considered banal in their commonness. Yet to deny that we have never been gripped by them – have been *moved* to tears of joy, sorrow, desperation or childish exultation – would be dishonest. When we have such universal experiences, and when the discourse of ordinary life is inadequate to express them, it is an archetypal experience. They are most commonly expressed through symbols, and to study human nature at its most basic level is to study the symbols of its culture(s), mythology, art, religion, architecture, drama, epic, ritual. The fact is that, despite the advancement of knowledge in various fields, human nature as such is really no different from what it was at the beginning of recorded history. We have absolutely no evidence that we are in any sense *better* than our ancestors. Life remains at heart the same – love, ambition, sexual desire, power, defeat, security, confusion, competition, betrayal, despair, and all their opposites and much more. In short, the stuff of life is unchanging.

Male, Female and Psychological 'Polytheism'

While Freud gave a rather neat psychological framework (id, ego, superego, etcetera) of the psyche, the reality, whether in the clinic or real life, is much more messy. It is, in fact, more in keeping with the pantheon of mythology, in which there is no single, permanent, perpetually ruling god. Different gods – male and female – have different domains and there is a constant intermingling of domains. Even the gods are human, behaving frequently in (in)human ways – for example, in the experience of jealousy and vicious anger. Mars, god of bloodshed and war, has a secret affair with Venus. Apollo, god of reason and learning, could be quite irrational with humans and other gods. The gods and goddesses, like ourselves, are multi-faceted. On one hand, they are benevolent and responsible for their various domains: agriculture, love, marriage, health, war, knowledge, death. On the other hand, they are quite capable of treachery, cruelty and caprice. In this they are very much like you and me and our consciousness as we *experience* it, in which different archetypes exit and enter in ways that are beyond our control: moods of elation, depression, fleeting thoughts of prurience and passion, saying and doing things we did not intend, from lying to over-eating to being haunted by conflicts of desire, betrayal and vengeance.

So our psyches are 'polytheistic' by nature, that is, they contain both male and female and, as the pantheon suggests, even these have many variations and styles. Pan of the flute also represents panic. Zeus and Apollo, while reflecting some major thrusts of male energy, also have to contend with Hermes and Dionysius, who express a more ambivalent idea of masculinity. Similarly, the Great Mother of distant antiquity is refined into different faces of woman, maiden, seductress, crone and matron. Artemis the huntress is quite different from the mature Aphrodite. Each has many faces and forms.

Within the archetypal perspective, the issues of whether gender is important *vis-à-vis* factors such as socialization take on a marginal importance. As is evident, the gods, whether Greek or Indian, present a range of masculine behaviours from Zeus to the bisexual Dionysius. Similarly, the female form is host to the huntress Artemis, Venus or Kali – to name just a few. Each is a *style* of consciousness, suggesting different perspectives on life, events, relationships; exhibiting many qualities shared by both sexes, and yet uniquely *embodied*.

The Literal and the Symbolic

Another way of understanding the significance of the archetype is to distinguish between the literal and symbolic. Since those two concepts will be referred to frequently, it is important to understand the basis of distinction.

Human existence functions as a unified whole but for heuristic purposes one talks of the 'mind–body' spectrum. That is, there is an awareness of body but there is also a complete *inner* world that we inhabit – consciousness – where body awareness recedes into the background. The first is literal, the second symbolic. To the extent that we are physical and creative beings, what is literally so is at some level symbolically true, and vice versa. This is the essence of the concept of the archetype, which can be expanded into the categories of the individual and the collective.

The collective, our social aspect, in order to adequately express itself requires the symbolic, something which will unite and yet be transpersonal. Symbols therefore are flexible: ambiguous and open-ended enough to 'receive' and respect individual differences. At the same time, in so far as we are hostage to the physical, the symbolic cannot but be expressed through physical means. That is, there has to be an image (such as a flag), sound, movement (ritual) or person, which gives form to the symbol. The content, in so far as it pertains to the individual, is literal and can even be precise. The form reflecting the collective is more open-ended, subject to variation, and can never be totally circumscribed. If this circumscription or pinning down occurs, the symbol loses its uniting 'power'; the individual (literal) becomes dominant, and diversity with its requirement of interpretation is excluded. But the power of the idea lives on in the individual in terms of affect.

From the Jungian perspective, the modern understanding of symbols – such as in anthropology and semiotics – although claiming to maintain this distinction, does not do so. Their interpretation of symbols is more an interpretation of signs (such as the matchstick figures for male/female public restrooms). This is allegorical, not symbolic. True symbols, those which abide over a considerable period of time, because they have an affective element capable of 'holding' a particular emotion or idea – the veil, the Kaba, Hercules, mother – can never be fully explained and will always have an element of mystery: an individually unknowable, transpersonal element. As Henry Corbin remarked, 'symbols say that which cannot be said in any other way'.[7]

The Myth of the Hero

The sort of thinking that dominates our ideas about religion, especially within the Western intellectual tradition, can be seen as flowing from the myth of the hero. The story of the hero is a universal one. It can be found in legends, myths and stories the world over and, its myriad variations notwithstanding, certain themes remain common. Typically, it is a story describing the birth of a boy in unusual circumstances where he is, for example, missing a parent, or is the long-awaited child of a royal couple, or perhaps is born in a very humble situation. The child is raised under conditions of ever-present danger and frequently exhibits early proof of superhuman powers. There follows a difficult journey or quest for treasure, or perhaps a special mission which brings him to a position of prominence. This stage involves a series of confrontations with a range of frightening forces and culminates in the hero's eventual victory and his being acknowledged as a ruler, unifier, redeemer and giver of laws. For some time after this, all is well until his final fall, when death comes to signal human mortality. Frequently it is either through loss of favour with gods or men, his fallibility to the sin of pride (hubris), through a betrayal, or as a heroic self-sacrifice. Some better-known examples of this hero figure are those of Perseus,

Hercules, Achilles, Prometheus, Superman and Rambo. (It is perhaps reflective of the age that modern figures like the last two refuse to undergo the final decline and fall.)

The archetypal story of the hero can be interpreted as an account of the development of consciousness, especially in the earlier stages of male adulthood. The initiation ritual and rites of passage in 'primitive' cultures can be seen as preparatory enactment of the attitude which is required for the process of separation from familial protection and of a symbolic death leading to a rebirth as member of the adult community.[8] The myth of the hero can also be understood as the emergence of the faculties of will and reason. Heroic tales emphasize these as the two pre-eminent qualities required for victory. Frequently, there is a violent experience during which the hero must undergo enormous tests of physical endurance. Similarly, he must plan complicated campaigns and carefully calculate his route to survival and eventual triumph. Tortuous initiation rites which test the initiate's capacity to survive under difficult circumstances reflect this psychic process of the development of the powers of will and reason. It is interesting to note in passing that the life stories of the founders of the monotheistic – and other – traditions bear close parallels to the hero myths: for example, Christ, Buddha and Moses.

The heroic story of the ascending, conquering male, is literally and symbolically evident as a vertical movement from South to North, from the Mediterranean era in which the earliest dominant deities were images of the Great Mother to the end of the Greek period and its domination by the heroic gods.[9] This 'upward' movement of the hero is parallelled in the domain of religion, in which Roman Catholicism and the significance of Mary is overtaken by the Protestant ethic in Northern Germany. It is important to remember that the foundations of modern science and other crucial, consciousness-changing technologies such as the printing press emerged from the North Germanic milieu. According to Jung, the hero myth was subsumed into Protestant Christianity, leading to the fusion of a purely masculine god with heroic (masculine) ideals of will-power and reason, along with a theological schema associated with light, height and law. He termed this mindset as the 'West's true religion … a monotheism of consciousness'.[10] It is a mindset which places overwhelming emphasis on singularity of meaning and renders invalid all other possibilities. Consequently it is unable to cope with ambiguity, paradox and the symbolic, which are as much a part of being human as they are of the divine.

Conscious Male, Unconscious Female

In psychological terms, the hero's ascent is evident in Freud's conception of personality. What we call ego is expected to be 'in charge', especially of the id and its demonic forces. The id is, of course, 'down below' (unconscious), containing all that is different from the ego's principles of will-power and reason. The diversity and multiplicity of the mythological pantheon, full of what Jung called 'the little people' of the psyche, are repressed and denied expression; they are seen by the heroic ego only as 'symptoms' of a dis-eased and dis-ordered mind.[11] In Jungian terms, the gods, and especially the goddesses, have become diseases. Significantly, then, the first two 'diseases' to be discovered were hysteria, which is classically a woman's disease (the wandering uterus), and schizophrenia, or multiple personality. It was almost as if the psyche's inherent diversity, including its feminine dimension as represented by the goddesses, erupted in protest, only to be labelled as 'symptoms' by the heroic ego and modern psychology, the latter now no longer a *logos* of the soul but increasingly a 'science' of behaviour, of a 'mind' residing principally in the brain.

Thus, given psychology's archetypal roots in religion, much of what we call psychopathology can be considered a secular term for 'heretical' tendencies. To the extent that it was primarily the goddess(es) (the feminine) which had been suppressed, it is no wonder, then, that across the world women tend to be given more psychiatric pills than men having the *same* condition.[12] Today, women in the US receive *twice* as many prescriptions for psychotherapeutic drugs, more multiple and repeat prescriptions, and more prescriptions for excessive dosages than men.[13] Given the poverty, lack of education and the power of modern psychiatry in the South, the situation here is much worse.[14]

The Freudian model, of a high fortress containing an ego based on rationality and will-power that surveys the scene 'below' (the feminine), finds its counterpart in the Cartesian mind–body conception and the dictum, 'I *think* therefore I exist.' The body is below the mind/brain, it is feminine (emotions/feeling) as opposed to the masculine head (thinking). Mind over matter.

All women must aspire to this essentially Western, male construction of what constitutes desirable criteria of mental health. These criteria, according to Hillman, are overwhelmingly masculine, Aryan, Apollonic, Germanic, positivistic, rational, Cartesian. They leave no room for anything different, feminine, intermediate, ambiguous, metaphorical/symbolic. To the extent that these criteria are disconnected from feelings and emotions, the equating of body/woman has covert religious implications. As Cooey points out,

> The body metaphorically understood as a land of emotions suggests an ambiguity of the body as both site for an artifact of human imagination, as well as human ambivalence toward the body, an ambivalence that saturates religious symbolism.[15]

Masculine North, Feminine South

Freud's ideas are inseparable from his historical and cultural context. The concept of the ascending hero-ego is a nineteenth-century one, based on the (now) primitive Darwinian idea of dominant over recessive characteristics. Similarly, the approach to the unconscious is fundamentally imperialistic, regarding the id as something to be tamed, taken over, colonized. Freud's classic description of the purpose of analysis and consciousness states: 'To strengthen the ego, to make it independent of the superego, to widen the field of perception and enlarge its organization so that it can appropriate fresh portions of the id, where id was there ego shall be. It is a work of culture.'[16] Likewise, whether in ideals of health, progress, development or science, alternative approaches are denigrated on the basis that they are not rational. The only value is placed on reason, power and 'hard' facts. This phallogocentricity is understandable, if one keeps in mind that the hero myth is an adolescent one, an age when the sexual impulse is at its peak in males. The metaphors of science reflect this impulse of power, dominance and/or male sexuality.[17]

As Hillman puts it, South is both an ethnic, cultural, geographic place and a symbolic one.[18] Thus 'South', is not simply 'out there', but within, as the unconscious which is 'down there, below'. Psychologically, it is those areas, emotions, experiences, perspectives which are (1) different from the (masculine) ego and its emphasis on power and rationality; and (2) inclusive not only of other cultures, but of women as a whole, whether North or South. South is the (soft) body, which needs to be ruled (or denied) by the (hard) head. South is nature and the 'other', which the colonial enterprise sought to 'rape', 'tame' or 'civilize'.

Monotheism of Consciousness

In referring to what Jung called the 'West's true religion … a mono-theism of consciousness', one must distinguish between a *belief* and an *attitude,* and one can exist without the other. Reference has been made to the 'polytheistic' nature of the psyche, the pantheon within. And when one studies the history of the monotheisms – and their earlier substance – this psychological polytheism is still evident. In Judaism, God is essentially unnamable and the Torah has a myriad faces, one for each Jew in exile. Similarly in Islam there are the proverbial 99 names of Allah. So we are talking here of a *psychological* monotheism which refers to a *literal* attitude towards what are primarily psychological/symbolic events. The heroic (Freudian) ego is unable to deal with dif-ference, diversity and the symbolic, and exemplifies this monotheism of consciousness.[19]

Monotheism, then, is not simply a religious perspective. In so far as the three traditions incorporate multiplicity within an ideal of unity (God, Yahweh, Allah), at a symbolic level it can be seen as a religious perspective *about* religious perspectives, talking of the unity among all religions. Monotheism of consciousness refers to a literal attitude towards symbolic events in which one vision, in this case the hero's, dominates and renders 'pathological' or 'heretical' what was/is a natural matrix of psychological and religious diversity. The resultant lopsided and exceedingly narrow vision of science, religion, self and society is evident at different levels and is part of the ethos of moder-nity. It was in response to this ethos, and particularly the loss of the feminine, that Jung wrote his well-known *Modern Man in Search of a Soul.*[20]

Such a 'mono' consciousness has no capacity for anything opposing its view, even though life at its most basic physical level is dual, witness the hormones that stream through our blood. 'Contradiction', 'ambiva-lence', 'opposite', 'inconsistent', are dirty words, a sign of mental weakness and demand 'resolution' into a singular frame of meaning and action. These ideas of singularity intellectually rest on the Cartesian assumption about the mind as separated from the body – even though medical phenomena such as phantom pain, and indeed modern psychiatry and its 'discovery' of psychosomatic illness, show that the separation is delusional. If anything, the body houses the 'mind' and modern medical research, especially on AIDS, gives the lie to the Cartesian hypothesis, particularly in emergent disciplines such as psycho-neuro-immunology. To the extent that this Cartesian consciousness is overwhelmingly heroic and masculine, it is particularly prone to pathologize or hereticize that which is most starkly different from it, namely the female and the feminine.

Feminine and Masculine Religions?

The problem, then, is not in the monotheisms *per se*; rather, it lies in the (heroic) consciousness which we bring to the study of religion. This is a totalizing consciousness, which sees things in terms of a legalistic, win/lose, either/or, black/white, monolithic perspective. Fundamentalism, thus, can be religious or secular. In both instances it involves a hypermasculine approach to the construction of both knowledge and meaning regarding self and other. Put another way, consider 'secularism'. This ideology places humans at the centre, believing in progress (upward) to a stage at which, through sheer will-power and reason, humans can live 'ethically'. Today we know the totalizing and violent side of communism. We know – through the Holocaust, communism, Palestine and Bosnia, not to mention incidents such as the mass killings of school children in Britain or the United States – that men are as ready to kill in God's *absence* as they are in His name. Rationality can lead as much to murder as faith. Fanaticism is not born with religion but has its roots deeper in the human psyche.

The problem, then, is of a *psychological* monotheism which makes a monolith of any religion – and, as discussed, this is an overwhelmingly literal and masculine way of looking at issues. To see things symbolically is implicitly to accept ambiguity and a wider spectrum of meaning. *Theos* (God) is the archetype of meaning, and literalizing narrows this idea, excluding multiple possibilities and narrowing the spectrum of meaning. Interpretation is a possibility in the presence of multiple meanings. But modern, masculine consciousness does not permit difference. We must agree with it or are labelled 'mad' or 'bad' – the former by modern psychology, the latter by religion.

All these ideas have to be unlearned by women (and men), especially because in most non-Western cultures such heroic ideals are not the norm. As we all know individually, we are not heroes. The heroic view separates everything, including faith, from reason. Once the separation is made, an inexorable process sets in and a further (heroic) 'leap' must be made to bridge this chasm. Ask a foolish question and get a foolish answer. For example, in a cover story on 'Evil', *Time* magazine posed the juvenile (adolescent) proposition, 'If God is all good and all powerful, why is there evil?' (10 June 1991). The fact is that Divinity Itself has never claimed that It is exclusively *only* kind and good. Whether in the mythic pantheon, or in the proverbial 99 names of Allah, or in the Chinese tradition, the concept of divinity is 'paradoxical', in which opposites exist *simultaneously* as part of unity – as they do, to repeat, even in our bodies, which have both male and female hormones and other dual features. The problem, then, is not with religion but in our lopsided and partial view of it – and of ourselves.

The question, then, is not if there are feminine and masculine religions. Rather, all religions are essentially diverse in their psychology *and* contain a bedrock of the feminine, literally and/or symbolically. Furthermore, from within the archetypal framework, they have been masculinized by a consistent and overwhelming patriarchy in culture and interpretations, frequently violently mutilated by male theologians and politico-religious leaders. As a saying attributed to Hegel states: 'What is required is a "monotheism of reason and heart, a polytheism of imagination and art".'[21]

The Feminine

What does this mean? To see it simply as an image of a goddess, especially in iconic religions such as Judaism and Islam, is to fall into literalizing and again into heroic thinking. Like anything else, 'feminine' is both literal and symbolic, but, as the earlier discussion on these dimensions suggests, in psycho-spiritual discourse the significance of the symbolic cannot be underestimated. Let us remember that images, too, are not meant to be taken literally. They are *containers* for ideas and emotions and religion is primarily a symbolic, psychological business, dealing with the life within and ideas of the unseen, particularly life after death. Thus, in order to talk of 'feminine' and 'masculine' in religion and culture, it is vital to think in symbolic terms, rather than just literally of man and woman.

Life is male and female. Both are essential, representing certain profound concepts as exemplified in the body which contains physical and hormonal elements of both sexes. The graphic representation of the Chinese Yin and Yang in a circle is a symbol of this totality. In Jungian terms masculine and feminine are psychological-symbolic concepts in which, for example, 'masculinity' may represent a certain type of reason, one that is penetrative and analytic. Similarly, 'feminine' represents a different sort of intellectual attitude, one that is receptive, poetic, more inner-oriented rather than an external, action-focused view. Another way of illustrating these ideas is through a symbolic view of the male and female body: the former representing the outer, penetrative aspect of the intellect; the latter its contemplative, generative and receptive capacities. One can speculate that this inner, symbolic and psychological dimension of the spiritual has been overshadowed, impoverished and ignored by modern consciousness. What is valued is the outer, material world – and even that is regarded as something to be owned, mastered and tamed.

The writings of many 'New Age' feminists, or others such as Luce Irigaray[22] who have been labelled 'essentialists', are also relevant to understanding the notion of the feminine as expressed in the term *féminité*. Their emphasis on the body, especially as women can (potentially) experience it (*jouissance*), runs counter to the stereotypes evoked of feminine 'passivity'. As Cooey observes, these writers are

> elevating biology as a source of metaphors that have enormous social and political implications. *Jouissance*, as a celebration of *féminité*, opens up an avenue to transcendence: of not only patriarchal institutions, but of phallogocentric constructions of subjectivity and spirituality as well ....[23]

Thus, keeping the metaphor of the female body in view, one can say that the creative aspect of the divine is 'feminine' – that is, it is the source of life, that which gives birth. From another perspective the (hu)man experience of the divine is feminine, in so far as it requires a psychological attitude of receptivity, and a passivity as related to a contemplative mode. This feminization of consciousness is the opposite of the heroic, masculine outlook, which overvalues mastery, control and action. Religious fundamentalism, then, can be considered a hyper-masculine and extremely lopsided response to religion, one which overvalues action to the point of violence and which is, naturally, anti-feminine in its psychology and, by implication, anti-woman.

In sum, the notion of the feminine is both an aspect of divinity as well as a psychological experience. All religions, particularly mysticism, incorporate this dimension in which human consciousness must put itself into a receptive state in order to experience the divine. This feminization of the psyche in religion is evident across numerous cultures. As Hillman recounts, such 'inner femininity' can be discerned in the religions of different cultures. In the Shamanistic traditions the shaman performs a symbolic change of sex, living as a wife to a man. The integration of the feminine through ritual is found in tribes in Siberia and Patagonia, and among Asiatic Eskimos. Hercules, the great exemplar, man of men, after completing his twelve labours served Queen Oomphale, becoming a servant to a woman. Similarly, in Hindu iconography, the female aspect or Śakti is worshipped along with the male and the centrality of the feminine is especially significant in Tantra. The Buddha's feminine characteristics are obvious as heavy, silent, full-bellied, soft-breasted receptivity. Huge ears reflect the attitude of 'taking in' and the lotus posture represents compassion, a 'soft' feminine virtue. The Sabbath in Jewish tradition is feminine, welcomed on Friday evening as a Queen, the Sekinah. And in Christianity there is the central figure of Mary, representing a passive mood to God's intention.[24] In Islam, the most often repeated attribute/Name of God in the Quran is Al-Rahman, the Gracious and Compassionate One. The etymological roots of 'Rahman' are directly related to those of 'womb'.

The feminine is essentially a constellation of a different consciousness. Today, it is all around us, rising again as archetype and evident in feminism, the empowerment of women, women's scholarship, in the increasing sense of unity with the planet, in ecological awareness, in the widespread urge to reconnect with the body and emotions, in the broad popularity of the Gaia hypothesis, in scientific ideas about chaos, dissipative structures and holism. The list could go on and on. The main point is that it is not an image, but a *consciousness* and it is this consciousness which must be reclaimed within the religious traditions.

Today, we are at a unique point in history where one is barely beginning to understand the 'mystery' of women's spirituality. This includes trying to unravel some of the many conceptual cobwebs and their tangled psycho-cultural history which prevent us from understanding not only religion *per se* but also its relationship with both maleness and femaleness. And before women (and men) can begin to understand and articulate the spirituality of women, they have to understand the history of their modern dominant analytic/intellectual vocabulary, which in its phallogocentricity devalues and pathologizes the domain of the feminine. If this chapter has not touched upon the masculine in similar detail, it is partly in the interest of brevity but also because, as it is, prevalent views on religion and psychology are generally dominated by the masculine perspective, both as an inner psychological attitude and as an exceedingly narrow and harsh vision of God. Such a macho and lopsided vision, as exemplified by fundamentalism, especially lacks the feminine aspects of creativity and compassion.

Finally, it is important to remember that, in accordance with the paradoxical nature of reality as reflected in the Chinese symbol of Yin/Yang, the feminine too has positive and negative aspects. Unfortunately, this has largely been forgotten by many women and especially by those feminists who choose to focus only on the positive – even though, here again, a woman's body reflects such a duality: on one hand, symbolic of the source of life, birth, nurturance; on the other hand, in its cycles of blood and then cessation also signifying decay, dissolution and death. Death, of course, is the ultimate mystery and thus the ultimate concern of religion. These dimensions are vividly illustrated in the awesome power of some of the Greek and Hindu goddesses. The negative aspects of the feminine, like those of the masculine, are also all too apparent, whether in the bitter infighting among and within various feminist movements or in the fascination – especially in the West – with the naked body of woman, now a globally visible image. Separated from the sacred, it becomes an image reflective of an infinite and insatiable fascination, to the point of obsession. If this were not the case, there would have been no multi-milliondollar pornography industry; a few images would have been enough. But because it is an archetypal image in modern consciousness, its endless variations show that it is above all a powerful *idea*, having both positive and negative dimensions, sacred and profane.

As yet there are vast gaps in our knowledge regarding women and religion. The theologian needs to understand the realities of the human psyche. The lay person needs to gain deeper and direct knowledge of theology and to understand the distortions brought about by patriarchy, not only in theology but also in key ideas regarding psychology itself, and especially the psychology of women and the spectrum of their relationship with religion. Because it is only when we have a deeper – more imaginative and yet more realistic – understanding of human nature that we can begin to understand the nature of religion. This is why Socrates' dictum 'Know thyself' continues to resonate with the sayings of the Prophet of Islam: 'Man's knowledge of *himself* comes before his knowledge of God – whosoever knows himself knows his Lord.' As the ancient myths and all religions teach us, when we look inward towards the pantheon within, each of us will discover both the feminine and masculine aspects of the human and the divine.

Notes and References

1   See, for example, *Time* magazine's special issue on the leading thinkers and scientists of the last century. It includes Freud but not Jung (29 March 1999). Or *Newsweek's* cover story, 'Freud's Enduring Legacy: How His Ideas Still Shape Psychotherapy' (4 July 1988).

2   Durre S. Ahmed, *Masculinity, Rationality and Religion: a Feminist Perspective.* (Lahore: ASR, 1994, 2001).

3   Gloria Steinem, *Ms*, 4, 5 (1994).

4   James Hillman, *Revisioning Psychology* (New York: Harper and Row, third edn, 1977), p. xi. While these, too, are mostly 'white males', the point, in any case, is not to dismiss Freud, Marx, etcetera, simply because they are men. Jungian and archetypal theory is fundamentally nearer to many non-Western conceptions of human nature and religion. The present framework is particularly relevant since it categorically acknowledges its strongest connections with among others, Islamic thought. As Hillman says, after Jung, 'the second immediate father' of archetypal psychology is Henry Corbin (1903–1978), the French scholar, philosopher and mystic, principally known for his interpretation of Islamic thought. He goes on to cite the close parallels in ideas of prominent Muslim mystics/philosophers with archetypal theory.

5   Giovanni Papini, 'A Visit to Freud', *Colosseum* (1934), reprinted in *Review of Existential Psychology and Psychiatry*, 9 (1969): 130–4.

6   Hillman, *Revisioning Psychology*, p. xiii.

7   Henry Corbin, *Creative Imagination in the Sufism of Ibn'Arabi* (Princeton:

Princeton University Press, Bollingen Series, 1987), p. 41.

8 Female rites of passage are different. Menstruation itself is a rite of passage. The rituals around it and other female rites are intended to evoke a different consciousness, more reflective than action-oriented.

9 James Hillman, *Archetypal Psychology: a Brief Account* (Dallas: Spring Publications, 1985).

10 C. G. Jung, *The Collected Works of C. G. Jung* translated and edited by Read, Fordham and Adler (London: Routledge and Kegan Paul, 1977), Vol. 13, para 15, hereafter *CW*. See also his *Man and His Symbols* (New York: Doubleday, 1964).

11 C. G. Jung, *CW*, Vol. 8, p. 209.

12 Muriel Nellis, *The Female Fix* (New York: Penguin, 1981).

13 S. Matteo, 'The Risk of Mulitiple Addictions: Guidelines for Assessing a Woman's Alcohol and Drug Use', *The Western Journal of Medicine*, 149 (1988): 742.

14 Durre Ahmed, *Masculinity, Rationality and Religion*.

15 Paula Cooey, *Religious Imagination and the Body: a Feminist Analysis* (New York: Oxford University Press, 1994), p. 42.

16 Sigmund Freud, *New Introductory Lectures on Psychoanalysis* (London: Hogarth, 1933), p. 106.

17 'The metaphors of science are, indeed, filled with the violence, voyeurism and tumescence of male adolescent fantasy. Scientists "wrestle" with an always female nature, to "wrest from her the truth" or to "reveal her hidden secrets". They make "war" on diseases and "conquer" them. Good science is "hard" science, bad science (like that refuge of so many women, psychology) is "soft" science, and molecular biology, like physics, is characterized by "hard inference".' Harvard biologist R. C. Lewontin, 'Women Versus the Biologists', *The New York Review of Books* (7 April 1994).

18 Hillman, *Archetypal Psychology*, p. 31. Also, 'Schism', in *Loose Ends: Primary Papers in Archetypal Psychology* (Dallas: Spring Publications, 1975).

19 It should be noted that Jung had a running battle with Christianity about these ideas and was frequently labelled a heretic by both Catholics and Protestants. On the other hand, while travelling through Africa, he was on more than one occasion called a Muslim, by Muslims. The anti-Christian label of heresy is similarly the frequent lot of post-Jungians such as Hillman.

20 C. G. Jung, *Modern Man in Search of a Soul* (London: Routledge and Kegan Paul, 1966).

21 Daniel J. Cook, *Language in the Philosophy of Hegel* (The Hague: Mauton, 1973), p. 62.

22 See Elaine Marks and Isabella de Courtirron (eds.), *New French Feminisms: an Anthology* (Amherst: University of Massachusetts Press, 1980).

23 Cooey, *Religious Imagination and the Body*, pp. 23–4.

24 James Hillman, *Insearch: Psychology and Religion* (Dallas: Spring Publications, 1984), pp. 105–7.

II

The Hidden Woman and the Feminine

5

The Forgotten Women of Anuradhapura
'Her Story' Replaced by 'History'

HEMA GOONATILAKE

Sri Lanka has the longest tradition of historical chronicles in the entire South and South East Asian region, the abode of roughly 1,500 million people. These chronicles cover nearly 2,500 years of history. Anuradhapura was the capital city of this history, and the major economic religious and cultural centre in the country up to the eleventh century AD.

The chronicles themselves put the beginning of this recorded history at the sixth century BC but modern historians have generally chosen to identify the third century BC as the beginning of the verifiable history of the country. It is from this time that the major monuments and inscriptions in Anuradhapura can be dated. The time before this has hitherto been considered as protohistorical and mythical. But recent excavations in the citadel of Anuradhapura have pushed the datable history back to the fifth century BC with the discovery of inscriptions dating back to this period. One such fragment of an inscription from the fifth century BC bears the word 'Anuradha', tantalizingly spelling out the first part of the name of the city.[1] Anuradhapura was known as the centre of *Theravada* Buddhism in the then Buddhist world. For example, it is referred to by name in a sixth-century AD inscription from the Dvaravati kingdom in present-day Thailand.[2]

Buddhism was introduced into the country in the third century BC, and a few years later the nuns' order was established. There is strong evidence that women had an influential role to play in the early cultural and religious history of the country as revealed by the chronicles and corroborated by rock inscriptions from the third century BC. The present chapter attempts to highlight the role of some of these forgotten women who created and shaped the history of Sri Lanka. (Tradition has it that the first ruler of Sri Lanka was also a woman. She went by the name of Kuveni and was conquered by Vijaya, a prince from Bengal, in the sixth century BC.)[3]

The *Dipavamsa* – a Woman-Centred History

The *Dipavamsa* (The Island's Chronicle),[4] a work dating back to the fourth century AD, records in detail the establishment of the nuns' order in Sri Lanka, the history of its development, its expansion to other parts of the country, and the spiritual and intellectual achievements of the nuns.[5] In contrast, a later chronicle of the sixth century AD written by the monk Mahanama, the *Mahavamsa* (or Great Chronicle), though based on the *Dipavamsa*, totally ignores the story of the nuns except for the initial description of the establishment of the nuns' order and a brief reference in the last chapter to two nunneries that flourished in the reign of Mahasena (274–301 AD). For this reason, it has been argued by some scholars that the *Dipavamsa*, the first chronicle preserved in Sri Lanka, was a compilation by the community of nuns.[6] The later chronicle, which provides only a 'male' history of the *Theravada* fraternity, appears to be a deliberate effort on the part of monk scribes to delegitimize the earlier contribution of the nuns.

The *Dipavamsa* chronicle, a fourth-century 'nuns' tale', is thus the earliest example of a recorded 'her story' in Sri Lanka, and perhaps anywhere in the world.

Sri Lankan Chronicles on the Introduction of the Nuns' Order

According to the ancient chronicles of Sri Lanka, the *Dipavamsa* and the *Mahavamsa*, the Emperor Asoka of India introduced Buddhism to Sri Lanka. He sent thirteen missions to different parts of the Asian region to propagate the religion.[7] To Sri Lanka, he sent his son, monk Mahinda, during the reign of King Devanampiyatissa (250–210 BC), to establish the order of monks there. Just six months after the monks' order was set up the nuns' order was established by Mahinda's sister, the nun Sanghamitta.[8]

It is noteworthy that there are significant differences of emphasis in the two chronicles as they depict these events. Although in both chronicles there is a special focus on the account of Sanghamitta bringing with her the southern branch of the Bo tree, under which the Buddha attained Enlightenment, the *Dipavamsa* contains extra accounts that show the authenticity and continuity of the nuns' lineage brought by Sanghamitta to Sri Lanka. This lineage goes back to the founder of the nuns' order, Pajapati Gotami, the Buddha's aunt. As illustrative of the correct continuation of this lineage, the *Dipavamsa* describes Sanghamitta's ordination ceremony and highlights the ecclesiastical roles played at this ceremony by the nun Dhammapala, her instructress *(upajjhaya),* and the nun Ayupala, her teacher *(acariya).* The *Dipavamsa* also gives an account of the group of ten nuns who accompanied Sanghamitta to Sri Lanka. Ten is the number of nuns required by the *Vinaya* rules to grant ordination to women.

What is of central interest is the variant narratives regarding the Sri Lankan nuns in the two chronicles. According to the *Dipavamsa,* it was these women (they later became nuns) and not the monks who were the first in Sri Lanka to attain *sotapatti* (the first step to Enlightenment) in responding to the first sermon delivered by Mahinda:

> When they heard that most excellent doctrine, princess Anula and her five hundred attendants ... attained the reward of *Sotapatti*; this was the first case of the attainment of a stage of sanctification which occurred in Sri Lanka.[9]

It is significant that this part of the narration in the *Dipavamsa* does not appear in the later chronicle, *Mahavamsa*. It is also significant that there is a detailed account of the request made by Anula to the king to arrange for the ordination, the arrival of Sanghamitta, her ordaining Anula along with her five hundred maidens, and her death. It is even more significant that the *Mahavamsa* speaks in glowing terms of Sanghamitta and her contribution to the propagation of the Buddhist faith in the country, but totally ignores the development of the order of the nuns.

'Her Story' Version of the Development of the Nuns' Order

The *Dipavamsa* provides a great deal of information, not only on the high spiritual attainments of the nuns, but also on the continuous development of the nuns' order and its spread to other parts of the country.[10]

The names of Saddhammanandi, Soma, Ciriddhi, Dasiya, Dhamma (who was well versed in *Vinaya*), Sobhana, Dhammatapasa, Naramitta (she was highly wise), Sata (she was versed in the exhortations of Theris), Uttara (the leader of a large group of nuns) and Sumana (who understood the true religion and its history) were among those who received higher ordination during the earliest phase. They taught *Vinaya*, *Sutta* and *Abhidhamma Pitakas* in Anuradhapura. Mahila (who kept the *dhutanga* precepts), Samantan Girikali, Dasi and Kali had come to Anuradhapura from Rohana (southern province of Sri Lanka) together with twenty thousand nuns during 161–137 BC, and taught the *Vinaya*, indicating that the nuns' order was widespread by that time.

The first group of nuns to resume the task of teaching the *Vinaya* after the troubled period of 102–89 BC included the names of Mahasona, Datta, Sivala, Rupasobhini, Dhammagutta, Dasiya, Sapatta Channa, Upali, Revata, Mala, Khema and Tissa. The king received advice from these learned nuns and provided them with whatever they wished for during this time. Mahila, the chronicle records, was a superior of nuns. Naga and Nagamitta taught *Vinaya* at Anuradhapura during 41–19 BC.

The *Dipavamsa* describes how various nuns had excelled in different sections of the canon, but the study of *Vinaya* was given the highest place. An element of continuity in the tradition of the study of *Vinaya* was emphasized. Nuns who had taken to the study of this teaching have been variously described as having 'great wisdom', 'great fame', 'cleverness' and other attainments. Some nuns were renowned as illustrious preachers of the *dhamma*, while others were known by their strict observation of the *Vinaya*. Two of the nuns, Sumana Mahila and Sanha, were said to have been endowed with *Abhinna* ('supernatural powers'). Many more names of nuns along with their special skills are mentioned.[11]

This recording of their own spiritual and intellectual achievements in the *Dipavamsa* is probably itself a response to concerted anti-woman representation by Sri Lankan monks dating back to an earlier period, when the canon was put into writing for the first time at the Aluvihara in Matale, Sri Lanka, in 29 BC. At this point, it is useful to draw special attention to the negative representation of women in the canonical texts and commentarial literature, against which the nuns may have been reacting. This negative representation, it should be noted, is in keeping neither with the equality of status afforded to women by the Buddha, as recorded in the same texts, nor with the contemporary social norms prevalent in Sri Lanka two thousand years ago.

The *Cullavagga* of the *Vinaya Pitaka*[12] records that the Buddha refused the request of his aunt, Pajapati Gotami, to grant ordination to women on three consecutive occasions. He consented on the fourth occasion only on the intervention of his attendant, the monk Ananda. The ordination was granted, however, on the condition that the nuns adhered to eight *Garudhammas* (special rules), in addition to other disciplinary regulations. Soon after entering the order, Pajapati Gotami asked the Buddha to remove the first special rule, which prescribes that even a nun of a hundred years standing must show respect to a monk who has just been ordained, to allow monks and nuns to pay respect to each other, not according to their sex, but by seniority. This was turned down by the Buddha. It is also alleged by the monk authors that the Buddha made the pronouncement that his dispensation, which was meant to last a thousand years, would now last only five hundred years because of the establishment of the nuns' order. This request by Pajapati Gotami is the first record of an institutional protest against male supremacy 'in the Buddhist Order, and perhaps anywhere in the world'.[13]

The outpourings of women against the ill-treatment by men recorded in the *Therigatha* (Psalms of Sisters)[14] during the time of the Buddha may be referred to here. These can be described as the first recorded expressions of women's liberation, although personal protests by women from the earliest human interaction almost certainly existed, though not recorded.

Misrepresentation of the Buddhist Spirit and of Social Reality

The character of the Buddha represented in the above accounts in the *Vinaya Pitaka*, written down in Sri Lanka, is not in keeping with what the Buddha taught, and with the principles according to which he organized the community of monks. The major principles that determined the status of a monk were seniority as a monk and spiritual and intellectual achievements. The status of the monk did not depend on his previous status as an individual in relation to social rank, caste, wealth or other criteria. Why was this same principle not applied to the community of nuns? Did the change happen in the hands of the scribes who recorded the particular episode of the ordination of women?[15] It appears so.

It is interesting to note in this context that the *Cullavagga* records that at the First Council (meeting of all monks), held three months after the death of the Buddha to codify the teachings, Ananda was accused by a section of the monks of helping with the admission of women into the order.[15] Several scholars, Horner[16] and Dhirasaekera[17] in particular, have discussed the issue, but adduced no conclusive evidence. Dhirasaekera has further pointed out that there is evidence that the monks continued to level criticism against the order of nuns even after its recognized success. The reason for this criticism was the fear of being eclipsed by the newer order. Dhirasaekera has cited a statement, ascribed to the Buddha in the Chinese version of the *Mahisasaka Vinaya*, in which the Buddha says that after his death the male and female lay devotees would have honoured the monks in many ways if there were only monks and no nuns in the order.[18]

None of these negative representations of women in the *Cullavagga* accord with the social norms prevalent in Sri Lanka at that time. According to inscriptions[19] and other records, women owned and disposed of their wealth at their own discretion. Some acted as leaders within communities of men and women; some even ruled the country – at times quite as ruthlessly as men. In a society where the relationship between the sexes showed wide variation and depended on the birth and social position of the individual, the low status given to women in the *Cullavagga* can be explained only by a deliberate attempt on the part of the monks who wrote down the canon to keep the nuns down. It is possible that many of the nuns, whose ranks included royalty and members of the upper strata of society, people who were used to exercising authority over both men and women, were not happy with the *Vinaya* rules imposed on them by the monks. This was why they soon sought to develop an institution independent of the monks.

It is clear that the nuns were reacting to the narration in the *Cullavagga* by writing their own version of the establishment of the nuns' order, its development into an independent institution, and the individual spiritual and intellectual achievements of members of the order. It is also clear that the monks' opposition to nuns – or even envy of them – continued because the monks could not monopolize the respect of the laity. The intense resentment on the part of the monks against the independent spirit of the nuns, as reflected in later texts, is of great relevance here.

The following translated extract is taken from a passage running to about seven pages in the *Samantapasadika,* a commentary on the *Vinaya Pitaka* written in Sri Lanka in the fifth century by Buddhaghosa, a monk born in South India:

> The Buddha formulated a decree that nuns should go constantly to monks (for guidance) without seeking opportunity for any other mode of action. Why? (Because of the) lack of wisdom or intelligence in women. Because women lack wisdom, listening to the *dhamma* is greatly useful. Therefore, the Buddha did so in order that they pay homage to monks, and lead a meaningful ordained life without proudly thinking 'It is what we know, that the monks themselves know.'[20]

The above statement presents a sharp contrast to what the Buddha said about the intelligence of women, and, in particular, about the spiritual and intellectual achievements of nuns. What is also clear from the above account is that the nuns had mastered the *dhamma* quite as well as the monks had during the Buddha's period, and that they had questioned or even challenged the superiority of the monks over the nuns. The response of the monks evidenced in Buddhaghosa's commentary is a vivid example of male chauvinism that transcends cultural, territorial and time boundaries. Female lack of intelligence and inferiority in intellectual abilities is an argument advanced by males from time immemorial to the present.

The Nuns' *Vinaya* Tradition and Teachers

In his recent research Gunawardana has thrown more light on this issue. He points to the likelihood that the community of nuns possessed their own versions of the *Vinaya* and their own distinct traditions of interpretation. He argues for the existence of an unbroken succession of teachers of the *Vinaya* coming down from the time of Sanghamitta. As importantly, he argues that this succession of teachers had no links with the line of teachers among monks, as given in the *Samantapasadika*. The *Samantapasadika*, which later became the authoritative guide for the interpretation of the *Vinaya*, is, in effect, the result of an attempt of a long line of commentators to develop a code of conduct for monks, with modifications to suit the changes in the local environment over the centuries. The same principle has not been applied here to the case of nuns: instead the interpretation in the *Cullavagga* is retained with more reinforcement, which, in effect, presents a sharp contrast to the contemporary social ethos.[21]

Evidence for the existence of different traditional versions of the *Vinaya Pitaka* of the *Theravada,* other than the only one available to us today, can be found in the *Samantapasadika* as well as in the *Vamsatthapakasini*,[22] the commentary on the *Dipavamsa*. The controversy between the *Mahavihara* and the *Abhayagiri* monasteries in relation to a punishment given to a nun, as it appears in *Samantapasadika*, is directly relevant. The *Mahavihara* version of *Cullavagga* has it that when the nun Mettiya falsely accused the monk Dabba Mallaputta of having violated her chastity, the Buddha inquired from the monk, and, on his denial, ordered that Mettiya be expelled from the order. The *Abhayagiri* version has it that the nun was expelled on the basis of her own confession, not just because of the monk's denial. The importance given to this issue of ecclesiastical justice is seen from the fact the *Samantapasadika* records that the king at that time, Bhatika Tissa (143–67 AD), commissioned the official Dighakaranaya to hold an inquiry, and the verdict given was in favour of the *Mahavihara*.

The *Vamsatthapakasini* provides evidence for the fact that different schools had their own versions of the *Vinaya*. The *Abhayagiri* monastery and the *Jetavana* monastery had distinct accounts, together with their own interpretations, and these were criticized by the *Mahavihara*. Based on this evidence, it has been suggested that the nuns had their own version of the *Vinaya*, together with a distinct tradition of its interpretation. The information discussed above and the lineage of *Vinaya* teachers given in the *Dipavamsa* reveals the fact that there was a long line of *Vinaya* teachers coming down from the time of Sanghamitta, and that it had no link with the line of teachers among monks, as given in the *Samantapasadika*. This evidence suggests that the nuns inherited a line of *Vinaya* teachers which was independent of the order of monks.

Sri Lankan Nuns as Propagators of Buddhism in Foreign Countries

It is of significance that later Sri Lankan chronicles do not refer to nuns who were engaged in missionary activities in foreign countries. The *Dipavamsa* mentions Sivala and Mahaniha as nuns who propagated Buddhism in Jambudipa (India) during a period of unrest in Sri Lanka in the first century after Christ. After the situation became normal, they returned at the orders of the king, and resumed their teaching work. A Sanskrit inscription assigned to the third and fourth centuries and found at Nagarjunkonda, a well-established centre of *Mahayana* learning in South India, refers to Sinhalese nuns from Tamrapanni (Sri Lanka) who carried out missionary work.[23]

Another event of great significance is not mentioned in any of the Sri Lankan records. According to the *Pi-chiu-ni-chuang* ('Biography of the Nuns')[24] compiled by Pao-chang in 520 AD, and biographies of Gunavarman and Sanghavarman, nuns from Sri Lanka went over to China in the year 429 AD to give higher ordination to the Chinese nuns. Earlier, these Chinese nuns had received ordination for the first time, but only from a monk. Thus, in the year 433 AD, three hundred Chinese nuns received their higher (second) ordination in the presence of over ten Sinhalese nuns headed by Tie-so-ra at the Nanking Temple.[25]

The rivalry between the *Mahavihara* (third century BC) school and other schools such as *Abhayagiri* (first century BC) and *Jetavana* (third century AD) had become more pronounced by the fifth century AD. There is reason to believe that the Sinhalese nuns who went to China were from the *Abhayagiri* monastery, an emerging centre of *Mahayana* activity at the time. The first group of Sinhalese nuns arrived in

Nanking in 425 AD, about ten years after the Chinese pilgrim Fa-hsien left Sri Lanka, having stayed there for two years; both events took place during the reign of King Mahanama (410–31 AD). Fa-hsien showed greater interest in describing the activities of the *Abhayagiri* monastery in his records. It is also to be noted that Fa-hsien took residence in Nanking, and undertook the translation of Sanskrit manuscripts – especially the *Vinaya* literature – into Chinese. It is probable, although not recorded, that he took the initiative in bringing the mission of Sinhalese nuns to China. Fa-hsien's records mention a Chinese merchant who made an offering to the *Abhayagiri* monastery, and it is to be noted that the Sinhalese nuns left for China in a merchant's ship. Another fact that supports the close connection between the *Abhayagiri* monastery and China is that King Mahanama (Mo-ho-non) sent a letter to the Chinese emperor along with a model of the Shrine of the Tooth Relic in 428 AD, and the Shrine of the Tooth Relic was under the care of the *Abhayagiri* monastery at the time.[26]

It is interesting to note a reference to a Sri Lankan nun, Candramali, described in the Tibetan and Mongol versions of the *Tripitaka* as a translator of Buddhist *Tantrayana* texts while living in Tibet in the eleventh century.[27] Thus it is possible that Sinhalese nuns found a more congenial atmosphere for their existence side by side with the order of monks under *Mahayana* or *Tantrayana* than under the *Theravada,* since the *Mahayana* has always been more open to new ideas and more adaptive.

Conclusion

The discussion above has sketched in the contribution made by the women of Anuradhapura in creating and shaping the religious and cultural landscape of Sri Lanka from the third century BC to the fourth century AD, the period when the *Dipavamsa* was written. In fact, the women of Anuradhapura were the pioneer historiographers in the country, and perhaps anywhere in the world. What is significant is their attempt to present their own version of the story – which can be called feminist historiography. I have also dealt above with the reasons for displacing a woman's perspective with that of a man's, both in the writing of history as well as in the practice of monastic life. This displacement also needs to be seen in the perspective of the relative equality of women in a Buddhist society.

It is clear that the Sri Lankan records that emanated from the *Mahavihara* of Anuradhapura, the only ones that are extant, after the fourth century, give only a partial or male-only history of the religious and cultural development in the country. After the *Dipavamsa*, no records from a woman's perspective have been found, either because women's voices were silenced by the monk's delegitimizing campaign, or because the nuns' writings have not survived.

Notes and References

1 S. U. Deraniyagala, *The Pre-history of Sri Lanka*, Vols 1 and 2 (Colombo: Department of Archaeological Survey, Government of Sri Lanka, 1992).

2 *Charuk nai prathet II* (Inscriptions in Thailand) (Bangkok: National Library, 1985), Vol. 2, p. 45.

3 *Mahavamsa*, translated and edited by W. Geiger (London: Pali Text Society, 1908), Chapter 7.

4 *Dipavamsa*, trans and ed. H. Oldenberg (London: 1879).

5 In the eleventh century, after the South Indian Tamil Chola invasion, the nuns' order disappeared, along with the monks' order. The monks' order was later re-established, but not the nuns' order.

6 G. P. Malalasekera, *The Pali Literature of Ceylon* (Colombo: Gunasena, 1958).

7 For example, he sent the monks Sona and Uttara to the region that covers Cambodia, Laos and Thailand.

8 *Mahavamsa*, Chapter 19.

9 *Dipavamsa*, Chapter 12.

10 *Ibid.*, Chapter 18.

11 *Ibid.*, Chapter 17.

12 *Vinaya Pitaka*, ed. H. Oldenberg, 5 vols (London: 1879–83), Vol. 2, p. 253.

13 Hema Goonatilake, 'Buddhist Nuns: Protests, Struggles and the Re-interpretation of Religious Orthodoxy in Sri Lanka', in Judy Brink and Joan Mencher (eds.), *Mixed Blessings: Gender and Religious Fundamentalism Cross-culturally* (New York: Routledge, 1994).

14 *Therigatha* (Psalms of Sisters), translated by C. A. F. Rhys Davids (London: Pali Text Society, 1909).

15 *Vinaya Pitaka*, Vol. 2, p. 289.

16 I. B. Horner, *Women under Primitive Buddhism* (Delhi: Motilal Banarsidass, 1975).

17 Jotiya Dhirasekera, *Buddhist Monastic Discipline* (Colombo: 1982).

18 *Ibid.*, p. 146.

19 S. Paranavitana, *Inscriptions of Ceylon*, Vol. I (Colombo: Archaeological Department, 1970), pp. 1–5, 43–4.

20 *Samantapasadika,* eds. J. Takakusu and M. Nagai (London: Pali Text Society, 1924–47), Vol. 4.

21 R. A. Gunawardana, 'Subtle Silks of Ferreous Firmness: Buddhist Nuns in Ancient and Early Medieval Sri Lanka and their Role in the Propagation of Buddhism', *The Sri Lanka Journal of the Humanities*, 14, 1–2 (University of Peradeniya, 1990).

22 *Vamsatthappakasini,* ed. G. P. Malalasekera (London: Pali Text Society, 1935).

23 *Epigraphia Indica*, 20 (Department of Archaeology, n.d.), p. 22.

24 *Pi-chiu-ni-chuan,* trans Li Jung-hsi as *Biographies of Buddhist Nuns* (Osaka: Tohokai, 1981).

25 Hema Goonatilake, 'The Dasa-sil-movement of Sri Lanka', *Sri Lanka Journal of Buddhist Studies*, 2 (Buddhist and Pali University of Sri Lanka, 1988).

26 Hema Goonatilake, 'The Impact of Some Mahayana Concepts of Sinhalese Buddhism', unpublished PhD thesis, University of London, 1974.

27 *The Tibetan Tripitaka*, Bkah-Hgyur, Rgyud III 3, Nos 37, 38, 39, 48, 50, Peking edition, ed. D. T. Suzuki (Tokyo-Kyoto: Tibetan Tripitaka Research Institute, 1956).

6

'Mother' Victoria Vera Piedad
as a *Mutya* Figure
A Study of an Archetypal Image of the Self

GRACE P. ODAL

This chapter stems from a humanistically oriented study in which the researcher/writer arrives at a proposition and generalization about an archetype of Filipino consciousness through an experiential, personal and inductive process of understanding. As a personal project, it is the individual and experience-based perspective of an arts-and-culture professor focused on a Philippines-based phenomenon. Simultaneously, it is an imaginative and creative synthesis of a particular culture-based phenomenon into the wider and global perspective of an archetype of the divine self.

The framework followed in understanding the concept of the *mutya* involves embarking on the 'journey of consciousness' approach, which is called, in Filipino, *pamamaybay* or 'sailing along, across, and on the edge of the water to some destination point and direction, done with or without the conscious awareness of the one sailing'.[1] This word is extended in meaning metaphorically and applied to a journey in consciousness in the mind and psyche of the traveller, in which the meanings and significance of the empirical and mental phenomenon being studied are derived from an unfolding of the various facets of a thing or concept as viewed from the multi-level perspective in the mind of the traveller. This is done by using the integrative, synthetic, analogical and associational tools of the imagination, called into play by the heart or 'cognitive feelings' as well as the intuition of the student-researcher-writer experiencing the total process. This process is what I call the *pamamaybay* approach to the study of the mind, psyche and consciousness of a people, based on a metaphorical study of their cultural constructs.

The thesis of this chapter is that the image of the Mother – which refers in my study to Victoria Vera Piedad of Pila, Laguna, Philippines – is one representation of the hidden contemporary figures of the Mother Goddess, understood as the primal, total God. In terms of Filipino experience, this image belongs to the archetype of the *mutya*, and that in turn is identical to the archetype of the cosmic and individualized Divine Self.

In this sense, the Mother Goddess, through her human, semi-human or divine historical medium, represents not only the Cosmic Mother, Mother Nature and Mother of the World, but also the Mother of the Nation (motherland), or the folk spirit of the people or the race. She may also be the spirit of a place, or the guardian of a place, a nation or a people. Marriage or union with her means union with the divine, in which one's *mutya* or divine self is born and realized at the micro and macro levels of reality.

A Personal Encounter with the Image of *Mutya* and Mother

It was in 1992 that I started studying the concept of *mutya* in Philippine culture. The first *mutya* figure I studied was that of the *Mutya ng Pasig* or the *Mutya* (Water-Goddess) of the Pasig River, as immortalized by a Filipino *kundiman* or love song composed by Nicanor Abelardo in 1926, based on a popular legend in the town of Pasig.

In January 1997, in the course of my field research in the Laguna de Bai region, I came across a small school for indigent elementary and high school students at Brookside, Pila. The school also had a free clinic service for the surrounding community. Attached to the school building was a chapel managed by a few resident priests who were running a small seminary adjoining the school grounds. The sign on the front gate read, 'Mother's Brookside Haven'.

The school grounds, the clinic, the chapel, the small seminary, and the small residential houses comprising Mother's Brookside Haven were then all made of native materials like bamboo and coconut lumber mixed with cement. The complex was headed and founded by a retired medical doctor – Dr Paul Domingo – the 77-year-old owner of the land who was also designated as the 'medium' of the place, through whom the spirit of the Mother was channelled.

I was brought to the place by two students of Filipino spirituality who thought that, since I was already in the vicinity looking around for data on the local interpretations of the *mutya* image, I might as well pass by Mother Victoria's spiritual centre to pay my respects to the nearest medium in that area. He might possess some knowledge on the subject that might enlighten me.

The car entered the gate of Mother's Brookside Haven one early evening in January 1997. Everyone had just finished taking supper. Dr Domingo, who was then resting in his domestic quarters, graciously consented to the interview. When I asked him whether he knew anything about the *mutya,* he said he knew nothing about it. I was so disappointed by his response that I thought of immediately leaving the place. But then he started telling the story of how he became a medium of the spirit who manifested bodily and was popularly called 'Mother'.

Since he was not directly talking about my subject of interest, I attended half-heartedly to his storytelling, listening merely out of politeness. As his long story dragged on, though, it began to dawn on me that the person whom he called 'Mother' was the same 'Mother' whom I had heard being mentioned by scholars who had made a study of certain Filipino mystical and spiritual groups. I dimly recalled, indeed, that her name had been fondly mentioned by friends who had been part of a nation-wide spiritual fraternity she had established in many parts of the Philippines, both while she was still in her physical body as 'Mother Victoria' and after she had assumed her spiritual form. This nation-wide fraternity was known through its acronym BROMOKI, or the 'Brotherhood of Mother's Kids'. I also vaguely recalled hearing people claim that she was still very actively at work, even if no longer in her physical body, channelling her messages and spiritual communications through various mediums all over the nation.

Despite my lack of concentration, two stories about 'Mother' captured my attention. The first story pertained to the idea that she was not born in the regular human way – from the womb of the human mother. Rather, she was literally 'brought down from the sky' somewhere in Cuyo Island, off Palawan. Her relatives were, in fact, unknown, neither did she have any records or stories of her parents.

The corporeal goddess

This information fascinated me because it connected her to the *mutya* tradition in the Philippines. One trait of the *mutya* figure, according to this tradition, is that he/she is mysteriously generated – born from the womb of nature itself – a spontaneous streaming forth of a baby from nowhere, very much like a gift of nature. This spontaneous generation directly from nature, of what appears to be a human being, implies the divinity inherent in the *mutya*. In fact, another characteristic feature of the *mutya* is that she is a god/goddess. Unlike other immortals, however, who are remote from humanity, the *mutya* figure lives among ordinary mortals, revealing her identity as a goddess to some of them; sometimes, she lives among humans as a goddess in disguise, apparently hidden and obscure, but paradoxically a popular, funny figure who is well-liked by people. Hence, the *mutya* figure usually lives hidden among ordinary people, sometimes transfiguring into her real divine identity, and, at other times, disguising it behind a despicable, rough and crude appearance and form. Similarly, Mother Victoria usually appears as an old woman in a nun's habit but sometimes transfigures as a very young and beautiful woman, an old bearded white-haired man, or a bent old woman beggar.

It would appear that, even if the *mutya* is a divine figure, she aligns herself with the day-to-day and mundane lives of humanity. Unlike other divine figures who are remote from humanity, a *mutya* figure even takes the form of humanity, lives as guide, healer and friend to mortals, and actively helps them towards their upliftment and evolution. In obscurity, Mother Victoria heals; she absorbs people's negative vibrations; and she teaches them the way towards perfection. She had even communicated with some members of the hierarchy of the Roman Catholic Church in the Philippines, and, despite their unfavourable response to her, she had managed to go on with her work in this unlikely context. According to Dr Domingo and other old-timers of his group, she had even written a letter to the Vatican in Rome, addressed to the then Pope Paul VI. She did not, however, receive any response.

The power of the *mutya* lies in her presence. Just as the stone-like figure of the *mutya* is an amulet, a talisman and a gem, so the *mutya* figure in human form also embodies, stores, carries and radiates power and energy. She is a presence so full of magic, charm and fine vibrational frequencies that those around her are transmuted by her mere presence and silence. Similarly, Mother Victoria is an embodiment of divine power. She carries the virtues of what her name represents: *Maria Victoria Vera Piedad* – which one may translate literally as 'Maria – the triumph of a true/genuine piety/spirituality'. Her being is a talisman, an amulet, a charm, a gem of a great power, beauty, wealth, wisdom, etcetera. It is a well-known story among the group that, on one occasion, when her favourite adopted son was extremely drunk and suffering severe adverse effects, she started showing signs of being drunk herself – while the son immediately started to recover. Moreover, Mother has an emergency number which serves as a means of availing help from her instantaneously. Her 'cosmic' call number 01230-6-4 is a hot line for those with emergency needs and who are in great desperation. According to the group's interpretation, 'zero' represents God as Alpha or the Beginning; 'one' represents God as The One Supreme and Infinite God; 'two' represents God as the Twin – The Woman-God and the Man-God; 'three' represents the Divine Trinity of the Father, the Mother and the Son/Daughter, represented by the triangle with an opened eye in the midst of it; 'zero' represents God as Omega or the Principle of the End; 'six' represents the union of God and the human, or the perfection of the human as depicted by the Star of David or the union of two opposing triangles-one pointing down and the other pointing up; and 'four' represents the four quarters of the earth, and points to the God-in-incarnation or God manifesting on earth.

The androgyne

The second story that fascinated me pertained to her having both male and female organs. According to Dr Domingo, a fellow doctor who examined Mother Victoria in Panabo, Davao City while she was on a fast, reported that Mother had an unusual case of appearing to have two organs – one male and the other female. Even Dr Domingo's wife, who was a retired nurse, remarked that once, while taking care of Mother in her weak moments, after she had deliberately absorbed negative energies from patients in her healing sessions, Mrs Domingo inadvertently passed over with her hand the organ part of Mother and felt to her surprise the shape of a male organ! Her sex and gender changes, as well as her identity swapping, are common stories among the believers of Mother. People talked matter-of-factly of how her appearance as Mother, with the familiar white habit and veil, would, without warning, change into the other figures I have mentioned – the old bearded man, the beautiful maiden or the decrepit and bent old woman beggar. This shape changing is reminiscent of the usual pattern in Filipino myths and legends in which the gods appeared to humans disguised as old male and female beggars, retiring hermits, clowns and tricksters, outlaws and bandits, as well as beautiful 'white' ladies or 'red' ladies. This shape-changing tradition is part of the context of the *mutya* figure in Philippine culture, a context that leads also to the conjunction of male–female traits and characteristics in her being. Though the *mutya* generally appears as a female of a highly evolved nature, she can also appear as a male figure. Thus she embraces, encompasses and integrates, within her feminine being and nature, the essence of the masculine.

The *Mutya* in Philippine Culture

What, then, is the *mutya*? It appears to be an archetype in Filipino consciousness – a register or pattern of energies, manifesting in a complex of ideas, expressive of a unified web and manifold forms of reality.

The word *mutya* is a pre-Hispanic, pan-Filipino term. It has various levels and subtle nuances of meaning. On one hand, it may literally refer to any charm stone or magical stone, or to a pearl, or to any precious, bright, dazzling gem or jewel of great value or symbolic of great virtues and powers. At another level, again, it may mean *any* magical object, person or thing. Its most usual appearance is as an odd-looking, freakish, extraordinary product of nature believed to be highly charged with potency and vibrations. It is always prized for its uniqueness and rarity. There are many kinds and essences of *mutya*, but each *mutya* has a specific and special function, virtue, capacity and power.

The *mutya* can appear in various boundless forms in the cosmos: there is the *mutya* in the mineral world, in the plant world, in the animal world, in the human world, and in the world of gods and divinities, etcetera. It can be a stone, or any fossilized plant or animal parts possessive of healing and magical potencies. It can also be any stone-like object found inside or attached to the skin, or even buried under the skin of any other stone, rock, mineral, plant, tree, flower, fish, insect, bird, animal, or even human. It can also be a stone, crystal or gem that may be swallowed and vomited through the mouth. It is used for luck and prosperity, as protection and shield, for divine assistance and blessing, for facility in thinking and good judgement, for health and healing, for guidance as well as for its possession of power and virtues.

On the human level and within the symbolic world of humanity, the *mutya* can refer to any unique, extraordinary or rare person, power, trait, virtue or value. It can refer to a great and unusual devotion or to a love that is sublime, profound, noble, sacrificial, devotional or intense; it is both spiritual and divine.

The *mutya* may also refer to the virtues of purity, virginity, holiness, innocence, childlikeness, nobility, and sanctity. It connotes the heavenly virtues of Faith, Hope and Love. On still another level, it is a model of excellence, the highest point in the development and evolution of any object, thing, idea or person. It suggests the realization and fulfilment of the destiny and nature of a thing or a person, or an awakening into her divine self or god self, a case of self-realization or god-realization. Hence, at the micro level, the *mutya* is the 'divine spark' within the human being and the created order; at the macro level, it is the 'individualized cosmic consciousness' in which lies the process and experience of merging and unifying with the whole universe. At the same time, one is maintaining and realizing one's identity and individuality, and this occurs simultaneously for and between the individual and the cosmos.

The *mutya*, moreover, refers to a transformative initiation process, very much like the one involved in the natural process of pearl creation or production. A grain of sand, a fleck of mud or a speck of dust enters into an oyster shell. The oyster gets irritated by the rough edges of the grain of sand lodged within its shell; so it releases a substance called nacre to enwrap the sand. The nacre coating is gradually smoothened in the process and develops into a translucent coat of gem called the pearl. Hence, from a grain of sand, this lowly piece of earth develops into a gem of light that is valued as a jewel, as well as for its healing and magical properties. In symbolic terms, the oyster shell refers to the body and the pearl refers to the evolving immortal spirit within the human being. The *mutya,* therefore, is the symbolic image of the divine self – or the God-within-the-human being merging and uniting with the cosmic self.

It is no wonder, then, that another connotation of *mutya* is that of a human-friendly goddess. She is identified with a local folk spirit, a spirit of the place, a spirit guardian of the place who protects and guards its treasures and guides its people. In this connection, the *mutya* is none other than the divine original spirit, the primal spirit, the genius of the place who is identified with the goddess of the waters, the original mother and source of humanity.

The association of the *mutya* with the primordial and original spirit explains the characteristic of the *mutya* as the mother–creator and source of life from whose watery womb emerged all life. She is also Mother Nature – the source of all the elements of life, namely earth, water, air and fire. She is, therefore, by extension, also the *Inang Bayan* (the Mother Country/Motherland) – the divine spirit who gave birth to the people of the place, or the animating, dynamic and creative spirit behind the nation – the folk spirit: the *Mutya ng Pilipinas* or the muse/genius/goddess of the Philippines.

The legendary context

In the Philippines, the most primal elements dominating the con-sciousness of the people appear to be the elements of water and fire. This is probably due to the archipelagic nature of the nation, as well as its volcanic substance and origin. Hence, the folk spirit behind this place would naturally be the *Mutya of the Waters*, usually embodied in the figures of the fish-woman, the water nymphs and sprites, and the mermaid. In the Tagalog region, she is popularly called the *Mutya ng Pasig*, or the *Goddess of the Pasig River* – immortalized, as I have men-tioned, in the *kundiman* composed by the Filipino composer Nicanor Abelardo in 1926.

Moreover, the *mutya* is also the original spirit of light and fire embodied in Filipino folklore in the form of dancing balls of light shining in the darkness of night. The *mutya* is also the ball of light or the stone of light carried by the King of the Cobras in its mouth, believed to be given as a gift to the pure of heart. It is also the balls of light owned and played with by the *tikbalang* (half-man, half-horse of the Philippines) under the shade of giant and ancient trees. Another *mutya* form is the cigar-like light seen by people emerging from the mouths of *Kapres* (tall black giants), or burning in them continuously. It also reveals itself in the form of animals and monsters that appear walking or running across fields at night. The banana plant called *saging sa tindok* has a blossom that is believed to drop a gem of light upon the earth, at the stroke of midnight on Good Friday during the Lenten season. The *mutya* also refers to the goddess of light, who has the habit of walking along river banks at night in the form of a woman radiating light. Furthermore, the *mutya* is also the great *Bulalakaw*, or the water-goddess who appears as a flashing comet or meteor across the sky at night, before embracing the earth as falling light over mountain-tops, hill-tops and large bodies of water.

In the *Manuscript Collection of Philippine Folklore* assembled by Dean S. Fansler at the University of the Philippines,[2] there is an account attributed to the Negrito people of Luzon reporting that *Mutya* is the name of the indigenous heroine of light and fire – a great magician and enchantress – who challenged both the sun god and the moon god. He/she emerged as a winner in the series of combats for supremacy that followed. In *Mutya's* combat with the sun god, the Negritos, who were then already existing upon the earth, were almost scorched by the heat that the sun generated, and this was how they became black in skin colour. This association with the sun and moon, as well as with the elements of fire and water, probably also explains why the Philippines is called the 'Pearl of the Orient', or, in local terminology, the *Mutya ng Silangan*.

But what does *Mutya ng Silangan* really mean? On the literal level, its meaning is indeed the traditional 'Pearl of the Orient' – that is, a pearl of great price arising from the watery depths. It also means, more metaphorically, 'the Gem of the East' – the precious, rare and special beauty, power, wisdom and treasure of the eastern seas. But it also means the 'Centre of the East', because one nuance of meaning of *mutya* is 'centre of attention' – hence the 'Sacred Centre of the East'. Furthermore, it can also mean the 'Light of the East' by association with the Sun of the East, the Rising Sun, the emerging light of morning in the eastern sky. She, therefore, is none other than the Sun

Goddess or the Goddess of the Dawn, the light arising from the darkness, from the muddy and the watery depths of chaotic night. It means, therefore, the light of resurrection, of new hope, new beauty, new power, new wealth and new love streaming from the East, symbolizing rebirth and new life. On the symbolic, mystical and spiritual level, the *Mutya* is the primal womb and tomb from which life is born, dies and is reborn; she is the primal goddess, the mother spirit and guardian spirit of the Orient.

On the esoteric side, the phrase *Mutya ng Silangan* has the connotation of a paradise, an Eden, a kingdom of beauty and wealth – a Paradise of the East or a Kingdom of the East that has vanished and faded away, becoming a lost, enchanted and hidden heaven. This acquires even greater depth and power if one views it from the millenarian perspective that connects the idea of a 'Paradise of the East' with local and folk interpretations among the various religious and spiritual communities scattered all over the Philippines. Of recent years, and increasingly in these times, more and more groups are revealing what they considered hidden knowledge from the past, attesting to the existence of a sunken civilization of great power, glory and magnitude buried underneath the Pacific Ocean, whose centre used to be somewhere between the Philippines and Indonesia. These local people – whose knowledge is based on a combination of folk/oral traditions, sacred revelations from spirit guides, and hidden supernatural writings and scripts secretly passed on from generation to generation – generally believe that the Philippine Islands are actually floating fragments of a sunken gigantic continent popularly called *Lemuria*, sometimes *Mu*, but with an undisclosed localized ancient name. Mother Victoria's writings reveal that *Mu* was an even more ancient and extensive body than the vanished continent of the Pacific Ocean now popularly called *Lemuria*.

Linguistic connections

As mentioned earlier, the word *mutya*, with its minor variants, is found throughout the Philippine Archipelago. For instance, in the Tagalog, Kapampangan, Ilocano, Bikol, Pangasinense, Cebuano, Palawan, Waray and Hiligaynon languages, the words *mutya*, *mutia* and *motia* are interchangeable. Another Tagalog variant is *mutika*, meaning 'precious stone'. In Mangyan and Tagbanua, it is *mutia*. In Manobo, it is *muntiya*.

In Maranao, it is *montiya* or *montia* and, sometimes, *motia*. In Maguin-danao, it is *muntia* or *muntya*. In Mansaka, it is *motya*. For the Tausugs, it is *mussa*. (Juan Francisco reports that there are other terms in Tausug that refer to 'pearl', 'gem' or 'jewel', and that these are *mucha, pamata, permata* and *parmata*.[3] In Cuyonin, to return to our long list, the word is *moya*. In all these Philippine languages, the word *mutya* and all its variations refer to the following range of meanings: pearl; gem/jewel; anything or anyone rare or precious, that is, unique; amulet, talisman, charm; bezoar stone; one and only; someone treasured, cherished; and love.

One cannot help noticing that the word *mutya* or *mucha*, in Tausug, appears to have some sonic resemblance to the name *Muchalinda* in Buddhism – the seven-headed *Naga* king who sheltered the meditating Buddha from the rain by forming a canopy above the head of the sitting Buddha. In terms of Filipino mythology, this could be read as the King of the Cobras revealing or yielding its great *mutya* through its mouth; or one may recognize the Buddha who is shaded by *Muchalinda* as none other than the *mutya* of the *Naga* King. Hence, the Buddha is also a *mutya* or the *Mutya* – an image of the realized self, the illumi-nated self, or the divine self.

Similarly, the *mutya* theme is a running motif in South East Asian arts and culture. In fact, similar themes can also be found in India, China, Sri Lanka, Korea, Japan and in the Pacific Islands. But, for the present purpose, I must limit discussion of the *mutya* theme to its usage in Philippine culture.

The centre

One 'side' to the mutya still remains to be discussed. This is its associa-tion with the idea of being 'the centre'. As was mentioned earlier, another meaning of the word *mutya* is 'centre of attention'. This is probably the reason why the Philippines – and Manila in particular – was called the 'Pearl of the Orient': it was once a centre of trade and commerce in the region, especially during the height of the Manila galleon trade.

Hence, *mutya*, in its meaning of 'centre-point', refers to the 'sacred centre', the holy point of origin of all manifold beings, the root from which all of life and creation emerged, and to which all shall once more return in oneness at the end of human time. It would then appear that *mutya* is a 'way of knowing' of an evolved and transformed state of consciousness. Hence, it is the 'jewel' or 'pearl' of consciousness, of awareness, or knowing and being, the gem of the divine self – in other words, the divine self that has achieved its essence, uniqueness and supreme identity.

It has been said that God is a circle whose centre is everywhere and whose circumference is nowhere. If this is so, then perhaps we can understand the *mutya*, being the centre of the circle, as potentially also containing everything: for it has no boundaries and it is everywhere and nowhere at the same time. Therefore, it has passed beyond the dualities of existence and contains everything – even light and darkness. It, therefore, embraces darkness and is embraced by darkness, which is really just the external form of the 'hidden light' – the eternal light dwelling in the darkness.

At this point, it becomes clear that the *mutya* does not just refer to the point of origin – the centre-point, the primordial, the spark of divinity within, the divine light – but also refers to the *Kabuuan* or the harmonious whole, embracing the male and the female, the sun and the moon, the positive and the negative, the light and the dark. It also refers both to the cosmos and to chaos, to the transcendent and the immanent, the Alpha and the Omega. In other words, the *mutya* is the archetypal image of the divine self that is on the level of an individualized cosmic consciousness – a self both unique and universal at the same time.

Mother Victoria as a *Mutya* Figure

Mother Victoria, as one historical embodiment of the *mutya* archetypal figure, is a multi-faceted character and a being of manifold personalities. Just as the *mutya* is a rare, extraordinary and unique figure, so is Mother Victoria. Her existence continues to baffle people, including her believers. Conventional norms, beliefs and ideas about God, about good and evil, about the laws of both ethics and morality – all are challenged by her. Her epistemology appears bizarre and out of this world. For instance, she has revealed that she had long existed before the physical embodiment of the historical Mother Victoria and that she would continue to exist even long after her. She has advised her believers, in fact, not to focus on her specific physical manifestations but on the spirit behind her embodiments – that is, her *diwa* (spirit and spiritual essence/identity). She is a master shape-shifter, and anyone hanging on to or becoming fixated upon one of her physical identities is bound to be confused and confounded. Mother Victoria is best understood through an examination of her attributes, personalities and traits, in order to get an overall idea of her as a *mutya* figure – a divine shape shifter who embodies in her personality as Mother Victoria the unity-in-diversity character of life and reality: that is, a unity of opposites, and a unity of everything and all things in her being. She is a living myth, and the people's intuitive understanding of her being is summed up in how she was perceived by bus conductors who used to encounter her often in Pila, Laguna back in the late 1970s: for them, she is *yong madreng jeproks* or 'the nun who looks and behaves like a hippie'.[4]

After considering the evidence of three published biographies[5] as well as the much more numerous oral accounts of the life of Mother Victoria from the various perspectives and experiences of their writers and observers, one can summarize her manifold being as a *mutya* figure in the following aspects: mother as healer; mother as teacher–guardian–guide; mother as cosmic female energy; mother as figure of great devotion; mother as talismanic and magical figure; mother as miraculous figure; mother as primordial water spirit and the Philippine water goddess; mother as goddess of light; mother as Image of divine beauty; and mother as sacred centre and spiritual centre of the Philippines.

Given these diverse dimensions, it can be said that Mother Victoria Vera Piedad has enriched and expanded the concept of *mutya* in Philippine culture. In addition to following the familiar patterns of the *mutya*, as exemplified in Philippine traditions, she has enriched and expanded the awareness of the people regarding this image by introducing and focusing on new elements in it through her individual life as Mother Victoria Vera Piedad. Below I offer some brief evocations of her contribution to the archetypal image of the *mutya* in Philippine culture.

The **Mutya** *as a trickster figure*

Traditionally, the *mutya* typifies and follows the conventional and ideal forms of beauty, power, truth, virtue and excellence. Mother, however, just like the trickster figure, poses a clear challenge to the conventional modes and ideals of goodness and excellence established by the *status quo*. First, though considered to be the manifestation of God, she came in the form of a small, old, brown-skinned and plain-faced woman who was not educated in the regular way of the school system, and who spoke ungrammatical and sub-standard English. Second, while she claimed to be one of the modern-day manifestations of the Blessed Mary, Mother of God, who had an angelic face and divine beauty as represented by her icons, Mother Victoria, on the other hand, turned up on earth in the form of an old, unglamorous woman, sometimes even disguising herself as a miserable, skinny and haggard-looking old beggar.

Third, she preferred mixing with the lowest classes of people – the poorest of the poor, the most uneducated, the most neglected, abandoned and forgotten, those whom she herself termed the 'scum of the earth' – rather than socializing with the rich, the glamorous, the famous and the intellectuals (who, nevertheless, pursued her with fascination). Fourth, she challenged the traditional image of virtue and the value of protecting the health of one's physical body, by appearing without compunction to people with tobacco inserted between her lips – a practice she said would keep her from the tendency to levitate, most especially during sleep! Hence, while smoking, she would sometimes speak in a witty, down-to-earth way, using the rough, vulgar language of street people, using swear words in a cavalier and comic manner.

Fifth, she has allowed Dr Domingo to use what appears to be the most lowly object of divination – a thing considered 'devilish' and 'dangerously demonic' by the conventional religious groups and institutions, the *ouija* board – as a public means of spiritual communication with Mother. Sixth, although Mother Victoria generally uses familiar Christian terminology in her communications, some terms and concepts outside the frame of reference of standard Christianity also feature in her contact – 'reincarnation', for example, or 'karma', or 'soul swapping'. This has bewildered many of Mother's traditional Roman Catholic believers, not to mention her fundamentalist, Bible-based Christian non-believers who consider Mother's believers as being 'lost', 'confounded', 'deceived' and 'led astray by the lies and subterfuges of the devil'.

Seventh, Mother talks about UFOs and the 'Legion of Light', of 'Masters', 'Adepts' and 'Initiates', as well as of the earth's crust, of rotation on its axis, of the galaxies, the cosmos, and of interplanetary, intergalactic communications, including those with discarnate spirits and dwarves, and with other beings and kingdoms of nature. All this, and more, keeps most people, visitors and believers alike, confused most of the time, but still deeply interested.

Mother Victoria Vera Piedad thus belongs to the underground world of non-institutionalized Philippine cultic groups – ironically termed a sub-culture despite its size – of unrecognized prophets, gurus, shamans and others, the 'underside' spiritual leaders who exist on the margins, boundaries and peripheries of life and society, and yet touch the most vital and elemental aspects of the inner life of human beings.

The Mutya *as a continuous living source of spiritual communications*

What is remarkable in Mother Victoria Vera Piedad is that though she belongs to this marginal level of 'superstitious, unlettered, vulgar and religious fanatics', she can easily and instantly shift from her popular manner of speaking – which is familiar, personal, jocose, witty, down-to-earth and humorous – to an elevated, literary, profound and formal tone. This frequently happens when she comes face-to-face with an educated person who has an honest-to-goodness existential/philo-sophical/metaphysical question to ask of her. She can also be prudent and indirect in her communicational style, preferring to speak in riddles and figures of speech for the sake of courtesy and politeness. But equally she can be direct and caustic in her manner, depending upon the attitude and mental set of the person consulting her via the *ouija* board.

Dr Domingo, who has the sole privilege of holding the glass as the medium during the spiritual consultations, says that he prefers to use the *ouija* board as a public and general means of communicating the messages of Mother, rather than the usual means of being in trance. He says he is comfortable using the *ouija* board and has been working with the glass since 1972. Even while Mother was still in the flesh, he was personally instructed to communicate with her, whenever she was out of Pila, not on the telephone, but through the glass. Even when Mother was within the grounds of Brookside, he would sometimes communicate with her, although she was physically in another room, through the glass. She claimed to be the spirit behind the glass handled by Dr Domingo. But the others were not allowed to use the glass. Visiting mediums of Mother coming from other parts of Luzon, the Visayas and Mindanao were specifically instructed by Mother not to use the glass for consultations. Each was given a different means of communicating with her publicly.

Hence, when Dr Domingo was out of Brookside, no one was authorized to use the glass as a means of public consultation with Mother. This reflected a general belief that, without the recognized channel for the glass, there was a great danger that another spirit pretending to be Mother would intervene in the process of communication. In the absence of a medium, the believers who could meditate and tune in with Mother on her level communicated with her spirit-to-spirit. Generally, these people were those who had had a longer experience of Mother's teachings and who had been taught by her, directly or indirectly, how to meditate in order to tune in with her or undergo telepathy with her. The general public, however, who as yet had no access to this inner guidance from Mother, and thus had no direct way of communicating with her, waited for the external vehicle of Mother's guidance – the open-to-the-public general consultation and spiritual communication held at least once a week at Brookside, Pila.

Spiritual communications are thus conducted on a regular basis (daily for residents of Brookside and weekly for non-residents), as well as on special occasions and feasts days of the Catholic Church. A special session involving personal consultation on a one-on-one basis can also be conducted at the request of a believer or a visitor and with the consequent approval of Dr Domingo, the medium. Certain other persons, aside from Dr Domingo, have official functions during such a session. There is a need for a *second handler of the glass*, usually a female, as a complementary and balancing force to Dr Domingo's handling of the glass. They sit opposite each other across the table on which the *ouija* board is placed. Together, with their hands lightly touching the glass, they follow the movements of the glass as it rolls across the *ouija* board. A *secretary*, who records the words and sentences formed by the gliding of the glass across the letters of the board, sits beside them. This secretary is accompanied by an *assistant secretary* who double-checks the reading of the letters, words and sentences by the secretary. Finally, a *reader* of the completed written text or message is assigned before the session starts. There is no permanent position in this secretariat except that of Dr Domingo, the medium. Any of Mother's believers could handle the glass with Dr Domingo – subject, of course, to his approval. But generally the task is given to a priest, although there is no rule saying that only priests are eligible to undertake it. The persons serving as secretary and assistant secretary are usually resident priests who exhibit speed and dexterity in reading the letters formed by the glass as it glides, sometimes nimbly and lightly, and sometimes slowly and heavily, across the letters of the *ouija* board. The reader, on the other hand, could be any believer capable of reading aloud and in a clear voice the scribbles of the secretary. The proceedings may start with a question coming from a member of the public attending the session. Sometimes, it is the glass that initiates the communication process with some opening statements and messages, even before anyone has posed a question. As the session goes on, anyone and everyone may pose a question silently to Mother without announcing it publicly in any way. Sometimes, in the process of the consultation, an answer to this silent question may arise from the recording, at which point the person whose question was answered without his/her verbalizing it may choose to keep the matter to himself/herself, or may disclose it to the group openly. Moreover, the statements of Mother may be understood simultaneously on different levels of meaning and interpretation, depending upon the depth of each person's experience and under-standing of life, the world and reality. Dr Domingo, being the medium, generally interprets difficult passages, but sometimes he leaves the interpretation open to the private understanding of each one in the assembly. Circumstances unique to each individual come into play as the medium guides each to his/her own private understanding of a specific message. At other times, however, the message is so literal and clear that people just seem to understand it easily, without any need for clarifying questions.

Dr Domingo does not communicate with Mother only through the glass. According to him, when he is not using the glass, Mother some-times shows herself to him in the form of an image, or else he hears a *bulong* or 'internal whisper'. Sometimes, she also speaks to him directly; sometimes, again, she makes herself known through dreams. Hence, his public communication is done through the *ouija* board glass, and the private communication is through an image, a whisper, an intuition, or even a dream.

Thick volumes of spiritual communication papers have been compiled between 1972, when Mother Victoria's message began to be heard, and the present. These papers contain erudite and esoteric revelations on matters pertaining to human affairs, but also include references to the most mundane chores, the management of daily community activities, and inter-personal relationships within and beyond the community. These documents have yet to be sorted out and classified systematically, and remain to be studied in detail.

The Mutya *as conductor of a terrestrial and cosmic orchestra*

In her human lifetime, Mother Victoria Vera Piedad established many spiritual centres in the Philippines that still exist today. These centres are located all over the three major island groups of the Philippines. They are found in Davao City and South Cotabato in Mindanao, in Iloilo City in the Visayas, in Brookside in Laguna, as well as in La Union and Pangasinan in Luzon.

These spiritual groups are independent of one another, have their own spiritual leadership, teachings, rules and stories, and have evolved independently out of Mother's own specific and particular teachings to them. Each centre has its own medium with his/her own distinct way of communicating with Mother. The centres have developed their own missions and outreach projects in their own and surrounding areas. No wonder that when I visited various centres in November 1997 I found other spiritual groups focused on Mother Victoria's teachings and linked to Mother's spiritual centres in the main areas of Luzon, Visayas and Mindanao. These centres are growing rapidly in number and magnitude, both in the city and in the provinces, but they are not necessarily interacting and coordinating with one another. In fact, when once or twice they have tried to coordinate their activities, these efforts have not been successful. But they all agree that there will come a 'right' time to embark on closer cooperation.

The centres in the Visayas and Mindanao have each produced a biography of Mother to compare with that of the La Union group in Luzon, which produced the earliest (1988) and the thickest biography so far. Meanwhile, Mother's Brookside Haven in Pila, Laguna has been preparing another biography, presented in the light of its own experience with Mother and from its own perspective of her teachings and mission. These spiritual biographies of Mother Victoria Vera Piedad speak of her mission to embody a form of unity established within the framework of diversity.

Mother at Brookside

Coming to Mother through the Brookside connection, I can only say that the mission Mother left behind for Brookside to continue remains the same, but also evolves through time. Thus the original spirit of the plan remains the same, but its form adapts to the times, gets transformed, evolves into other differentiated forms, but still exhibits the same spirit encountered in the beginning. Hence, the beginning ties up with the end in the process of renewal, transformation, change, metamorphosis and evolution. The question is inevitably raised of who remains faithful to the original spirit of the vision and the dream; this could only be answered by Mother, or perhaps within the spirits of the people concerned.

Meanwhile, many people have come to Brookside and gone away again – the rich, the glamorous, the wise, the academicians, the writers, the artists, the unlettered and the poor. Those who chose to stay on at Brookside after the usual 'honeymoon period' with Mother continue, in spite of obstacles, the task she has left them. The difficulty appears to centre on how people understand, practise and realize Mother's teachings, revelations and prophesies. People are changing as the years pass, and so inevitably is the understanding of Mother's teaching and mission.

Within Brookside there are sub-groups of individuals. Among the visitors to the community are still other groups with various degrees of awareness of Mother and her mission. Intentions and expectations clash within Brookside and also with the visiting outside groups, which are trying to link with it. However, all the individuals and groups presently converging at Brookside seem to feel the influence of a pervasive unifying force: the belief that Mother Victoria is orchestrating everything that happens in all her missions. Everyone waits for the realization of Mother's revelations and prophecies, especially at the dawn of a new millennium.

Mother's Vision

Mother has declared that the coming age – the Age of the Holy Spirit – is actually the Age of Woman. Using Christian terminology, Mother speaks of the Old Testament as a product of the Age of God the Father; the New Testament as a product of the Age of God the Son; and the coming Third Testament as the product of the Age of the Holy Spirit, which is declared to be the Age of Woman. In astrological terms, this seems to correlate with Western astrology's Age of Aquarius, or even with the 'New Age'.

Mother says that she is not only the embodiment of the Holy Spirit, but also embodies the 'Blessed Name' – that is, the Father, the Son and the Mother, all at the same time. She also says that she manifests herself in various forms of gods, goddesses, saints and gurus, all over the world, both ancient and modern. This is probably the reason why Mother Victoria aims to realize a Universal Sovereign Catholic Church. According to her, the meaning of the word 'Catholic' is not 'Roman Catholic' nor 'Greek Catholic' but a truly 'Catholic' or 'universal' church that would include Islam, Hinduism, Buddhism, Taoism and all the other religions.

This is probably also the reason why she is known to express in her spiritual communications her desire to build a 'spiritual cathedral' composed of individual human edifices. Here she might be invoking the notion of a universal cathedral of human hearts and spirits, welded into One while at the same time freely expressing their own individualities.

Mother places great emphasis on the value of human freedom. Though she guides and gives counsel to people regarding their lives, her help is not perceived as a 'dictatorship of the spirit' but as a spiritual partnership. Similarly, she has always stressed the significance of unity among all believers. She worked it out once by calling for a yearly spiritual congress which would be a national assembly of all faiths in the Philippines. This call picked up momentum for a while, and for several years a number of spiritual groups in the Philippines congregated annually at Brookside in Pila, Laguna. Most of the groups that supported this significant initiative came from the 'underside' of society. There were also some rich, glamorous and wise people who came to watch and see for themselves whether something significant and substantial would develop. But owing to the natural human desire of wanting to be 'number one', the spiritual congress ended up in chaotic splinters. The individuals, the people and the groups have still to learn that true unity is not born out of uniformity, but as the convergence of differentiation: in this process no one individual nor any one group can enforce its own identity and procedures over others. Each individual or group makes a unique contribution to the whole through its own *mutya* or gift of uniqueness, identity and essence.

To prepare for a national and global spiritual networking, and to push for greater human evolution, in 1989 Mother Victoria Vera Piedad, against much resistance from the intellectual groups at Brookside, established the Victorian Order of the Resurrected Christ – a new order of male and female priests and bishops (single or married, rich or poor, educated or uneducated) that is independent of the Roman Catholic hierarchy. These female and male priests either volunteered to be made priests, or were chosen, asked or requested by Mother to be part of her ecumenical and interfaith order of priests. She herself, as head of the Victorian Order, ordained the priests through the *Supremo* (Head Bishop) as the channel and officiating priest. Mother has not fully declared her reasons for this move, but some believers say that it is hoped that these priests will complement the work of the traditional priests of the Roman Catholic Church. This creation of a new and unconventional order of priesthood by Mother Victoria is interpreted by the present Supreme Bishop of the Victorian Order as an improvement of the original BROMOKI groups established by Mother all over the nation, since the latter is a fraternity of kids (BROMOKI, as I have mentioned, is the acronym for Brotherhood of Mother's Kids) whereas the Victorian Order signifies the growth and maturity of believers from Mother's 'kids' to Mother's 'priests'.

Mother states in her spiritual communications that she chose the Philippines as one of the countries in the world in which she would manifest herself because the country could serve as a trigger point in world development. Folk traditions, as it happens, also foretell that the Philippines will serve as a beckoning and signalling light to the coming of a new spiritual order. Some cultic groups believe that the Philippines will serve as one of the spiritual centres of the world, a kind of New Jerusalem that will serve as an inspiration and a model to the world. One can note in passing that United Nations surveys over the last few years have indicated that the Philippines is the most spiritual country in the world.[6]

The return to roots

Cognizant of its responsibility to the whole world as a trigger point, the Victorian Order of the Resurrected Christ at Brookside, Pila, Laguna struggles to realize its own destiny by working out its own unity within the Order, with the old BROMOKI members all over the Philippines and the world, and also with those among Mother's sympathizers and believers who have chosen not to become priests. This work of unity is being pursued by looking for the common ground upon which everyone can unite. This common ground is believed by some to be found in following the message of Mother Victoria to go back to the indigenous roots of the nation – to reconnect with its origins and cultural heritage, and so to build the present and the future on the solid foundation and basics of the past. The Order is now slowly veering away from the celebration of Holy Mass, a rite derived from the Roman Catholic Church. It has already adopted full-moon and sunrise festival rites derived from indigenous practices. It holds a neo-indigenous ritual festival every third Saturday of the month at the lakeshore of the Laguna de Bai, attended mostly by street children. This ritual is performed to develop a sense of communion with the place, its people and its environment. The festival aims to effect a spiritual healing of the people and the increasingly polluted environment. On the national level, it aims to effect a moral recovery and renewal for the whole nation.

The Order's religious programme thus includes the indigenization of religious rites, the holding of neo-indigenous ritual festivals for the renewal of the environment and humanity, and mass prayer for the healing of people, afflicted souls and discarnate spirits, as well as the healing of all nature. These activities also have a social dimension. The Victorian Order has opened a cultural heritage programme for the children of two communities it serves: Pagalangan and Banca-Banca, Victoria. This programme teaches children their long-forgotten local indigenous alphabet, revives Philippine folklore and mythology, and provides appreciation and knowledge of their community arts and culture.

As all these developments continue, the expectations of people within the community have been intensified by another phenomenon: UFO sightings have become a familiar experience at Brookside. Many still remember the prophecy that some day, near the end of the old or the start of the new millennium, a UFO-assisted 'Grand Lift' would occur. In preparation for this, people see to it that they purify their *kalooban* (inner life) by adopting a healthy, simple, pure and harmonious lifestyle.

Postscript

'I go back to the very beginning and start all over again on another level. I am a dancer and love dancing. Since I first came to know Mother in January, 1997, the *mutya* that I had come to study as a mythical symbol acquired flesh and blood right before my eyes, dancing to the rhythmic mysteries of life. Dancing out the letters of the past, the present, the future …. I never knew the value of such motion and such stillness. I, too, am a dancer of sacred mysteries, trying and yearning to achieve oneness with the Divine flow, praying that my body will become transparent enough for the Light to pass through, for the body to be fluid enough to respond to the minutest "energy", to make it quiver in devotion, or jerk in ecstasy, to make my body a temple and vehicle for the *mutya*.

I have found a home in a community, not the best and the most spiritual, I know, for I see in it the most common flaws of struggling humanity. But I have learned to accept it as my place of assignment to realize the goal of unity within diversity, and to practise Mother's "Three Virtues to the Holy Path", namely, Charity, Humility and Patience.'

• • •

The above was written in 1997. It is now 16 April 2001. I am presently outside the Brookside community, and have been on extended leave of absence since May 1999. Outside Brookside, I am not a bishop nor a priest. Yet I feel that Mother's ordination is a never-ending ordination. Priesthood, I realize, is not a matter of being recognized by popular and dominant religious institutions. Priesthood is a matter of consciousness. One need not necessarily go through a ritual to become a priest. But since I was personally invited by Mother, both indirectly through the spiritual communications at the board, and through the direct invitations of the priests of the Victorian Order, I still passed through a priestly ordination – that of Mother's ritual of priestly ordination held on Easter Day of 1997. Moreover, my 'licence' as a priest is still effective until the end of 2001. But whether I will renew it or not is immaterial to me now. I believe that, even outside the Brookside Community, I am still a priest of Mother, both from the ritual point of view and in my consciousness of that commitment originally established with Mother. The unbelief of others cannot take this conviction away from me. And whether I renew the licence or not is just a matter of legality for me, as is the matter of my choice to continue practising this function officially in the context of the Brookside community. Outside of Brookside I remain, unofficially, a priest of Mother Victoria even without the licence.

I had to leave the community, however, because at one point it ceased to be a community for me. Differences over interpretation of Mother's teachings arose. There was a growing preference for uniformity of opinions over a healthy discussion of these differences and the agreement to disagree on matters fundamental to the uniqueness of each person. A no-discussion approach in dealing with ticklish issues was favoured over the discussion approach. Healthy questions to counter any suspected abuse of power by the medium were avoided and considered dangerous and hostile to the maintenance of unity and order in the group. Moreover, the indigenization programmes I had initiated had been halted after some top leaders had expressed fears that 'pagan' elements had obtained influence in the Victorian Order. I was also up against an excess of caution about being ahead of one's time in promoting the indigenization of Roman Catholic-based rituals like that of the Holy Mass, and, tired of swimming against the stream, I had to give way. Feeling the weight of resistance from the top leadership, and seeing the openness of other spiritual communities outside Brookside to my indigenization programmes, I decided to take leave of absence from Mother's Haven to prevent a collision. Instead, I focused my energies on continuing my cultural heritage and indigenization programmes elsewhere. Now, along with the teaching and practice of anthropology, I am a freelance ritual art performer, doing my sacred and ritual dances in three forms: dancing alone in the midst of nature;

dancing with some fellow ritual dancers; or dancing with the participation of the community, people's organizations and local government and non-government institutions.

My concept of community has expanded: I no longer understand it as merely a collection of people in one geographical area, but rather as a group of people who choose to work together on the basis of awareness and consciousness of their mission in life. Hence, a community is not determined by number alone; even a group of two or three could still be a community if there is 'one flow of communion within them' and if their lives have impact on the beings and lives of people and the environment around them.

I believe that the spirit behind Mother Victoria led me to Brookside in the course of my research on the *mutya* for me to meet her historical being and find in her one of the embodiments of the living myth of the *mutya*. She made Brookside my spiritual school and training ground. When I had learned all the essential lessons I needed to learn, she made me 'graduate' from this school and expanded my tasks on a wider scale. My one-woman ritual group *Sayaw-Bathala* (The Dance of God Within) teamed up with other networking ritual arts groups in *Teatro Katotohanan* (Truth Theatre) and *Pandayang Babaylan* (Workshop of Priests-Ritualists). To this extent, Mother has guided me all the way from the individual sphere, to that of the community, the national and now, with the publication of this chapter, even to the international sphere. Now I know that the local is also universal, and that the One is also the (diverse) Many.

Notes and References

1 This approach, called *pamamaybay*, is what I am developing as a research methodological framework for my doctoral dissertation titled 'Images of the *Mutya* in the Pasig River, its Suburbs and Other Water-based Systems of the Philippines'. See Grace Odal, '*Mutya*', in Teresita Obusan (ed.), *Roots of Filipino Spirituality* (Quezon City: Mamamathala Inc., 1998); Grace P. Odal, 'Pagtuklas sa Mutyang Sarili: Paglilimi sa Isang Pamamaraang Panloob', in Teresita Obusan (ed.), *Pamamaraan: Indigenous Knowledge and Evolving Research Paradigm* (Quezon City: Mamamathala Inc., 1994).

2 Dean S. Fansler, *Manuscript Collection of Philippine Folklore* (Diliman, Quezon City: University of the Philippines, Filipiniana Section, ca. 1922), no pagination.

3 Juan R. Francisco, *Indian Culture in the Philippines: Views and Reviews* (Kuala

Lumpur: University of Malaya, 1985), reprinted in the Philippines by the author, 1987, p. 12.

4 Cielo Buenaventura, 'Unusual Spiritual Congress: a Journey to "Motherland"', *Philippine Panorama*, 12 May 1985, pp. 24–31.

5 See Ma. Isabel S. Aniez, *The Last Testament to Mankind*, arranged and ed. Jane F. Almora (San Fernando, La Union: Silent Wings Club, Inc., 1988), p. 310; Bella Sombong Falcis, *The Last Drop* (Iloilo City: BROMOKI Universe at the Cross of salvation, 1996), p. 136; *The Promised Comforter God the Holy Spirit, Rev. Mother Victoria Vera Piedad, Blessed Name No. 0123-6-4 Jesus Joseph and The Second Coming of Jesus Christ and the Manifestation of God the Holy Spirit, the Third Order of the Holy Trinity* (Royal Valley, Km. 7, San Juan Village, Bangkal, Davao City: Universal Catholic Cathedral, Inc., undated, *ca.* 1997?), p. 267.

6 Serafin Talisayon, 'Patotoo: Concepts of Validity Among Some Indigenous Filipino Spiritual Groups', in Teresita Obusan (ed.), *Pamamaraan: Indigenous Knowledge and Evolving Research Paradigms* (Quezon City: Mamamathala Inc., 1994).

Additional Sources

Interviews with Most Reverend Alfonso Gonzales (1997–8) and Monsignor La Chica (1997–8).

7

Suprema Isabel Suarez

SR MARY JOHN MANANZAN OSB

In a consultation of Asian women theologians in the Philippines in
1985, the participants came to the conclusion that 'there is a religious
root to women's oppression'.[1] This radical bias against women is true
of all institutionalized religions. The remarkable thing, however, is that
when women claim their right to religious experience and venture to
set out on this spiritual journey, many reach the highest peak, transcending the oppressive element of religion. They even become gurus,
teachers and spiritual leaders, who number men among their followers
and spiritual children. There are today many such living women gurus
and spiritual leaders. One of them, the subject of this chapter, is
Suprema Isabel Suarez, the head of a religious group called Ciudad
Mistica de Dios (CMDD) in the Philippines. Before introducing
Suprema Isabel, it will be helpful to describe the context in which she
lives and works.

The Sacred Mountain of Banahaw

The mountain of Banahaw, which is in the southern Tagalog province
of Quezon, has always been considered a sacred place of pilgrimage
even before the coming of the Spaniards. In those times it was a place
of worship and offering for the *babaylanes* (women priests). Vitaliano
Gorospe writes:

> From pre-Hispanic times, Banahaw has always been a spiritual center – a
> geological dynamo that radiates an intense vortex of energy which
> inevitably attracts clouds that bring rain to nurture the mysterious moun-
> tain. Banahaw is a mysterious place because it attracts mystics and those

who in one way or another are searching for God or contact with the divine. It gained popularity through numerous reports of miraculous cures that happened on the mountain. But Banahaw continues to expand its influence beyond the rituals of structured religions and religious cults, attracting mystics and psychics, mediums and yogis, thousands of religious pilgrims, and, in growing numbers, a new generation seeking to develop and enrich their prayer life and spirituality.[2]

At present, Banahaw is the home of about 30 religious groups that have in common some elements such as the integration of Catholic Christianity with folk religiosity, nationalism and the worship of the *Mahal na Ina* (Sacred Mother). The biggest and best-organized of these groups is the Ciudad Mistica de Dios.

The Ciudad Mistica de Dios

The founder of this religious group was Maria Bernarda Balitaan, born in 1876, when Spain still ruled the Philippines, at a time of growing nationalist consciousness in the country. Among her attributes are a mysterious birth and mystical experiences which include travelling to the planets and also to the Throne of God. Her birth is considered to be the dawn of the Age of the Mother. She is supposed to complete the work that was left unfinished by Christ. In her early twenties she gathered a group of followers who were won over by her wise teachings and healing abilities. Maria Bernarda Balitaan was ostracized by her own family, persecuted by the authorities and put in prison several times on charges such as insanity, disturbing the peace, usurpation of priestly duties and impersonation of religious persons. Her followers, later on, formally founded a *Samahan* or *Kapatiran* (Brotherhood/Sisterhood) akin to the *Hermandad* or pious groups founded within the Catholic Church during Spanish times.

This religious group, while retaining many of the teachings and rituals of the Catholic Church including the Mass, combined them with indigenous symbols, rituals and language during their ceremonies and prayers. The main celebrants of the rituals are women priests, who perform their ordinary work during the day. They believe in the Trinity, but with a fourth person, the *Bathalumang Ina* (God the Mother). They talk of God as Father, Mother and Son, with the Holy Spirit binding them all.[3] The God Mother is sometimes identified with the Blessed

Virgin Mary and at other times with Bernarda Balitaan herself. They also believe in the sainthood of some patriots like Dr Jose Rizal.

The group is millenarian in nature because they believe in the coming of the Armageddon. History is divided into three periods, the period of the Father, that of the Son, and that of the Mother. The time of the Father was the time of pre-history, the period of the ancestors. Evil and sin are thought to have started during this period. With the birth of Jesus Christ came the period of the Son, which continues until the year 2000. Those whom Jesus left behind to continue his work have not accomplished their duty; in fact, they have led the people astray, just as the male leaders of the Church are doing at present. Though the age of the Mother has already come with the birth of Bernarda Balitaan, it is not yet fully accomplished. The coming of the millennium and of the Mother will mean the end of the present power structure, the separation of the wicked from the good, and the establishment of a new order. Mt Banahaw is seen as the *huling daungan*, a refuge for those who are to be saved. It will be the New Jerusalem.[4]

In preparation for this last event, people should embrace regimes of good conduct and enhance their spiritual lives. The 'prayer life' is mainly communal, characterized by daily, weekly, monthly and yearly rituals. The 'never ending prayer' is accompanied by the *dose-dose* of 12 men and women, who form a continuous chain of prayer in the church and religious processions and pilgrimages (*pwesto*) to different sites of worship in the mountains.

In view of the coming global judgement, the group emphasizes the values of the sisterhood/brotherhood that include equality, sacrifice, service to others, care for nature and the centrality of women.[5] There are communal undertakings such as a cooperative store, cooperative farming and a transport service; group resources are shared by all. According to members, the millennium will be accomplished when woman becomes the *Bathalumang Ina*, as well as *ministra* (priest) and *ate* (older Sister) to all.[6]

Suprema Isabel Suarez

Early Years and Vocation

Isabel Suarez, a handsome woman with natural dignity, was born in 1940 to the family of Amador Suarez, one of the leaders of the CMDD.

Just as a mysterious birth from a crystal ball was attributed to Bernarda Balitaan, similarly Isabel was supposed to have stayed in her mother's womb for 21 months. Even as a child she showed signs of being clairvoyant, and incidents of her foreseeing accidents happening to her relatives were common.

When she finished high school, she came to Manila where she intended to study medicine. In an interview, she relates how she wanted to go to college but every time she was about to enrol, she was visited by a grave illness which made her vomit blood. During one of these bouts, it is known that she said she was nearing death. Her father, who was at her bedside, said that she fell ill because she was not meant to go to a 'material school' but was destined to do God's work. She still persisted in trying to go to school until a visionary experience convinced her that she was indeed called to another vocation. Isabel Suarez told her father she was ready to join the CMDD.

Although told by the doctor not to get involved in any strenuous activity, on her first all-night vigil and *puwesto* she stayed with the group throughout their long walk to the different sites of worship. She consoled herself by thinking that if she died in the process at least she was doing the will of God. After her decision, her surrender to God was so complete that she never looked back, and devoted herself utterly to the service of God.

When the Suprema Victory Ebry died on 16 December 1963, the community chose Isabel Suarez as their Suprema. She was just twenty-three years old and new to the movement, and therefore was reluctant to accept the title of Suprema. However, after nine days of prayer offered by the community, and after she recognized divine signs confirming that she was indeed the right choice, Isabel Suarez acceded. In an interview, she comments on her election:

> When the second Suprema died, the elders met to choose the next Suprema. They saw me in a vision, and that was that. I was hesitant at first, after all, I was only 23 years old at the time. But it was not up to me, nor was it up to them. They had a vision, you see.[7]

Functions as Suprema

Suprema Isabel Suarez is the highest spiritual leader of a community that has about fifty thousand members, some of whom live outside

Banahaw. She is responsible for the temporal and spiritual welfare of her followers and also has administrative, ritual and educational tasks.

As the temporal administrator, Suprema Isabel is bound to maintain unity among the members, go on missions/visits to the different communities, and ensure that the community has enough to live on. Her more important work is providing spiritual leadership and spiritual guidance.

She is called 'Mother' by all and is also the community's main teacher. This she does through individual consultations and also through public lectures that she gives every Saturday and on special occasions. The weekly lectures last up to three hours and the usual topics are unity of the community and precepts such as spiritual life, self-knowledge, prayer, consciousness, sacrifice, humility, truth, hope, etcetera. Nationalistic songs sung by the community are usually the prelude to the lecture.

The lecture delivered on the birthday of the founder, Bernarda, usually determines the theme of the lectures to be delivered during the rest of that year. However, the structure of the talk remains familiar to her followers, since Suprema Isabel always narrates different events from the life of Bernarda and talks about adherence to her precepts in current times.

The Suprema presides over all important and official rituals, including those of the 'Feastday of Bernarda' and the 'Holy Week' with its 'Seven Last Words'. She has been trained as a priest but she seldom says mass now because of her other work. On the important feasts, she wears a formal vestment and a tall crown.

A unique role of the Suprema is in the *Paglangkap*, the ritual in which the Suprema acts as a medium for her departed father (Mamay) and for Bernarda Balitaan. This happens about six to eight times a year. There are various rites and gestures involved in this process but the main part is the communication of the messages and advice of the two departed leaders. Witnesses have testified that during these communications the face of the Suprema undergoes a change. Future events are sometimes foretold and Suprema also goes on astral travel during this rite.

These activities are supposed to prepare the members for the end time and the fulfilment of the covenant. To complete and complement her role as spiritual leader, Suprema Isabel Suarez has developed

strength of character and a deep spirituality which Arche Ligo has
described in the following words:

> Because of her role in the community, Suprema has to nurture a deep spir-
> ituality and develop a moral strength to lead her community into the
> millennium of the Mother. She participates regularly in the daily prayers of
> the community. It is said that she also goes to pray in the natural spots
> sacred to Ciudad Mistica de Dios.[8]

She also fasts and does *suplina*, a form of self-flagellation. Sometimes
she goes into trance, where God, or the spirit of Maria Bernarda, or
that of her father, Amador, takes over and gives her messages. Therefore, whether in the midst of prayer or some rite, she always listens
closely to the *Santong Boses* (Holy Voice) for messages and direction.

Since there is a lot of wisdom and knowledge behind her words,
members and friends of Ciudad Mistica de Dios seek her out for counselling, healing and advice. Outsiders, including myself, can attest to
her integrity as a female religious leader. She is simple, devoted, gentle,
unassuming, hospitable, accommodating, and just. People around the
community, including politicians, respect her and hold her in high
esteem.

Conclusion

Although we cannot call the CMDD a feminist organization nor
Suprema Isabel Suarez a feminist, she and her organization do have an
important role in the women's movement in the Philippines, especially
in the area of women and religion. There is a definite and conscious
feminine perspective, not only in the theology of the group but also in
its leadership. The God-image is inclusive, the importance of the role
of women is emphasized. There is a preference for women leaders, not
only in the administrative but also in the ritual aspects of their lives.

Notes and References

1 Proceedings of the Asian Women Consultation, unpublished MS, 1985, p. 1.
2 Vitaliano Gorospe, *Banahaw: Conversations with a Pilgrim to the Power Mountain*
   (Manila: Bookmark, 1992), p. 17.
3 Arche Ligo, 'Elements of an Indigenous Feminist Spirituality in the Popular

Religion of Ciudad Mistica de Dios', unpublished Masters thesis, De La Salle University, Manila, 1998, pp. 112–22.
4   *Ibid.*
5   *Ibid.*
6   *Ibid.*
7   *Sunday Inquirer Magazine*, Manila, 8 October 1995.
8   Arche Ligo, 'Elements of an Indigenous Feminist Spirituality'.

8

Parallel Worlds of Madhobi Ma, 'Nectar Mother'
My Encounter with a Twentieth-Century Tāntric Saint

MADHU KHANNA

In contemporary discourse, many feminist scholars have been engaged in a careful re-examination of the constructive and positive role that religion can play in moulding current feminist concerns. In Asia, despite the constraints posed by an overtly patriarchal society, women scholars are beginning to redefine the personal narratives of women saints known in Asian history,[1] in the hope that such empowered female figures may provide a model for the empowerment of modern Asian women. Moreover, research into female saints in Asia has demonstrated how often they embody unifying streams of religious consciousness and, with very few exceptions, may be advanced as inspiring examples of inter-faith unity.

In studying the social concerns of women in India, greater emphasis used to be laid on examining the mainstream Brahmanical paradigm dictated by the law givers of ancient India. However, modern research has conspicuously proved that the lives of several non-Brahmanical religious groups and non-Hindus are not governed by the ideals articulated in the Brahmanical law codes. A woman's lived experience often reverses the path set out in the scriptures. To interpret this highly volatile socio-religious scenario within which women reconstruct their lives, it is necessary to pay closer attention to two categories with reference to which the personal narratives of women are assembled. First, there are the traditional roles (such as wife and mother) that women are meant to follow unconditionally. These define her *strīdharma*, a traditional code of injunctions motivated by choiceless action. Second, there is the vast silent area of a personal code of action which a woman invariably negotiates within the prison of patriarchal constraints. We may call it *svadharma*,[2] an action motivated by free choice. It is obvious that these two categories are in conflict with one another and to a modern mind may appear irreconcilable. In this chapter I shall examine the manner in which the overwhelmingly patriarchal codes get inverted or subverted and redifined in ever new ways in the extraordinary world of Madhobi Ma, 'Nectar Mother', a twentieth-century Tantric saint.

It has been observed that a woman who lives as a saint dies as a woman.[3] The question I would then pose is, what is the Hindu response of a Tantric woman saint to this observation? Taking my inspiration from what is described as the irreconcilable conflict between the *strīdharma* set out in the law books, and one's *svadharma*, an action dictated by personal choice, I propose to explore some hidden dimensions of this ambiguous terrain with reference to the life of a Tantric woman saint. In order to examine this proposition, I explore several dimensions of her extraordinary life: her miracle birth, the role of a woman guru in Śākta Tantra, and the religious life of this woman who is regarded by her devotees as an incarnation of the goddess.

Madhobi Ma (Mother Madhobi), whose name means Nectar Mother, is a woman of extraordinary calling. She is unusual among Indian woman, for she combines several roles: a wife, a mother, a Tantric priestess, a detached renunciate, a healer (*vaidya*), a guru and a female preceptor.

The Tantras of all denominations – Hindu, Buddhist, Śaiva, Śākta – attach a strong significance to the role of a spiritual preceptor or a guru. In the Tantras, the guru occupies a special place as someone who shares unity with the sacred mantra and the adored deity. There can be no genuine transmission of power, it is said, unless a spiritual transmission of cosmic energy, technically known as *Kuṇḍalinī Śakti*, has taken place from a guru to the disciple. This transmission may be visible and gross – as when it takes place through an initiation ceremony of *śaktipāt* or transmission of energy – or it may be subtle, as on recorded occasions when the preceptor, by means of mere touch or a gaze, awakens the dormant spiritual force in the disciple. Another significant feature of the Śākta Tantra is that women preceptors are regarded as the supreme vehicles of spiritual wisdom and transmitters of spiritual energy. They are empowered to play powerful religious roles of leadership.

Tantric conventions hold that a female preceptor is a perfect vessel of the great archetype of the goddess eulogized as the dynamic energy of the cosmos. Although the Vedas recognized the contribution of semi-divine woman preceptors, called *rishikās* or *brahmavādinīs*, it is in the Tantras that they found their fullest expression. In the textual tradition, Tantric scriptures are often cast in the form of a dialogue in which the goddess Pāravatī or Bhairavī assumes the form of a teacher who is also a source of revelation. Though not frequently, some traditional hagiographies record the names of female preceptors who were a part of specific religious sects. The female preceptors occupy as significant a place in Tantric ritual as their male counterparts. In all the vast liturgical literature of the Hindus, it is specifically in the Tantras that we find a hymn solely dedicated to the female guru, which is to be chanted before the worship of the goddess commences. In the hymn from the *Mātrkābheda Tantra*, the female guru is described as a 'saviour who carries the disciple from the bonds of the world' (*bhava-bandhanaparasya*); she is also the supreme mother, the bestower of knowledge and liberation, identical with the holy trinity.[4] To her devotees, Madhobi Ma represents all the qualities that a true guru is supposed to embody. She stands as one of the most influential forces in a disciple's life. The bond between her and the disciple has an umbilical strength. She is perhaps one of the few female preceptors who has been given the authority by her five male preceptors to take the chair of guruship.

A Miracle Birth

Madhobi Ma's father, Sasadhara Chowdhary, was an aristocractic *zamindar* and an heir to the well-known Chowdhary clan. The family owned estates of agricultural land in Hasanabad, East Bengal, now in Bangaladesh. His wife was one Kamalnayani Devi. The couple, blessed with wealth and fortunes, were devout Hindus with strong spiritual leanings. The family had a rare blessing from a Muslim Sufi saint, Pir Syed Ali Akhtar Bade Baba, who over the years became their family preceptor and spiritual guide. Kamalnayani gave birth to thirteen sons. For the preceding seven generations no daughter had been born to the family. One day, a dejected Kamalnayani Devi went to the sacred grove of the Sufi Pir and begged the boon of a daughter that would lift the curse from the family.

Her pledge was soon to be fulfilled through an extraordinary event that was to take place in her life. One day when she went to pray at the grave of the Sufi saint, Bade Baba, a halo of light came from the sky and entered into her through a wound on her left wrist. She returned home and related the incident to her husband, but he brushed it aside as hallucination. When this incident occurred, Kamalnayani was fifty-five years of age. Soon, she was to discover that she had undergone a miraculous conception and was to give birth to a child. Thirteen months passed after this miraculous event. The birth, when it came, was as mysterious as the conception, defying natural laws. On the epoch-making day, 11 May 1954 (*Bikram Samvat* 1361, according to the Bengali calendar), she went to her courtyard for evening devotion and fainted on the floor. A bundle wrapped in a thin membrane rolled down between her legs. While the women of the family assisted in the natural birth of a baby girl, a rainbow appeared in the cloudless sky.

After a few days the child was taken to the grave of the Sufi saint for a thanksgiving ceremony. Kamalnayani picked up the bundle of joy and offered the child to him. Just then a halo of light appeared and a voice seemed give notice of a higher intention: 'I shall take her back, when the time comes.'

The child was named Ranu and was brought up in the midst of comfort and luxury. The pampered Ranu became the apple of every-one's eye. But she was often a little distant, and abstained from the usual childish pranks. Communicating with unearthly powers, perhaps, she was observed to live in a world of her own. Seeing this inclination, her parents took her to a hermit, who proclaimed that she would be a saint and devote her life to the deliverance of humanity.

In 1969, the family was struck by tragedy. Eleven of their thirteen sons expired within a year, which caused them a great deal of distress. At the tender age of sixteen, Ranu was married to a commoner working in Delhi. But this event, instead of plunging her into conjugal bliss, made her even more detached from the cares of the world and she secretly yearned for a formal initiation (*dīksā*) that would set her on the right path.

Thereupon began the tension of a housewife yearning for the passionate life of the spirit, which is free and spontaneous. She realized that emotional turmoils are the testing ground of a devotee, necessary for the purification of the spirit. While internally, she had cut her bonds with the life of a householder, externally she did not disassociate herself from her husband and her family. A son named Ravi was born to her. Later, another son, Siddhartha, and a daughter Dipa were to become a part of her 'worldly family'.

Ma's family reverses the Hindu ideology of a hereditary family whose members are connected through the blood line. Her spiritual family consists of several members who are not her blood relations. This spiritual family has been bonded on the basis of ideology and a common philosophy of life. Entry into the group is strictly on the basis of spiritual competence and is confirmed through ritual initiation. According to Ma, the guiding principle of the true family was that it helped the inmates to live in harmony with the truth of life. Even the fragrant flowers, foliage, birds, fishes and rabbits that formed a part of the ashram were part and parcel of the spiritual world. Ma believed that since no element in life was inanimate, all the creatures from the plant and animal kingdom were conscious and in some spiritual way integral to her family.

Spiritual Lineage

Ma's early mystic experiences came from the Pir guru of the family, Bade Baba, who has, since her birth, been close to her in different bodiless forms. Sometimes he has appeared in dreams, sometimes as a voice, at other times as a thought form or simply in direct non-corporeal contact. His invisible presence is felt by Ma almost every day in one form or the other. He has been her most trusted guide and has shown her the way to move beyond the daily tribulations of existence. Out of his early guidance evolved her formal initiation into Śākta Tantra, which began to unfold from 1973. Ma's personal spirituality became fully manifested through the multiple initiations she received from the year 1973 onwards. It is necessary to record these in summary form.

At the age of nineteen, on 23 March 1973, Ma received her first initiation at Tarapitha, a small rural village in Birbhum District, West

Bengal. The temple of the goddess Tārā, the presiding deity, stands there above the village houses. Near the temple, running alongside the river Dwarka, lies a sacred grove of ancient trees which is the local *smaśāna*, the cremation ground. The grove is full of small huts and houses, made of mud with thatched roofs, where several Tantric hermits live in seclusion. The presiding deity of this temple, the goddess Tārā, is of great significance to the Buddhist and the Hindu Śakta pantheon. Tārā, as a manifestation of Śakti, has her dual aspects of being both creative and destructive. She is the divinity of passage. She protects and saves and, like a boat, carries her devotees to the shores of enlightenment. The goddess claims her own cult and is also one of the goddesses in the circle of goddesses known as the *Daśamāhavidyās*. Tārā shares an intimate connection with goddess Kālī, and represents the combined totality of fierce, benign, and motherly traits. It is observed that, both Tārā and Kālī are *jāgrata* (awake) goddesses[5] – that is, they rise to the occasion and are fully awake to the needs of humanity in the Kālī age.

Madhobi Ma's first initiation took place in this renowned sacred centre and was conducted by a Tantric saint, Shankar Khepa, a great devotee of Tārā, who gave her the Tārā mantra and imparted the holistic sacred knowledge of various disciplines such as astrology, palmistry, Ayurveda and the secrets of Kaula Dharma, the Left-Hand practice of Tantra. It was Shankar Khepa who gave her the name of Madhobi Ma, along with the mystic connotations of her name. The letters *Ma* stands for 'Mother', *DHA* for *Dharoni*, 'the bearer of creation', and *BI* for *Bishva Brāhmanda*, 'the whole universe'. Her name reflects her character and mission in life, her identification with the mother of the universe who is born to deliver souls from the round of existence.

Also in 1973, she visited Kamakhya in Assam, a well-known Tantric pilgrimage centre presided over by the goddess Kamakhya. There, she received initiation from the famous guru Ramnikanta Deva Sharma into the worship of the goddess Tripurasundarī. This is a lineage (*paramparā*) that traces its authority to the *miśrakrama*, or the combined traditions that came from Kerala and Assam. Thereafter followed a powerful infusion of *śaktipat*, which constitutes an awakening and transference of the cosmic energy lying dormant in us, known as the *Kuṇḍalinī Śakti*. Madhobi Ma, in recalling this

Table 8.1 Spiritual Lineage of Madhobi Ma

Dates	Name of Guru	Deity	Place
11 May 1954	Syed Ali Akthar Bade Baba – a Sufi Saint & Vishudhananda		Hasanabad Bangladesh
23 March 1973	Shankar Khepa	Tārā	Tarapitha, Birbhum, W. Bengal
1973	Ramnikanta Deva Sharma	Bālā Tripura- sundarī	Kamakhya, Assam
1974	Narayana Tirtha (Gufa Baba) (disembodied state)	Kundalinī	Gomukha
1982	Ganesh Narayana	Aghora Śiva	Chirawa, Rajasthan
1985	Swami Keshavananda	Krishna	New Delhi

Mode of Dīksā	Special features of Dīksā
Mystic experience in which Ma talks to him directly	Spontaneous transmission
Mantra Dīksā Tārā Mantra	Kaula Dharma based on Kaula Tantras, knowledge of Astrology, Palmistry, Ayurveda and Kaula Darśana
Śrīvidyā Mantra with pūrnābhiśekha	Miśra Krama, Śrīvidyā with Kerala and Assam traditions
In disembodied form as Śaktipat	Kriyā Yoga
Ādyā Mantra	Aghora Panthi Dīksā
Krishna Mantra	Vaisnava of Ramanuja Sampradāya

experience, explains the opening out of the subtle centres through her initiation:

> After the ceremonies, Ramani Baba gave me a ritual chalice (*pātra*) filled with holy substance. I brought it to my lips and sipped a few drops from the chalice. Then I felt a strange sensation, as though my personality, the me in me, does not exist any more. I exist only as a channel of *prāna*, life energy. I do not exist in my sensations and in and through my identities any more. I was not a person with a name and body, I was simply a ball of energy which had touched infinite heights of splendour. The 'I' does not exist, but the 'I' as a *prāna-ksetra*, the zone of energy. I blinked for a few seconds and felt drugged under the pressure of energy. For some time I lay silent in that state. Then I woke up and walked towards the underground shrine of Bhairavī. It was midnight and the moon reflected a silver river of light. I followed the shadows and came down the stairway towards the shrine. I felt as though I was being followed by Vama Khepa of Tarapitha. He held my hand and led me by the side of the silvery pond with the shimmering moon. I felt Baba's presence intensely. A sound reverberated and my crown centre (*sahasrāra*) split open. The 'I' that seemed dead opened out to another world. A conscious atom of light sprang up into a deep blue haze of light, then into a band of magenta light, then pure and luminous white light. In that radiant halo of light, I saw all the forty gurus of my lineage, standing before me in their transparent bodies. Then my guru said, 'Now you are ready for practice of *Kapāla-bheda*, the breaking out of the crown of the head for astral flight.'

Later, another mystic transmission took place in the high caves of Gomukha, a place of sacred pilgrimage in the Himalayas. This time the initiation was conducted by a disembodied guru, Gufa Baba, a Tantric living in the caves in the high mountains, who was named Narayana Tirtha. In 1982 she received another initiation on the worship of Kālī, in its extreme Aghora or esoteric aspects, from Swami Ganesh Narayana of Chirawa, Rajasthan. And finally, in 1985, Swami Keshavananda, a well-known *smārta* guru of Krishna-*bhakti* fame, gave her the Krishna mantra. Hence, between 1973 and 1985, in a span of twelve years, she had been ordained by five gurus from different sects (see Table 8.1). During this period the contribution of Bade Baba, the Muslim Pir, never declined but only heightened her spiritual experience. Ma often says, 'I am like the seven musical notes, six came from my gurus, and I, the seventh, completed the *Sura*, the song of the spirit.'

Through the mysterious and inexplicable forces of destiny, Ma's spiritual lineage has an eclectic quality. It was a spiritual amalgam of various sects often antagonistic to one another, yet fusing together in one spiritual experience. Contradictions get merged in the life of enlightenment. Like the great rivers in the Indian landscape that meander through the country and finally dissolve into the ocean, multiple streams of spiritual initiations merged into her, in the oneness of beatific knowledge.

Let me substantiate this further. First, there is a coming together of the mystic knowledge of the Sufi saint, Syed Ali Akthar, a Muslim Pir, with the mainstream Hindu and esoteric tradition. At a deeper level, there is a co-mingling of three major streams of Hindu religiosity: the moderate Śaivas; the extreme Śākta traditions (such as the practice of Aghora Vidyā and the Kaula *Sādhanā*, generally considered to be outside the Vedic fold); and, finally, the tender loving tradition of emotional *bhakti* represented by Krishna. This is the second level of synthesis achieved by her initiation.

The third level of synthesis consciously introduced by Ma, at a more popular level in her temple, is to bestow reverence to Christ during Christmas, and to invoke the compassion of Buddha on Buddha Jayanti day.[6]

The coming together of Hindu and Muslim traditions in one saint has historical roots. Several centuries earlier the saint tradition, with personalities like Kabir (c. 1448), and Guru Nanak (d. 1539), had rejected an exclusivist religious consciousness and appealed to the value of experience over dogma. They preached a religion of Hindu–Muslim unity founded on universal brotherhood. We also know of the famous Maharashtran saint, Eknatha (d. 1599), a theologian of great devotion. He wrote satirical dialogues, among them the *Hind-Turk Samvād*: in the set of dialogues which make up this work he expounds the transcendence of caste through devotion[7] and lays bare the universal element of both religions.

It may be argued that an exclusivist sectarian identity, by and large, does not fit within the ethos and structure of Indian society. Ma's case is yet another example of Hindu Muslim unity overriding caste distinctions. Ma's *sādhanā* incorporates several sectarian streams of the Hindu universe. The synthesis often pours forth in her religious expression. When Swami Keshavananda asked her how come she was interested in the path of Vaisnava *bhakti*, as she is a staunch Śākta, Ma broke into a song:

Should I call Him (the Absolute) Krishna or Kālī?
Śyāma (Krishna) or Śyāmā (Kālī)?

ami Krishna boli na Kālī
Śyāma boli na Śyāmā

Saying this, she announced that she would hold a *Hari-nāma-kirtan*,
or group chanting of the holy name of Krishna. On that occasion, it is
recorded, Ma spontaneously slipped into an ecstatic trance state
(*bhāvasamādhi*), sometimes assuming the stance of Chaitanya; at other
times she adopted the stance of Kālī engulfed by an electric blue haze,
playing Holi with Krishna. In her mystic experience, the Śākta and the
Vaisnava had merged.

What is to be observed here is that in the world of mystic experience, the religious boundaries are never rigid. Religious experience
defies analytical categorization and is not a sealed entity. It is more akin
to a fluid river which flows in many directions and fuses several streams
in the divine trance of the mystics. Ma told me once that when a
person attains enlightenment one has no sect, no caste, no creed. One
is beyond distinctions, beyond man–made limitations. 'I show the universal path for all,' she continued. 'Can light that dispels darkness, have
a *Dharma*? It illuminates all.' It is not surprising, therefore, that devotees
of all castes, from all sects and from all countries often throng her
ashram.

Religious Roles of Madhobi Ma

The divine physician

All spiritual healers act simply as a channel of the divine cosmic energy,
which is harnessed through several esoteric means and then transmitted
as healing energy. All over the world, healing has been a prerogative of
female deities who are the divine vehicles of the healing energy. It is
widely held that the divine feminine alone has curative powers to heal
and to bestow life. Ma is gifted with mysterious healing virtues, and
she plays the part of a divine physician like our goddesses Durgā and
Śīta, or Isis of Greece.

Contemporary high–tech medicine splits mind and body into two
separate entities that are unrelated to one another. Modern medical

practice does not recognize the role of the psychological dimension in healing. In traditional therapies of eastern origin, the treatment of disease is shaped by a holistic view of a person where mind-body and spirit form an integral whole. This holistic view of the mind-body as one unit operates within the larger context of the interrelationship of humans to the cosmic rhythms. Behind the interrelationships that sustain the mind-body cosmos, there are exclusive structures of philosophy of healing that have been developed, conventionalized and projected through practice.

The modes of healing followed by Ma were numerous. Ma would heal through prayer, meditation or occult medicine,. Sometimes she would apply esoteric therapies that she had received from her gurus. Sometimes she would heal by mere look, by mere stroking and touching, by tying consecrated threads on wrists and around the neck, by soft and gentle rhythms of mantra chants, and by *prānic*-transmission. At other times, she would look at the horoscope of the patient and prescribe Ayurvedic medicines, or else rituals to ward off the disease. On some occasions she would use clairvoyance to diagnose and detect the cause of ailment, and heal purely through the power of prayer.

I have seen Madhobi Ma playing the role of a divine physician. Like so many of our goddesses, she healed people of all ages, castes and social groups. I saw her healing the diseased and the wounded. I saw her showering grace on the sick and the decrepit. I saw her opening the psychic chest of medicine for those in quest of spiritual wholeness. In this role, Mother becomes Tārā, the saviour, who has the power to heal body, mind and soul, a comforter of the sick and the bereaved and a protector of all. Ma's capacity to feel the physical, mental and emotional pain of others was touching. She healed unconditionally until it 'hurt' her body. On several occasions there used to be a transference of disease which she would absorb into herself. One day I questioned her about the nature of sickness and disease. She said:

> Diseases are like persons. They possess a spirit-body and a soul. No human being wants to own such beings because they bring pain and torture to the body. These beings, like us, need salvation and freedom from the bondage of life. I told them, come to me, I am your mother, make my body your own home....

This attitude of reverence towards death, healing and disease is unique, for the saint tends to 'parent' disease. This attitude is seen as an act of mercy and a safe haven from the harsh and aggressive realities of life.

Tārā Bhāva: the divine incarnation of Goddess Tārā

In some Śākta circles woman gurus are accepted as an incarnation (avatāra) of the divine goddess. The Hindu notion of avatāra recognizes that the divine can assume multiple incarnations in either animal or human forms. It is believed that the goddess assumes a human form in the life of a woman saint. The divine incarnation begins to manifest in a woman saint's life partly by grace and partly by virtue of the power (Śakti) they accumulate through their practice. While appearing ordinary and plain, the female saint acquires certain extraordinary traits that in some sense resemble the divine manifestation of the goddess. Whatever one does when the incarnation is manifest through the person is looked upon as instance of the divine sport (līlā) of the goddess, who chooses special persons as her emissaries on the earth.

To her devotees, Madhobi Ma is no ordinary being but manifested traits of a divine avatāra when she was possessed by the energy of the goddess Tārā, whom she reveres. Saints and mystics have been magnetically drawn to the image of the goddess. In the mental landscape of saints, the goddess may assume many guises: of a healer, a miracle worker; as a friend, as a superwoman. One form of intimate interaction of the goddess with women Śākta saints is the way she enters the bodies of the saints, and uses them as a mechanism of her own power (Śakti). In the technical language of the anthropologist, this form of experience is described as divine possession. The incarnatory possession of the goddesses is never looked upon as an affliction but as a form of divine grace. This is the most direct way through which the presence of a higher level of consciousness is felt and recognized by the devotees. This is the way in which the great goddess grants a beatific vision to her devotees: through a direct one-to-one communication, without the intervention of another person.

It is widely recognized in the living tradition of Śāktas that the goddess enters her chosen devotee in countless ways.[8] She may possess through the power of thought (*vicāra-Śakti*): in this mode she causes the person to think and act in a particular way, through ideas and messages that are alien to the devotee. On the other hand she may enter the devotee as a doer and make her act in a certain way, or be an instrument of her action. In this altered state of goddess presence, the person is not ego-bound, and has no volition or free will. The mystic is at that particular moment a higher instrument of cosmic will. In the altered state of goddess awareness, there is no difference between the divinity and the chosen devotee. The subject and object of adoration are united and share an identical spiritual space. The altered state brings about a dramatic change in the agent followed by total oblivion and self-forgetfulness of the present state. In the ritual context, the divine cosmic power flows into the human vehicle in a variety of modes. The goddess may come when incense is burnt or a lamp is lit; when the holy name is sung; when an icon is worshipped; when a powerful and energized sacred centre is visited; when a holy book is read; and almost always on a special festival, when the goddess descends to earth to protect and bless her devotees.

My spiritual encounter with Ma reached a new high when I saw her incarnate and divinely possessed by the *svarūpa* of the goddess Tārā, physically, mentally and psychically. It was during the winter months, when the days were short and the nights long. One day in the evening while we sat chanting the name of the goddess during a *kirtan*, Ma fell into a deep trance. Her head began to sway gently and her body moved round and round in rhythm with the holy chant – a sign to indicate that the goddess Tārā in her energy-body (*Śakti-svarūpa*) had entered her body and had begun to conduct her movements. Ma's eyes were shut and her lips bore a benign look. Slowly and suddenly, the corners of her mouth got stained with a red blood-like substance and the liquid began to stain her mouth. Ma tightened her lips and gave an ecstatic smile. Slowly, the ruddy liquid was over-flowing from her mouth. She then opened her mouth wide, and out came her lolling blood-stained tongue. Here was a human icon of goddess Tārā, her live incarnation embodying her most important attributes in physical form. Soon her right hand rose up and her fingers curled into the goad posture (*ankuśa-mudrā*). After a while her left hand was poised in the gesture of fearlessness (*abhaya-mudrā*), then the latter changed to the boon-bestowing posture.

Ma's earthly personality was magically transformed into Tārā, the saviour; in human form she embodied the iconic marks of the goddess Tārā, the lolling tongue and the arms raised in *mudrās* – all this while the devotees continued to loudly chant *Bam Tārā, Bam Tārā*. Then her principal devotee went up to her and worshipped her as a living embodiment of the goddess who had entered into Ma's body to give *darśana* to her devotees. Although Ma's Śaktihood had never been doubted, the experience of divine possession was awe-inspiring, full of wonder, invoking the power beyond the immediate which finally warrants submission and total surrender on the part of the devotee.

This experience would repeat itself over and over again almost twice a week for a period of nearly three months. The devotees considered these to be stolen moments from the vision of eternity. Although divine possession may not be followed by miracles, for the devotees the sight itself was a blessing which purified them and strengthened their faith. Sometimes small mementoes would spontaneously fall from her hands, such as a locket, a *Rudrāksa* bead, a red thread, or a flower. This was followed by a soft aromatic fragrance that engulfed her body. After a while Ma would slowly regain her wakeful consciousness and be her normal self again. She had no memory of her previous condition. All she was aware of was that she had entered a blissful state. She explained it through the analogy of the plug and socket. She said, 'When my consciousness is plugged in, the cosmic current flows through me.'

Mother love

The most universal of all images and archetypes, glorified throughout centuries, is the power of mother love which expresses itself through unconditional giving and compassion. Explaining this, Jung says that

> mother love is one of the most moving and unforgettable memories of our lives, the mystical root of all growth and change. The love that means homecoming, shelter, and the long silence from which everything begins and in which everything ends. The mother carries for us that inborn image of the *mater matura* and *mater spiritualis*, of the totality of life of which we are all a small and helpless part.[9]

Mother love expresses itself in certain qualities, such as nourishment, protection, unconditional love, perseverance, mercy, tenderness,

PARALLEL WORLDS OF MADHOBI MA, 'NECTAR MOTHER' 151

forbearance, forgiveness and compassion. It may be said here that all goddesses reflect these eternal feminine virtues. In our human terms, we seek the protection of mother love all through our lives and instinctively respond to it when we encounter it. It is not out of place to say that in some infinitesimal way most of us symbolically live like embryos outside the womb, waiting to connect with the umbilical cord that has been physically severed at birth.

My own encounter with Ma proved to me that her greatest virtue and power lie in her qualities of mother love. An uninterrupted stream of unconditional love pours forth from her unreservedly without distinction. Although the mother image existed in all women, Ma is the 'mother of all mothers' in human form and embodies the benign feminine virtues of the goddess. It is interesting to observe that, for women who came to the ashram, Ma's motherhood was a perfection of their conscious self, a bigger, greater and more perfect Ma, while for men the mother image projected a latent mythological ethos, a symbol of motherhood rather than the mother herself as experienced by women.

Motherhood to many modern women also typifies the world of family life, which involves giving birth, rearing children, domesticity, house management and holding together the moral values which uphold the welfare of the family. In all these domestic roles, women often become passive receivers and lose their individuality and sovereignty. None of these was an obstacle to Ma's spirituality. It seemed to me that the motherhood of Kālī, Tārā and Tripurasundarī had entered into her and, in some mysterious way, transformed the overt passivity of womanhood to the active and dynamic attributes of a goddess. I learned from her that motherhood spiritualized, rather than being a disqualifier for a modern woman like myself, is often an avenue to, and a vehicle for, significant religious expression. Further, the maternal values of mother love are identical with the universal values of spirituality. In some forms of Buddhist meditation mother love meditation is consciously integrated so that it builds up an attitude of mothering towards all beings.[10] This experience, or way of being, is universalized in religious experience. Womanhood, its ordinary concerns invested with sacred values, is revealed as a state more powerful than we readily understand today.

Conclusion

The remarkable life of Madhobi Ma, who is at once a wife, a mother, a detached renunciate and a healer, challenges the normative ideal of *strīdharma* as it contains her *svadharma*. We may conclude by pointing out that there is a weaving together of several parallel worlds of Madhobi Ma that appear to be contradictory and fail to conform with the Brahmanical paradigm of womanhood. In Madhobi Ma's case there is unity between her domestic role as a wife and mother and the role of a detached renunciate. Both these roles coalesce in her life and intermingle. While her arranged marriage to a man of her parent's choosing represents her as one who passively gave in to her role designed by the codes of *strīdharma,* her relentless pursuit of a spiritual career dictated by personal choice (*svadharma*) reverses and subverts the normative Hindu ideal chalked out for women. According to the orthodoxy, the woman is subordinate to her husband. In the case of this saint, all the inmates of her spiritual family, including her husband, are her disciples and, from a purely spiritual perspective, they are subordinate to her as she is the source of divine power.

Once again, the normative ideal of motherhood finds a new expression in the life of this saint. In Ma's case her feminine qualities and motherhood have been enhanced to such a degree that she transcends her worldly identity as a human mother. She is regarded as the Mother of all mothers. She is both the physical mother and one who embodies the universal goddess, the abstract feminine principle who harmonizes and plays multiple roles. Rather than the death of the human woman in her, there has been a creative rebirth of the mother essence which is expressed through her spirituality. She has successfully woven her parallel worlds without sacrificing one to the other. Her motherhood has empowered her not to die as a woman, as Hawley points out, but to transubstantiate the human limitations.[11]

We may say that a woman saint may express her motherhood in various dimensions until her mother essence merges with the mother consciousness of the eternal feminine embodied as the goddess. Her powerful spiritual presence in her goddess Tārā incarnation confirmed her status as an extraordinary channel of divine grace. For each of her devotees she is a different person. At the same time, she is the embodiment of the Universal Mother, beyond human reach. In this respect she has certainly conqured the limitations of *strīdharma* through her choosen path, her *svadharma*.

Finally, Madhobi Ma's initiation by a Muslim Pir and several Hindu gurus make her life a unique example of inter-faith unity. Her adoption of a family bound by spiritual purpose reverses the notion of a traditional family bound by a hereditary blood line. Furthermore, the extraordinary life of this Tantric saint reverses the orthodox view that debars woman from playing powerful leadership roles in the religious sphere. As described here, Ma's life in many instances deconstructs the essentialist theory of gender inequality. We have to look at such personal narratives of woman more seriously than we have in the past.

Notes and References

1 For some notable examples of studies on Hindu woman saints, see A. K. Ramanujan, 'On Woman Saints', in John Stratton Hawley and Donna Marie Wulffe (eds.), *The Divine Consort Radha and the Goddesses of India* (Boston: Beacon Press, 1982), pp. 316–24; Lisa Lassell Hallstrom, *Mother of Bliss – Anandamayi Ma* (Oxford: Oxford University Press, 1999). Kathleen Erndl, *Victory to the Mother: the Hindu Goddess of Northwest India in Myth, Ritual and Symbol* (New York: Oxford University Press, 1993) gives an exposition of living women who emulate the image of the goddess in religious experiences. Judith Cornell, *Amma Portrait of a Living Sage* (New York: William Morrow and Harper Collins, 2001) is the biography of Mata Amaritananda-mayi from Kerala.

2 I use the word *strīdharma* in the technical sense to denote the normative ideals of Hindu woman set out in the *Dharmaśāstra*, treatises on obligatory duties for men and women. For a concise discussion see Hallstrom, *Mother of Bliss*, pp. 56–71. The word *svadharma*, through used in a technical sense in Hindu scriptures, has been used here to denote personal choice in action.

3 Hawley and Wulffe (eds.), *The Divine Consort,* p. 23.

4 *Ibid.*, Chapter 7, pp. 17–22. On *Śākta* woman gurus, see *Kaulajñāna Nirnaya*, ed. P. C. Bagchi (Calcutta: Calcutta Sanskrit Series 3, 1934), Ch. 22: verse 10; *Śāktānandatariangini* by Brahmanandagiri, ed. S. P.Upadhyaya (Varanasi: Sampūrnānanda Viśvavidyālaya Yoga-tantra-granthamālā, 11, 1987), Ch. 2: verse 31; *Tripurārnava Tantra*, ed. S. P.Upadhyaya (Varanasi: Sampūrnānanda Viśvavidyālaya Yoga-tantra-granthamālā, 12, 1992), Ch. 1: verses 196–7; *Mātrkābheda Tantra*, ed. Ram Kumar Rai (Varanasi: Varanasi Tantrika Texts Series, No. 1, Prachya Prakashan, 1983), Ch. 7: verses 14–44; cf. Hallstrom, *Mother of Bliss*, pp. 130–5, 143–4.

5 Alan Morinis. *Pilgrimage in the Hindu Tradition: a Case Study of West Bengal* (New Delhi: Oxford University Press, 1973), p. 175.

6 Ma's biography is discussed briefly by some of her devotees. See Vijay Pal, *Sri Sri Madhobvi* (pamphlet in Hindi) (New Delhi: Matrika Ashram, n.d.); Siddheshwarananda, *Snehamaygi Ma* (Matrika Ashram, n.d.).

7 Carl Ernst, *Eternal Garden: Mysticism, History and Politics at a South Asian Sufi Center* (Albany: State University of New York Press, 1992), p. 34.

8 See Erndl, *Victory to the Mother*, pp. 105–34.

9 C. G. Jung, *Aspects of the Feminine* (Princeton: Princeton University Press, 1982), p. 121.

10 For discussion of motherhood in religious experience, see John Powers and Deane Cartin, 'Mothering and Moral Cultivation in Buddhist and Feminist Ethics', *Philosophy East and West*, 44, 1 (January 1994): 1–18.

11 Hawley and Wulffe (eds.), *The Divine Consort*, p. 26.

9

'Real' Men, Naked Women
and the Politics of Paradise
The Archetype of Lal Ded

DURRE S. AHMED

The present, seemingly endless celebration of cultural and religious differences is in danger of being rendered meaningless if it implies abandoning the significance of that which is shared and which unifies. With the worldwide rise of religious fundamentalism, it is imperative to search for frameworks which unify rather than divide. Utilizing a Jungian framework, this chapter is about a remarkable woman in whose life and work both these dimensions of diversity and unity merged into a creative and powerful message encompassing Hinduism and Islam.

Biographical Background

The earliest recorded mention of the Kashmiri mystic known as Lalla is in 1654, in the book *Asrar-ul-Abrar* (The Secrets of the Pious) by Baba Dawud Mishkati.[1] She is also known as Lalita, Lali, Laleshwari, Mai Lal, or Lal Ded. Accounts of her exact date of birth vary from the beginning of the thirteenth to the middle of the fourteenth century AD.[2] This extreme variation would suggest at the outset that one is dealing with the stuff of legend. Yet, there is no doubt that such a woman existed in Kashmir. Not only is she mentioned in numerous historical accounts but there is a corpus of poetry attributed to her. Her verses are considered to be some of the finest and most profound in the spiritual poetry of the subcontinent and are acknowledged as such by sages and scholars alike. This revered status is especially high in her native land and among users of the Kashmiri language. Apart from the widely popular verse, numerous sayings and proverbs attributed to her have remained part of the vernacular Kashmiri idiom right up to the present, 'the sayings of Lalla being the current coin of quotation in Kashmiri'.[3]

While her date of birth is unclear all historians agree that Lalla was born no later than the middle of the fourteenth century into a Brahmin family. She was married at a young age and according to Brahmin custom was (renamed) Padmavati by her in-laws. Beyond this, facts merge into events that should be seen not as 'fictions' but rather as archetypal components, as they occur in innumerable spiritual narratives, including Lalla's.

For the young Padmavati, marriage was a miserable experience. She suffered greatly at the hands of a tyrannical mother-in-law and was the victim of constant scolding and unkind behaviour. Instead of a regular meal, she would be given rice thinly spread over a stone. The Kashmiri proverb *hond ma'rytan kina kath Lalli nalavath tsali na zanh* is a reference to this sort of harsh treatment ('They may kill a big sheep or tender lamb, Lalla will have her lump of stone all right'). Such humiliation was borne with fortitude, her main source of sustenance being meditation. On the pretext of fetching water, she would seek out a quiet place and meditate in solitude. On one occasion when she returned, her angry husband struck the water pitcher on her head with a stick. It broke to pieces but the water stood frozen above her head and eventually collected into a pond which, according to the Persian chronicler, Pir Ghulam Hasan,[4] came to be known as *Lalla Trag* – the Pond of Lalla – and which dried up in 1925–6. It is still known by the same name.

The episode of the pitcher marked a turning point in Padmavati's life since it had exposed her spiritual powers. She left home to embark on an inner journey which remains one of the most dramatic in the history of religious mysticism. From here on she is known as Lalla and this is how she refers to herself in her poetry. The most sensational stories pertain to her wandering around nude, and her encounters with various persons in this state of nakedness. Kaul refers to the work of scholars who speculated that it was this state that led to the name Lal Ded (Grandmother *Ded* Lal) because in Kashmiri *lal* refers to the flabbiness of the lower belly. Kaul himself disputes this, however, pointing out that she referred to herself as Lal, Lali, etcetera, in a period prior to the stage of the naked, wandering ascetic, and that Lali in Kashmiri means 'mad':

> My guru gave me but one precept
> 'From without withdraw your gaze within,
> And fix it on the inmost Self'
> I, Lalla, took to heart this one precept,
> And therefore naked, I began to dance.[5]

By all accounts, as Kaul puts it, the 'most famous and most persistent legends' about Lalla are related to this state of nakedness. Citing classical sources, Kaul describes one:

> Once an open-air performance … attracted a large crowd. Lal Ded's father-in-law too was there and he saw her standing nude among the spectators. He reprimanded her, and led her into his house to put on some clothes and cover up her shame. She protested, saying that there were no human beings about, only goats and sheep; and asked him to look out of the window. He was dumbfounded. There were only sheep and goats there ….[6]

But the most famous story concerns her encounter with the Persian/Iraqi Sufi Mir Sayyid Ali Hamadani, popularly known in Kashmir as Shah Hamadan and considered to be one of the greatest patron saints of Kashmir. As the story goes, when Lalla was asked why she wandered around naked, the answer would be: 'Because there are no men in Kashmir.' One day, somewhere near Srinagar, she saw Shah Hamadan approaching and realized that here was a *real* man and ran to hide herself in a grocer's shop. However, she was turned away because of her scandalous state, whereupon she jumped into the nearby baker's oven (*tandoor*). The poor baker was stunned, even more so when he saw Lalla emerge from the burning oven fully clothed in green-coloured garments of Paradise.

One version has it that this transformation took place under the aegis of Shah Hamadan, another attributes it to Lalla alone. Others mention the story only to dismiss it as a fabrication, while some consider it authentic but *vis-à-vis* an unnamed man, not Shah Hamadan.[7] Whatever the precise nature of the story, it is generally accepted as true in spirit and, in any case, is never refuted to deny her nakedness. True or false, it remains the most renowned legend associated with her, indelibly enshrined in the current Kashmiri proverb *ayeyi wa'nis gay iandras* ('She [Lal Ded] had gone to the grocer but [instead] arrived at the baker.') In short, like all legendary spiritual figures, Lalla's life was full of miraculous and strange phenomena but she is renowned above all for her dramatic appearance and poetry.

Like her birth, her death was also legendary. In one version the end came behind the wall of Juma Masjid at Vejibror, 28 miles south-east of Srinagar, where she literally disappeared in a flash of light.[8] According to a *rishinama* tradition, one day Lalla sat in a large earthen-ware vessel and placed another on top. When finally the upper vessel was removed, there was nothing there. In this version, too, she was gone without a trace. As Kaul says, 'It is a matter of surprise that there should not have been a *samadhi* (temple) or *maqbara* (tomb) to mark the place where her body was cremated or laid to rest.' Similarly, there is no monument, nor are there relics in a region renowned for wide-spread sacred memorabilia; the only thing close to such commemoration is the now dry pond. Given the present internecine strife in Kashmir, one does not know its state, either: the chances are it too has gone from sight. In other words, there is really nothing concrete to 'show' that Lalla ever existed.

Yet Lalla was a fact. That there was indeed such a person is corroborated by some of the greatest saints of Kashmir, both Hindu and Muslim, and subsequently by numerous hagiographers and historians. But the greatest witness is the *Lalla Vaakh*, a collection of profound spiritual poems and verses which have been studied by numerous scholars. It is important to note that these verses live on in the oral tradition of the Kashmiri language and have a stature similar to the poetry of Meera, Kabir, Bulleh Shah, Baba Farid, Guru Nanak and other great mystic poets/saints of the subcontinent.

Lalla Vaakh

The word *vaakh* in Kashmiri is both singular and plural and means 'verse saying'. As is typical with such poetry, it is primarily an oral tradition: it is rarely collected and written down, and, when it is, there is a spectrum of disagreement regarding authenticity. Nevertheless, there are numerous collections of the *Lalla Vaakh*, many with commentaries. Apart from many editions within India, the Englishmen George Grierson and Lionel Barnett attempted a collection in 1920, *Lalla-Vakyani*, or the *Wise Sayings of Lalla*, as a monograph for the Royal

Asia Society.[9] Similarly, there is Richard Temple's study, *The Word of Lalla*.[10]

All these studies confirm that Lalla occupies a significant position within the history and development of the Kashmiri language. Not only is there no disagreement about her being chronologically the first of the 'modern' Kashmiri poets, but many rank her as 'the maker of modern Kashmiri language and literature', with Grierson going as far as claiming that her *Vaakh* is the oldest specimen of recorded Kashmiri language.[11]

A *vaakh* is usually a four-line stanza, complete and independent in itself, of a generally loose metre, rhymed and unrhymed. Western translators sometimes refer to them as 'songs', but for most native speakers it is their spiritual intensity which is primary. In the West, the closest literary equivalents of such poetry are the Songs of Solomon and the Psalms of the Old Testament, which is why, perhaps, Grierson and others saw them as 'songs'.

The *vaakh* itself is in the great tradition of spiritual versifying of the subcontinent. The reader encounters not an organized set of narratives but rather a collection of intensely experienced realizations. These range from reflections on the transitory and ephemeral nature of existence to rapt expressions of yearning/desire/love for the Divine as grasped through metaphors. Like those of many rebel saints, Lalla's verses do not set out to preach any particular creed yet contain biting criticism of organized religion with its emphasis on power and external trappings and rituals. Similarly, the ruling establishment is criticized severely.

Yogni or Arifa?

For those not familiar with the Kashmiri language and unable for this or other reasons fully to grasp the depth of the poetry, the figure of Lalla nevertheless merits interest for two reasons. The first is the nature of the legends that surround someone who, by all accounts, was not just a spiritual poet *par excellence* but a woman whose span of experience ranged from the commonplace to the sublime (from the fate of a Brahmin who married and suffered the usual travails of mother-in-law and husband, to a 'renunciation' which was not exactly the sort commonly associated with women mystics). The legends and stories around her are rather unique, even in a domain in which the unusual and bizarre are common. The naked figure set against a background of the legendary beauty of Kashmir presents a powerful image: it evokes an unbridled, intense passion which is clearly not sexual. Yet the nakedness speaks of femaleness, as does the cryptic story about the 'real man'.

The second reason why she is a figure requiring our attention is the peculiar position she occupies within the scholarship on Hinduism and Islam and the history of these religions in Kashmir. The literature on Kashmir and its saints is vast and this is not the place to present even a cursory survey of the subject. But a brief review of some of the best-known general texts and some of the main ones on Lalla herself will demonstrate the controversial nature of this remarkable woman. The main controversy in a nutshell is: was Lalla a Hindu or a Muslim? Was she a *Yogni*, or – to use the term that Sufis/Muslims apply to a woman who has attained gnosis – *Arifa*? A few examples will demonstrate the difficulty of deciding the case.

In an extensive study of Lalla and her poetry by Jayalal Kaul, the author claims that Lalla was an adherent of the Trika School of Kashmiri Saivism, a branch of Hindu mysticism that arose in Kashmir during the thirteenth and fourteenth centuries. However, as Kaul himself points out, the earliest recorded mention of Lalla is in a 1654 chronicle by a Muslim, Dawud Mishkati. Kaul also states that, while there were Hindu chronicles in Sankskrit written earlier than 1654, none of these mentions Lalla, perhaps because 'she had thrown all conventional respectability to the winds and roamed careless of dress and decorum'.[12] As Dawud Mishkati pictured her, Lalla 'was one of those who wander in the wilderness of love, wailing and lamenting for the beloved', and he refers to her as Lalla *Arifa*. Mishkati uses such Islamic spiritual idioms to describe Lalla as, 'she was a knower of the path of the Valley of Truth (*haqq*)'. The author cites the Muslim *shaikh* (spiritual master), Nasir-ud-Din, as having written about Lalla:

> Passion for God set fire to all she had
> And from her heart rose clouds of smoke
> having had a draught of *ahd-e-alast*
> Intoxicated and drunk with joy was she
> One cup of this God intoxicating drink
> Shatters reasons into bits....

Ahd-e-alast refers to a passage in the Quran (VII, 172) about the contract between God and the human souls: '"Am I not your Lord?" God said. "Yes," said they' (*alastu birabikum, qalu bala*).

The main point here is that the first extremely reverential acknowledgement of Lalla's spiritual status is *not* in the Sanskrit/Hindu chronicles but in Persian/Muslim hagiography: as *ahd-e-alast* implies, Lalla was described in purely Islamic terms. Similarly other Muslim writers do not consider her Brahmin ancestry as something to fuss over, comparing her to the great Muslim woman saint, Rabia of Basra.[13] For example, the *Tarikhi-Hasan*, a generally well-acknowledged history of Kashmir written by a Muslim in 1885 and cited by Kaul, states:

> The saintly lady Lalla *Arifa*, a mystic of the highest order, was a second Rabia … this chaste lady was born in a Brahmin family in the village of Sempor. During the early days of her life she was under the influence of an extraordinary spell of ecstasy – she was married at Pampor. (p. 5)

Another chronicle says: 'Bibi Lalla *Arifa* was one of the perfect saints and a second Rabia of Basra.' Similarly, there are numerous stories about her having become a Muslim through Shah Hamadan, or one Muslim saint or another. An undated (perhaps nineteenth-century) pamphlet in Lahore claims she became a Muslim at the hands of the Persian Sufi saint, Sayid Hussain Samnani.[14]

These Muslim chronicles are mentioned by Kaul in order to establish Lalla's spiritual status in the history of Kashmir. However, in narrating/citing this history, Kaul's emphasis is on showing how, in fact, the Muslims were mistaken and that Lalla was actually very much a Saivite Hindu. To prove this point, he undertakes detailed analyses of various Muslim accounts of Lalla, juxtaposing them with other historical events such as the dates of rule of various kings, which are further compared with legendary anecdotes about Lalla such as the broken pitcher and jumping into the oven. Weaving his way through this uneven combination of the strictly factual and the imaginative, Kaul attempts to demonstrate either that the chroniclers were unreliable because certain dates/events had been wrong, or that – because by the seventeenth and eighteenth centuries Kashmir had overwhelmingly converted to Islam – it suited the Muslim orthodoxy to portray Lalla in an Islamic idiom.

Kaul's attempt is not a new one. As late as 1885, Pir Ghulam Hasan said in his history *Tarikh-i-Hasan*: 'The Hindus say that she is one of them. The Musalmans claim that she belongs to them. The truth is that she is among the chosen of God. May God's peace be on her!'[15] Thus, while it is indeed possible that Lalla was 'claimed' by the Muslims, the Hindu 'possessiveness' of Lalla is equally evident, whether in Muktenanda[16] or in Kaul's analysis of how and why Lalla's *vaakh* had entered not only vernacular Kashmiri but also the Sufi world. As Kaul states:

> [the *vaakh*] became part of the repertoire of the itinerant village minstrel and later still, of our *Sufiana Kalam* Kashmiri classical music, to be sung as sacred invocation at the start of the *Majlis-e-m'arfin'*, the assembly of *Sufis* and spiritual seekers. As more time passed and the language gradually and imperceptibly underwent change, many words became obsolete and difficult to understand. The people, a majority of whom had by now become Muslim, lost all touch with the past tradition, and much of what Lal Ded had said, many words and phrases of her *vaakh*, their nuances and rich philosophical and *yogic* connotation, became meaningless to them. (p. 34)

Includers, Excluders, Intruders

The debate as to what creed Lalla 'actually' subscribed to is compounded further by Richard Temple's *The Word of Lalla*. This study, along with Grierson and Barnett's *Lalla Vakyani*, has received considerable critical attention from Indian and Kashmiri scholars, Hindus and Muslims. The criticism is twofold. Typically, Kaul first faults Grierson and Barnett for not distinguishing Lalla's authentic *Vaakh* from various interpolations. Second, the Englishmen are criticized, along with Temple, for not having discerned the finer points of different Vedantic schools and practices. Thus, for example, Kaul suggests that Lalla was not a *Hatha Yogni* as Grierson and company imply. Rather, according to Kaul's analysis of the *Vaakh*, she belonged to the Kashmiri Saivite Trika School. The analysis of scholars such as Kaul relies on an enormous knowledge of the intricacies of different esoteric practices in various Hindu traditions and subtraditions. It should be added here that if one considers the entire corpus of research on Lalla as a whole, Hindu/Muslim claims on Lalla are not exactly symmetrical. Nevertheless, the pattern is strongly present.

Interestingly, beyond the 1960s, the writing on her, by Muslim and Hindu scholars alike, has been steadily moving towards establishing her as a 'pure' Kashmiri Saivite.[17] One can only speculate that the reasons for this 'strengthening' of the Hindu claim and a corresponding Muslim 'surrender' may have to do with the creation of Pakistan in 1947. Of course no author sees this as such, the credit being given by all sides to modern methods of historical research. These, it can be argued, reflect a particular masculine narrowness of vision, and an either/or, separative consciousness. Within such an approach, whatever the scholarly protagonists may or may not have succeeded in 'proving' about Lalla is secondary to the fact that, in the process of academic argument, they end up presenting each tradition (their own) as a little more rigid, a little more exclusionary. It is a pity, because it can be argued that both traditions have in fact an inherently and powerfully inclusive dimension. If this was not the case, there would have been no dispute to begin with. In any case, the post-1950s scholarship on Lalla presents an interesting contrast to the majority of earlier endeavours in which all sides, including 'outsiders' such as Temple and Grierson, tend towards a more inclusive vision, seeing more similarity rather than difference.

In contrast, the modern academic specialist remains influenced by various degrees of orthodoxy when it comes to seeing Lalla in the context of a fusion between Kashmiri Saivism and Islamic Sufism. Earlier, perhaps less 'rigorous' studies were more comfortable with the idea of hybridity. Thus R. K. Parmu's *A History of Muslim Rule in India* states that Lalla preached against the existing Saiva religion as it was practised by the Tantric gurus – 'she preached harmony between Vedantism and Sufism, good Hindu and good Muslim'.[18] Parmu also states that

> though originally Hindu, she was greatly influenced by Islamic Sufistic thought. It is commonly avowed by Muslims in Kashmir that her verses after her contact with Shah Hamadan and other Muslim saints are more expressly reflective of Muslim thought.

Similarly, in *Daughters of Vitasta*, Premnath Bazzaz says that she brought about a 'synthesis of the two philosophies' (the Trika and the Islamic Sufi) and this synthesis 'was given to the world in poetic sermons by wandering minstrels through the rest of her life'.[19]

Sir Richard Temple had also pointed to the various similarities in Sufi and Hindu Yoga practices, and sees in Lalla a synthesis of the two. As he states:

> although Lalla was a Saiva Hindu and her turn of thought and feeling was distinctly that of her own religion, yet there is much in them of this tendency of the Sufis, which is in fact almost Hindu Upanishadic idealism.[20]

He adds that Lalla 'quickly and deeply absorbed' Sufi thinking from her contact with her 'contemporary and friend, the Persian Sayyid Ali Hamadani, the Muslim Apostle of Kashmir'. (This is the same figure of the story of the burning oven, 'the real man'.) Similarly, another historian states that 'Lalleshwari's association with Shah Hamadan was due to an identity of the faith of Sufis and Hindu mendicants and saints in Kashmir'.[21]

In summary, until about four decades ago, Lalla's religious/spiritual identity was ambiguous. Prior to the 1960s, there is a substantial body of work which highlighted the commonalities of her philosophy *vis-à-vis* Hindus and Muslims. As will be discussed shortly, this intertwining runs deep.

Cultural politics

A final postscript is in order concerning some recent developments which are illustrative of various themes discussed so far. The claims and counterclaims on Lalla continue, in spite of historical pronouncements on her 'definitive' identitiy. In 1995 a private Pakistani television company (NTM) broadcast a play on Lalla by a well-known woman playwright, Fatima Suraiyya. Titled *La Se Ill-'allah Tak* ('From *La* to *Ill-'allah*'), it suggested, through a play on words, that Lalla's journey began as a Hindu and culminated with Islam (*Ill-'allah* being the last words of the Muslim *kalima*). Given the name Lalita, the story unfolds along variations of familiar motifs from her life. Ill-treatment from in-laws makes Lalita question her belief and ardent devotion to Śiva, and relevant verses are recited from the *Vaakh* as questions addressed to Śiva (such poetic queries are, in fact, an inherent part of a particular genre of a spiritual protest poetry, as for example in the poetry of the well-known poet of the subcontinent, Iqbal). As a review of the play explains, disillusioned by Śaivite Hinduism, Lalita meets two renowned Muslim saints, Syed Shaikh Ali Ramzan and Shaikh Hussain Samnani, and, after much soul-searching, she embraces Islam. According to the playwright, it was after this (allegedly) clear-cut conversion that the name 'Lalle' (which means 'mad' in Kashmiri) was given to Lalita by Hindus.[22]

The implications are self-evident. Thus, while the controversy may have been 'resolved' academically, it remains alive at the level of cultural politics. Given the longstanding hostility and violence between India and Pakistan over Kashmir, Lalla has resurfaced as a symbol of the dispute. Seen in the context of the prevailing political and religious culture of Pakistan and its oppression of women in the name of Islam, it is ironic that Lalla is claimed as a Muslim. At the same time, in spite of its political undertones, it is noteworthy that the claim for Islam has come from the pen of a renowned and respected woman author. Interestingly, however, the play never refers to the defining feature of Lalla's legend, the period of nudity.

The debate on the merits and demerits of the scholarly work on Lalla will continue and the purpose here is not to undertake an academic review and assessment. It is, rather, in the first place to highlight the fact that, from the Islamic point of view, until a few decades ago the issue of Lalla being a Muslim was rarely contested; and, if it was, it was left unresolved in view of the perceived similarities and a fusion between certain schools of Islam and Hinduism.[23] Second, the purpose here is to present a woman having complex and controversial views on religion. Finally, the aim is to draw attention to the fact that, amidst all the scholarly hair splitting, there is hardly a comment on how, for over four centuries, a seemingly stern and puritanical monotheism claimed as its own, and acknowledged with reverence, the spiritual greatness of a woman who was given to roaming around naked.

The Rishis

There is a deeper historical level to the controversy around Lalla which has to do with the Rishi movement in Kashmir. Like Lalla herself, this movement remains difficult to define in 'purist' terms. The word *Rishi* in Sanskrit means 'the singer of sacred hymns' and, in general, it came to mean a saint or sanctified sage. Persian historians, such as Baba Dawud Mishkati, suggest that such a Hindu ascetic order existed in

Pre-Islamic times but was eventually absorbed into Sufism. (Mishkati's chronicle, as we have seen, is also the first to mention Lalla.) According to most modern scholars, the Rishis came into prominence during the late fourteenth and early fifteenth centuries. Some see it as 'an indigenous Sufi order' which developed along the traditions of Buddhist renunciation and Hindu asceticism.[24] Another authoritative text on the history of Sufism in India states:

> The cross fertilization of Sufi beliefs with those expressed by Lalla through-out her verses led to the establishment of the Rishi order of Sufis in Kashmir. Its founder was Shaikh Nuruddin Rishi who, according to some authorities, was born on April 9, 1378.[25]

All available sources, Muslim and Hindu, do agree on one aspect – namely, that the person most responsible for this order, which was firmly established and flourishing by the fifteenth century, was a man known in Kashmir as Nand Resh or by the Muslim name of Shaikh Nuruddin. Many chronicles, including different *rishinamas,* also mention the legend of Lalla and the birth of Nuruddin. As Kaul describes it, apparently the infant refused to take milk from his mother's breast. Lalla happened to pass by and spoke to the baby: 'You were not ashamed of being born; why are you ashamed to suck?' Whereupon the baby began to drink the milk.[26] In the television play, this episode relies on an even more dramatic twist. Lalla intuitively 'hears' the baby crying and sets out for his village. She locates the baby and places her own finger in his mouth and milk flows forth. The infant's mother then gives her the title of *Arifa.* Beginning with this, Nuruddin himself evolved into a semi-mythical figure with all sorts of legends and miracles associated with him. Within the Sanskrit and Persian chroni-cles similar debates were common as to his 'real' religion.

Despite the legendary stories, like Lalla, he too was a real person. Whereas the name Lalla as such has no religious connotations, Shaikh Nuruddin's Islamic link is established with his name, which means the Light of Religion. But he was/is also referred to as Nand Resh or Nand Rishi. Beyond this, again, depending on how orthodox or liberal the view, he is criticized or revered accordingly. Kaul sees him as the 'chiefest guru' of the Kashmiri Muslim saints, the Rishis:

> Her (Lalla's) great younger contemporary, the founder of the indigenous order of Muslim Rishis of Kashmir, the famous saint Nand Rishi, speaks of

her with sincere reverence and from that time to this, other saints and poets, Muslim and Hindu alike, have expressed their affection and esteem in memorable words. (p. 29)

The general consensus on the Rishis is that they were widely revered throughout Kashmir by both Hindus and Muslims. They were well known for their simple lifestyle, ascetic practices and spiritual powers; and they were also extremely influential at the popular, mass level. The story of Lalla and the infant Nuruddin is a symbolic enactment of this genuinely indigenous form of Sufism. To quote one of the leading modern authorities on the subject:

> The cross fertilization of *Sufi* beliefs with those expressed by Lalla through-out her verses led to the establishment of the *Rishi* order of *Sufis* in Kashmir. Its founder was Shaikh Nuruddin Rishi …. [He] and his disciples preferred to call themselves *Rishis* not *Sufis*. Of his many disciples Bamudin, Zainud-Din and Latif-ud Din were Brahmins by birth and had become Muslim under the influence of their *pir's* intense spiritualism. The stories of their conversions are like many others concerned with mystic conversion, but all consistently portray Shaikh Nuruddin as a spiritual beacon to Kashmiri Muslims and Hindus alike.[27]

A Hindu/Muslim Syzygy

While the historians aim to provide a chronology about Shaikh Nuruddin and Lalla, the popular legends and early chronicles suggest otherwise. Some of them show Lalla and Shaikh Nuruddin as contem-poraries who had extended spiritual discourses.[28] This has led to a com-plicated knot at the core of Lalla's legend and an interesting mirroring *vis-à-vis* Shaikh Nuruddin, the principal confounding factor being a body of verses attributed to the latter. Once again, one is plunged into scholarly hair splitting. There is no doubt that there are great similarities to Lalla's *Vaakh*; and comparisons have been attempted showing their complementary nature. For example, Kaul claims that the *Nur-Nama* has in it verses ascribed by Grierson and Barnett to Lalla. There seems to be a sort of inextricable intertwining here of Lalla and Nuruddin, and this in turn has made her character more complex and difficult to separate in terms of the Hindu/Muslim issue. As Rafiqi states:

> Indeed it was not the Muslim saints who influenced Lalla, but she who influenced a section of the Kashmiri Muslim saints, the *Rishis*, through

Nuruddin .... Though the tales of Nuruddin's encounters with Lalla may be taken as hagiological fabrications, at least they reveal that Nuruddin was popularly considered to have had some association with Lalla. The similarity of their sayings and teachings would suggest this was more than mere association and that Lalla was, in fact, an initial and important source of inspiration for Nuruddin.... The personalities of Lalla and Nuruddin are so mixed up that it is impossible to separate them. But there seems little doubt that Nuruddin drew inspiration from Lalla, even if he actually did not become her disciple. (pp.145–7)

Interestingly, in the same way that Kaul acknowledges the profound similarities between Sufism and Lalla's philosophy as it comes through in Lalla's *Vaakh*, but insists that this does not necessarily 'make' her anything other than a Saivite, Rafiqi puts up a similar 'defence' of Shaikh Nuruddin. One can assume that this was/is in response to the Muslim claim of Nuruddin's greatness:

While Nuruddin was influenced by Lalla, her influence did not make him a Hindu saint in the guise of a Muslim Rishi. His sayings show that he believed in the fundamental principles of Islam.[29]

Like Lalla's, Nuruddin's message was one of simplicity and sincerity. He too was a rebel, who spoke of Divine love and was against the tyranny and oppression of the ruling class, state or religious. He was imprisoned by the ruler for such views and was a champion of religious tolerance:

We belong to the same parents
Then why this difference?
Let Hindus and Muslims (together)
Worship God alone.

Similarly, the historical consensus on his poetry and its impact on Kashmiri are virtually identical to Lalla's:

Nuruddin's message was not confined to one race or class but addressed to mankind as a whole. He expressed his thought in simple language. His verses had an immediate appeal to the unlettered masses. Allusions to his sayings and verses both by Muslims/non Muslims of Kashmir are common even today and have become almost proverbial.[30]

The Rishi movement is unique within Kashmiri Sufism and has been frequently compared to the Bhakti movement. Whereas the vast majority of Sufis from the fifteenth to the seventeenth centuries came to India and Kashmir from Persia and Central Asia, the Rishis were very much 'children of the soil'. As Rafiqi points out, while they did indeed convert to Islam, they were essentially inspired by the local environment, having hardly any knowledge of Arabic and Persian:

> The *Rishis'* inspiration ... was almost wholly popular. They preached love of mankind and did not concern themselves with Islamic missionary activities ... and kept themselves aloof from the ruling classes .... They did not claim any *Sufic* ancestry and did not hesitate to borrow the ideas and practices of the Hindu ascetics ... especially those of the *Saivites* of Kashmir ....
> (p. xviii)

There is thus a sort of closing of the circle and there really is no way of knowing the 'truth' about Nuruddin and Lalla: who was born first, who influenced whom, who said which verse and what precisely their creeds were *vis-à-vis* Saivism and Islam. A comparison of the verses attributed to Lalla and Nuruddin suggests that it may be impossible finally to decide the authorship of many of their shared sayings.[31]

The point here is first to recognize this deep intertwining of what are undoubtedly two distinct traditions. Simultaneously, however, Lalla and Nuruddin form a sort of syzygy, fused in such a way that the common features dominate to an extent that makes boundaries impossible to discern. Second, one must remember that, regardless of the most impeccable scholarship, the lived reality of the daily existence of ordinary people and their perceptions should be definitive considerations. Religion lives in the world, not in the universities where it is endlessly dissected and, as such, rendered lifeless. As Cooey has stressed, the fact that scholarship is both a discursive practice and a constitutive act has implications for the researcher and subject. In the context of religion, there is a 'scholarly bias towards textual and elite manifestions' at the expense of the oral, visual and popular. Similarly, women's practices and roles frequently have been ignored or subordinated to those of males, 'reflecting the androcentric assumptions of the male and female scholars rather than the values of the communities being studied'.[32]

The precise definition which scholars attempt to bring to Lalla's religion(s) is in a sense beside the point, for such precision was really of no consequence to the vast majority of Kashmiris. For them, she and

Nuruddin were simply great saints to be venerated. This is evident in the way their figures, ideas and verses were, and remain, intertwined; absorbed into Kashmiri language and consciousness. The popular indifference to the theological specifics of such saints is still evident at thousands of shrines across Pakistan and India. If today there is a degree of polarization, it has less to do with the religions themselves and perhaps more to do with the consequences of modernity and the politics of the postcolonial state. The role of modern scholarship cannot be ignored, either.

• • •

So what is one to make of Lalla? As we have seen, there is very little that can be categorized as 'facts' about her life, and we are left with legends in which it is difficult to discern 'pure' historical truth. The desire to disentangle this material and get a linear history, a narrative thread, frequently becomes a rather destructive sort of scholarship which establishes its theses through a *reduction* in the scope of possible meaning. Once the historical tapestry is unravelled, all one is left with is a heap of threads. Rarely are these rewoven into something as intellectually and aesthetically satisfying as the original material. Ultimately what one is left with are overt or implied claims to 'pure origins', and the claim on originality always entails a heightened sense of exclusivity. As the review of research on Lalla suggests, one is never free from individual bias and modern methods of 'investigation' frequently lead to virulent and destructive academic culs-de-sac. The Babri Mosque episode, one must remember, was fuelled and justified on the basis of such a modern approach to archaeological and historical scholarship. Once the literal truth of the historicity of certain bricks was 'established' by experts, the edifice was reduced to rubble.[33]

Image and Archetype

An alternative view of Lalla is possible by setting aside the arguments on dates, chronology and differing theological visions. In this conceptual clearing one may, for a moment, simply focus on the image as it has come down through the centuries in the collective imagination: the image of a mysterious, naked woman. But, before proceeding further, one needs to be clear what in this context is meant by image.

In the psychological imagination, an image is never 'just' an image. Rather, it is a formal idea. Today, of course, we tend to think of ideas as things which we 'have', whereas in fact they frequently reflect a powerful independence. Obsessions and compulsions are obvious, albeit extreme examples. The ancient Greeks, and many other cultures, saw ideas as *persons* in the notion of personification, in which the visual image was in fact a representation of an idea. The power of the idea is still evident in language when we speak of being 'gripped' by, or 'wrestling' with, an idea – one which we may either 'get' or which may elude our 'grasp'. The etymology of the word 'idea' itself suggests a dual meaning: as not only 'that which one sees' but also 'by *means* of which one sees'.

As Carl Jung demonstrated, the images of mythology are essentially archetypal in character, representing ideas, emotions and situations that have eternally (and powerfully) been part of the human condition, providing meaning to the spectrum of experiences and emotions that we call 'life'. As discussed elsewhere,[34] meaning can be constructed both literally and symbolically, the former having more to do with outer, material, concrete existence and the latter with our inner, psychological self. These concepts are similar to Sloek's categories of *mythos* and *logos*,[35] and to what Frithjof Schuon has called the 'metaphysical transparency of phenomena'.[36] That is, a phenomenon can be 'read' at a deeper (unconscious) or higher (metaphysical) level, beyond its literal reality, at a more symbolic, psychological level. In short, as the word 'imaginative' implies, the image, as a literal form or cognitive construction, is a carrier of meaning; not just in what it presents but also in what it re-presents. It is primarily in this psycho-symbolic sense that the images of Greek or Hindu mythology can be seen as 'real'.

The archetypal image, then, functions as a 'constellated' form, involving conceptual constructions similar to those required in perceiving the star forms of the night sky; in which each star (the literal) combines with others to form a larger 'picture' or constellation. As a whole, it provides a focus which enables one to 'see through' the outer/physical towards the metaphysical and psychological. It is within this primarily Jungian conceptual framework that some of the preceding historical material about Lalla will be explored as I attempt, in what remains of this chapter, to move beyond the disputes as to what was her 'real' religion. Such an archetypal framework, indeed, may better explain not only why she was/is a subject of academic controversy but also, perhaps, what *she* meant about 'real men' and her state of nakedness. Her historical and spiritual ambiguity, along with many other elements of her story, suggests that we are dealing primarily with an archetypal symbol as constellated through some rather intriguingly literal elements.

Paradise Lost

The notion of an earthly Paradise is common to many parts of the world and in the subcontinent this has traditionally been Kashmir: 'Paradise on Earth'. The idea of paradise is itself archetypal, speaking as it does of a haven/heaven wherein humans may find perfect peace, harmony and beauty. It is a symbol of the end of 'the quest', the goal of life, and is a universal motif expressing a universal human yearning. The modern *Shangri-La* is a contemporary expression of this archetypal idea.

It is perhaps no coincidence, then, that along with Kashmir's legendary beauty it is also renowned for its numerous saints and sages, Hindu, Muslim and Buddhist. While the first Muslim rulers of Kashmir did not emerge until the middle of the thirteenth century, Muslim settlements were known to have existed as early as the eighth century.[37] Over the following centuries, for reasons ranging from invasions and war, to the seeking of a spiritual sanctuary of great beauty, or a refuge from the Mongols, Kashmir became a destination for numerous Muslim mystics, especially from Persia and Central Asia. By the end of the sixteenth century and the height of Mughal rule in India, Kashmir had become a major spiritual centre.

By then Sufism in Kashmir had developed along two broad lines, the orthodox Muslim *silsilas* and the more indigenous Rishis. As Rafiqi points out in a passage cited earlier (see page 169), the Rishis drew on 'almost wholly popular' sources in the course of preaching 'love of mankind' and 'values associated with … liberal and generous attitudes'. For these they did not look so much to Sufism as to the 'ideas and practices of the Hindu ascetics, especially those of the Saivites of Kashmir'.

From an archetypal perspective, the Indian subcontinent can be called a 'fateful' place. Like the mythic *uroboros* representing totality in the image of a serpent with its tail in its mouth, this part of the world is the point of a fateful convergence: the coming round, full circle, of the cycle of religions in the meeting of the *first* major religion, Hinduism, and the *last* major representative, Islam. The culture which flowed from such an archetypal merger is epitomized in a music, art and architecture of exquisite beauty and depth.

Monotheism and Polytheism

This image of completion/totality is evident in the inner and outer aspects of the two religions, Hinduism and Islam. In discussing the psychology of religion, I have elsewhere referred to the concepts of monotheism and polytheism which can be viewed as *both* psychological attitude and religious belief.[38] Each can exist without the other. That is, one can have a polytheistic belief but a 'monotheistic' consciousness/attitude – as, for example, in fanaticism. Or, one can believe in a monotheism and have a 'polytheistic' attitude/consciousness – that is, a consciousness of equally valid, multiple perspectives. In sum, there is unity of God and diversity of divine manifestation. The basis of such a psychological 'polytheism' is evident even in the strict monotheism of Judaism in which the Torah has a myriad names, one for each Jew in exile. The proverbial ninety-nine names of Allah similarly reflect, in Islam, the inherent diversity of divine attributes. The uroboric merging of Hinduism and Islam in the subcontinent – personified by the syzygy of Lalla and Nuruddin in Kashmir – suggests this interlocking between inner and outer, between Hindu 'polytheism' and Islamic 'monotheism'. The Bhakti movement in the Indian plains and the Rishis in Kashmir are just two examples of this unique fusion.

The Politics of Paradise

Apart from being a locus of the closing of the *uroboros*, Kashmir also occupies a rather special place from another, albeit lesser known perspective; the focus of a rather peculiar strain of scholarship which needs to be mentioned briefly. The majority of these scholars are British, French and German and the thrust of their documentation and analysis is quite dramatic and relatively unknown. I will refer very briefly to some of the main ideas.

For example, a large body of ethnographic, linguistic, archaeological, cultural and anthropological writing suggests that the area from Central Asia/Afghanistan to Kashmir is populated not only by Aryans and other races but also by those of Hebrew descent. Starting with Joseph Wolff's *Account of a Mission to Bokhara in the Years 1843–45*, there has been a steadily growing body of work which, in a cumulative fashion, has generated various hypotheses about what indeed seem to be unusual linkages with the Hebrews. While it is impossible to condense all of this extensive material into any coherent summary, one must reiterate and emphasize that this is not some sort of lunatic fringe, but a group of well-respected scholars/researchers who represent different disciplines and a body of scholarship spanning more than two hundred years. One can only speculate that the reasons for the current obscurity of this body of work have little to do with its authenticity and may possibly reflect the politics of knowledge in modern academia. Many women scholars are familiar with political constraints of this sort. Thus, however strange this body of knowledge may seem, one can only point to bibliographical sources and leave the reader to assess its relevance and validity within the context of the present discussion.

Holger Kersten's *Jesus Lived in India* is a controversial but fascinating exposition of what is undoubtedly an elemental and strong linkage between different cultural aspects of Kashmir, and aspects of Hebrew culture.[39] Among many other unusual ideas, Kersten suggests that Jesus may be buried in Kashmir. The connections that he draws range from the startlingly factual to the tenuous. It is all the more interesting since Kersten is not promoting any religious agenda as such – that is, he is not trying to 'prove' anything regarding Judaism, Christianity or Islam. On the contrary, his book is within the framework of Buddhism. However persuasive or bizarre one may find these ideas, the fact is that Buddhism too is very much part of Kashmir, the Ladakh area being primarily Buddhist even today.

The point here is not to discover what was the literal truth of things: whether Jesus is actually buried in Kashmir; whether the Afghans/Pathans/Kashmiris are one of the tribes of Israel or not, and so on. It is, rather, that over a period of centuries, in the popular and collective imagination, Kashmir seems to have become a point of convergence for the major world religions, as is evident not only in the work of eighteenth- and nineteenth-century scholars and explorers, but also, as Kersen notes, through indigenous narratives emanating from Buddhist, Muslim, Hindu, Jewish and Christian sources. Thus, the attempt here is not to establish the literal truth but to discern a spiritual and symbolic *idea* and a different set of meanings underlying historical 'facts'. In order to understand what the *idea* of Lalla 'means' one must first place her image *within* the meaning of her mythic context.

Paradise regained

That context is Kashmir, a truly archetypal land, unique in its heritage of being 'seen' as not only a literal paradise, but also a place of significance *vis-à-vis* Buddhism, Islam, Christianity, Hinduism and Judaism. To reiterate, yet again, what matters is not whether all this is 'true' or not, but that these strands are there, if only in the imagination of a large number of people, including 'outsider' scholars. As the critic Northrop Frye pointed out, the primary question about a myth is 'not is it true? The primary question is something more like, do we need to know this?'[40] Given that our usual sense of day-to-day experience is actually quite fuzzy, the unusual metaphors of myths and archetypes provide a striking contrast, and thereby a focus which may offer a sharper view of self, culture and society. The same can be said of history as cause and history as story, and it is through this latter type of narrative that one can perhaps reach a better understanding of Lalla.

Thus, Lalla's meaning is to be found first within a powerful archetypal tapestry whose warp and weft are the literal and the symbolic, manifested in a region imagined as paradise in which towering mountains bear Old Testament names such as 'The Throne of Solomon' (*Takht-e-Sulaiman*) and 'The Prayer Mat of Moses' (*Musa ka Musulla*). In this Olympian landscape, one may glimpse the figures of god-like men, the saints representing the diverse facets of their Creator. And in this pantheon of religious diversity, as the ovum is to sperm, Lalla is the only woman of comparable stature. Without going into the complexities of Islamic cosmology, one can nevertheless note that, at one level, Muslims such as Rumi and Ibn'Arabi have conceived of the Truth, or the Absolute (Divinity), as expressed more comprehensively in the feminine principle. At creation, Adam was born from a feminine soul.[41]

> [T]he Feminine is not opposed to the Masculine ... but encompasses and combines the two aspects, receptive and active, whereas the Masculine possesses only one of the two .... This intuition is clearly expressed by Rumi: Woman is beam of the Divine Light/she is not the being whom sensual desire takes as its object/she is Creator, it should be said/she is not creature.[42]

Seeing Lalla from within this archetypal perspective, then, is to see in a diferent light not only religion but even such things as politics and culture. The archetypal religious tapestry of Kashmir spans at least three thousand years and is coloured with the hues of five great faiths; and one can read a larger narrative at work beyond the individual narratives of specific religions. Lalla herself becomes a microcosm of this narrative in the uroboric fusion of Hinduism and Islam, a human locus of the coming around of the circle of religions in the life of a woman who, one must reiterate, was as real as she was mythical. The words of Pir Ghulam Hasan bear repetition here, and given the archetypal nature of Kashmir itself, today they apply to the land as much as to Lalla: 'The Hindus say she is one of them. The Musulmans claim that she belongs to them. The truth is that she is among the chosen of God. May God's peace be on her!'

It is precisely because Lalla-Kashmir is a locus/symbol of an archetypal unity that she and her land have become an object of claim and counter-claim between India and Pakistan. It was perhaps no coincidence that, in his intense desire to posses Kashmir, the first Prime Minister of India, Jawaharlal Nehru, compared the territory to the body of a beautiful woman.[43] As such, she may never yield to any final 'possession' by what is, ultimately, a fragment of the whole. Perhaps, in any case, the idea is not so much to possess Truth as to contemplate It.

The Eternal Feminine

As Henry Corbin has pointed out, this particular ideal of Truth has frequently been depicted in the 'form' of a woman by Muslim poets and philosophers such as Rumi and Ibn'Arabi, while prominent Muslim mystics have obtained 'the highest theophanic vision in contemplating the Image of Feminine Being … the apparition of the Eternal Womanly as an Image of the Godhead'.[43] This conception of the Divine or Eternal Feminine is synonymous with the notion of Sophia (wisdom) as she appears in the Judaeo-Christian tradition. Corbin linked many of these ideas in Islamic cosmology with parallel concepts in Jung's writings, particularly the latter's work on the archetype of the feminine or great goddess in different traditions – for example, in the idea of Sophia or the Hindu concept of Śakti. In Jungian terms, the feminine as 'creative principle' encompasses the whole world and this primordial 'image' forms the all-embracing bedrock of human religious conciousness.[44]

As suggested, Lalla's 'meaning' resides in the interweaving of the literal and the symbolic. Whereas ultimately the symbolic must take precedence because of its greater capacity to contain meaning (because of ambiguity), the importance of the literal cannot be entirely dismissed since it too must reflect, in however fragmentary a manner, the larger symbolic truth. We have already glimpsed this inherent harmony and interconnection between Lalla and Kashmir, and between the symbolic and literal in the context of our subject: in the renown of Kashmir as paradise, the literal and imaginal traces of different religious cultures, and in major episodes of Lalla's life – from the breaking of the water pitcher (water being the symbol *par excellence* for spirituality and the Divine, and the water remaining 'contained' above her) to the devotee of Shiva nursing (initiating) the infant Nuruddin. All these 'facts' and events can be read as different narratives, not only from the perspectives of Hinduism and Islam but as psycho-spiritual metanarratives. In every case, however, the symbolic reading has an uncannily literal underpinning.

Real men and women

In discussing notions such as the Divine Feminine, it is important to remember that we are dealing primarily with symbols which, because of human perceptual limitations, do indeed have a literal dimension. However, to the extent that they have to do with the life within, with ideas of the unseen and life after death, their psychological substance is essentially symbolic. Thus, in the context of religion or archetypal psychology, feminine and masculine are primarily symbolic terms, not man or woman. As such, they are both aspects of Divinity as well as the human. For example, in Islamic thought, the attributes of God can be regarded in terms of *Jalal* and *Jamal*, that is, names which evoke God's majesty and beauty, and which in turn, reflect 'masculine' and 'feminine' qualities.

The naked image of Lalla also speaks of certain psycho-spiritual dimensions of gender relationships, especially her claim that she wandered around unashamedly because 'there are no men in Kashmir' – till she met one, as some would say, in a Muslim saint. While others have disputed this man's religion, the main point is that at some time she met someone whom she considered a 'real man'.

As a psychological symbol, masculinity, among other qualities, may represent a certain type of intellectual attitude, one that is penetrative and analytic. Similarly, femininity may refer to a more receptive and inwardly focused attitude. As explained elsewhere, the human experience of the Divine requires a feminization of consciousness, irrespective of gender.[46]

Within this perspective, a 'real' man is someone (male or female) who has developed such a psychological and spiritual capacity, among others. The contemporary emphasis in Western culture on the need for males to become more 'sensitive', 'in touch with feelings', etcetera, is a pale and literal level of what in Lalla's view was a 'real' man. Her lament that there were no 'real' men in Kashmir can be understood from within such a psychological framework.

In a more theological and spiritual vein, an excellent analysis of these ideas and ideals of gender in Islam can be found in Sachiko Murata's *The Tao of Islam*.[47] Without going into the intricacies of Islamic Sufi theology, it should nevertheless be evident that Lalla's perception of the absence of 'real' men in Kashmir is essentially a reference to the psychological *and* spiritual conditions of her social context. From this perspective, despite or perhaps because of the violence, there are still no 'real' men in Kashmir. Trapped between different brands of militant machismo and violence, the devastation of the land and its people continues. Lalla's pond dried up a long time ago. Her eclectic message stands susceptible to suspicion and misperception by those locked in, and desirous of locking in others, through considerations of power and politics.

The irony, of course, is that both the countries which have claimed and ravaged Kashmir aspire to represent high religious ideals.

Commenting on the profoundly symbolic and providential encounter between Hinduism and Islam on the subcontinent – 'the junction of the primordial with the terminal' – Frithjof Schuon has suggested how these two different religious can learn a great deal from each other in terms of spiritual attitudes:

> Islam offers its geometric simplicity, its clarity and also its compassion, while Hinduism brings its influence to bear by its profound serenity and by its multiform and inexhaustible universality.[48]

The subcontinent today is devoid of both compassion and serenity, and the paradise of Kashmir has become the eye of an impending (nuclear) storm, which, if unleashed, raises the spectre of hell on earth. But however terrifying that prospect, this destructive momentum is also indicative of other, larger processes: of life, death and rebirth, and the archetype embracing them all, that of the Great Mother.

The Great Mother

One key dimension of the Eternal Feminine is that of the Great Mother, an ancient, some would say *the* most ancient of archetypal images/ideas known to humanity.[49] An all-embracing whole, like Her namesake Mother Earth/Nature, she creates, sustains and encompasses the cycle of life/death/regeneration, presiding over each of these domains through a myriad facets. Durga/Kali, Sophia, Demeter – to name just a few – are all dimensions of the Great Mother as conceived over the centuries, in pre-history across cultures, and in almost every known religion. Lalla's image, yet again quite literally, evokes this ancient archetype.

There are, as such, no descriptions of Lalla's body as being sensually attractive: if anything, great emphasis has been placed on her ascetic life style and disregard for physical appearance. There is only one reference to physical proportion and this is in Kaul's discussion of the possible reasons for the change of name from Padmavati to Lal Ded, which is the name preferred by Kaul. As he points out, in Kashmiri, Lal Ded means 'grandmother Lal'. He also gives examples of scholars who interpreted a particular *vaakh* as referring to the 'flabbiness of the lower part of her belly (*lal* in Kashmiri) increased in size and hung loose over her pubic region'.[50]

This description of Lalla is in resonance with numerous archetypal images of the Great Mother (Grandmother?) as she appeared in the pre-history of many cultures: its archetypal composite is of a mature and independent woman, frequently a 'faceless' or veiled figure of generous proportions, full-bellied, with pendulous breasts as exemplified in the 'Venus' of La Salle and Willendorf.[51] Thus, even the most physically literal element of Lalla's story resonates with her symbolic substance as an incarnation of a powerful and unifying archetype. Simultaneously, her 'image' can be understood psychologically, enveloping numerous 'feminine' dimensions ranging from love and wisdom to compassion and grace. This literally organic integrity between name, image and idea encapsulates a symbolic but extremely vivid and graphic portrait of the Eternal Feminine and the all-embracing Great Mother.

As we have seen, beyond the literal, there is very little that one can 'really' know about Lalla. But then, perhaps, Lalla is not meant to be treated as a figure who can be 'classified' and 'done' through dates and sundry linear analyses. It is tempting to do so, because her reality is not in doubt. But to 'prove' anything beyond that is to miss her point, her message and meaning. One primary meaning lies in the fact that someone like her really did live in Kashmir, the form hinting at the existence of an eternal archetype, and beyond this we cannot go: her existence–as–image *is* her meaning. The legends and the poetry adumbrate this message but as through a prism, offering symbolic glimpses of what cannot be said in any other way. As Norman O. Brown thinks, the truth is always ambiguous and poetic,[52] and in Lalla's case this is again literally so: for her truth is carried in her ambiguity of faith(s) and in her powerful verses which live on in the language of Kashmir.

The final element which suggests her archetypal nature and divine connections is in her death. Like her birth, her death is also outside the grasp of chronological time. In the television play, Hindus and Muslims become locked in dispute about whether she should be cremated or buried. There are various versions of an extraordinary exit, but no concrete evidence. Reminiscent of another powerful archetype – Christ – one day, she simply disappeared. Reverting to Hindu/Muslim categories, Kaul states incredulously: 'it is a matter of surprise that there should not have been a *samadhi* (temple) or *maqbara* (shrine) to mark the place where her body was cremated or laid to rest'.[53] Thus, the very absence of a literal shrine or grave again suggests the primarily non-literal manner with which one must approach what is at the same time, a literal reality. In a place where there are numerous graves and memorials of spiritually heroic males – a reminder of our mortality – there is no place suggesting the end of Lalla and the Eternal Feminine.

Notes and References

1   Baba Dawud Mishkati, *Asrar-ul-Abrar* (Persian manuscript), Srinagar. As cited in Jayalal Kaul, *Lal Ded* (Delhi: Sahitya Academy, 1973), p. 3.

2   Kaul, *Lal Ded*, p. 3.

3   A. Q. Rafiqi, *Sufism in Kashmir from the Fourteenth to the Sixteenth Century* (Delhi: Bharatiya Publishing House, n.d.), p. 145.

4   Pir Ghulam Hasan Khuyihom, *Tarikh-e-Hasan*, No. 9048 (1885), as cited in Kaul, *Lal Ded*, p. 26.

5   Kaul, *Lal Ded*, p. 12.

6   *Ibid.*, p. 15.

7   *Ibid.*, pp. 13–21.

8   Pir Ghulam Hasan, as cited in Kaul, *Lal Ded*, p. 26.

9   George Grierson and Lionel Barnett, *Lalla Vakyani*, RAS monograph, Vol. 7 (London: 1920).

10 Richard Temple, *The Word of Lalla* (Cambridge: 1924). See also Swami Muktenanda, *Lalleshwari: Spiritual Poems of a Great Siddha Yogni* (New York: SYDA Foundation, 1981).

11 As cited in Kaul, *Lal Ded*, pp. 60–7.

12 *Ibid.*, p. 3.

13 Margaret Smith, *Rabia: the Life and Work of Rabia and Other Women Mystics in Islam* (Oxford: Oneworld, 1994).

14 Kaul, *Lal Ded*, pp. 17–23.

15 *Ibid.*, p. 15.

16 Muktenanda, *Lalleshwari*.

17 See, for example, A. A Rizvi, *A History of Sufism in India*, 2 vols (Delhi: Munshiram Publishers, second edition, 1986).

18 R. K. Parmu, *A History of Muslim Rule in India (1320–1819)* (Delhi: Peoples Publishing House, 1969), p. 107.

19 Premnath Bazaz, *Daughters of Vitasta* (New Delhi: Pamposh Publications, 1959), p. 129.

20 Temple, *The Word of Lalla*, p. 79–81.

21 R. K. Bamzai, *A History of Kashmir* (Delhi: Metropolitan, 1962), cited in Kaul, *Lal Ded*, p. 71.

22 *The Herald* (Karachi), August 1995, p. 120.

23 This is not to say that male Muslim historians have not done the same or seen

her in the context of Hindu/Islamic affinities. See, for example, Muhibbul
Hasan's *Kashmir Under the Sultans* (Calcutta: 1959). However, Rizvi, *A History
of Sufism*, disagrees with Hasan.

24 Rafiqi, *Sufism in Kashmir*, p. 134.

25 Rizvi, *A History of Sufism*, p. 350.

26 Kaul, *Lal Ded*, p. 28.

27 Rafiqi, *Sufism in Kashmir*, p. viii.

28 Kaul, *Lal Ded*, p. 18.

29 Rafiqi, *Sufism in Kashmir*, p. 152.

30 *Ibid.*, p. 158.

31 *Ibid.*, p. 149.

32 Paula Cooey, *Religious Imagination and the Body: a Feminist Analysis* (New York:
Oxford University Press, 1994), p. 123. Also relevant in the context of Lalla
and Kashmir is Gerald Larson, 'Discourse about "Religion" in Colonial and
Postcolonial India', paper presented to the Critical Theory Group at the
national American Academy of Religion meeting, Kansas City, 24 November
1992, cited in Cooey, p. 123.

33 Critics have made '... a defence of archaeology against political misuse. The
archaeological discoveries which are supposed to prove the demolition of a
Rama temple by Babur actually show no more than the logic of a politics
which destroyed Babri Maijid on 6 December 1992'. From a book review of
D. Mandal, *Ayodhya Archaelogy After Demolition,* http://www.resurgenceonline.
com/pictures/issues.htm. See also, 'A Closer Look at Ayodhya Issue', World
Archaeological   Congress,   May   1998,   Papers   in   Session   7,
http://www.wac.uct.ac.za/croatia/s7.htm. Also, Robin Coningham and Nick
Lewer (eds.), *Archaeology and identity in South Asia: Interpretations and
Consequences* http://interarch.ac.uk/antiquity/indiaintro.html.

34 See Durre Ahmed, 'The Literal and the Symbolic', in 'Women, Psychology
and Religion', p. 75 above.

35 J. Sloek, *Devotional Language* (translation) (Berlin and New York: Henrik
Mossin, 1996).

36 Frithjof Schuon, *The Essential Writings of Frithjof Schuon* (New York: Amity
House, 1986), p. 267.

37 Rafiqi, *Sufism in Kashmir*, p. 1.

38 James Hillman, 'Schism', in *Loose Ends: Primary Papers in Archetypal Psychology*
(Dallas: Spring Publications, 1975). Also Durre Ahmed, 'Monotheism of Consciousness', in 'Women, Psychology and Religion', p. 80 above.

39 Holger Kersten, *Jesus Lived in India* (Shaftesbury: Element Books, 1986). See
extensive bibliography therein.

40 Northrop Frye, *Myth and Metaphor: Selected Essays 1974–1978*, ed. Robert
Denham (University of Virginia: 1991).

41 'As to woman being both active and receptive, Ibn'Arabi explains further the
point that the Absolute is contemplated more perfectly through a woman ...
man exists between two feminine principles. The Quran states: "And He
created from Adam his mate and out of the two He spread innumerable men

and women" (4:1). Commentators, referring to this verse say: "The wife of Adam was feminine, but the first soul from which Adam was born was also feminine."' T. Izutsu, *The Key Philosophical Concepts in Sufism and Taoism – Ibn'Arabi and Lao Tzu, Chuang-Tzu*, cited in Laleh Bakhtiar, *Sufi: Expressions of the Mystic Quest* (New York: Thames and Hudson, 1976), p. 22.

42 Henry Corbin, *Creative Imagination in the Sufism of Ibn'Arabi* (Princeton: Princeton University Press, 1987), pp. 159–60.

43 As quoted in Josef Korbel, *Danger in Kashmir* (Princeton: Princeton University Press, 1965).

44 Henry Corbin, *Creative Imagination*, pp. 159–60.

45 C. G. Jung, *Aspects of the Feminine* (Princeton: Princeton University Press, 1982).

46 See Durre Ahmed, 'Women, Psychology and Religion', Chapter 4, pp. 70–87 above.

47 Sachiko Murata, *The Tao of Islam* (Albany: State University of New York: 1991).

48 Frithjof Schuon, *Sufism: Veil and Quintessence* (Bloomington, Indiana: World Wisdom Books, 1981), p. 38.

49 Erich Neumann, *The Great Mother: an Analysis of the Archetype* (Princeton/Bollingen: 1972).

50 Kaul, *Lal Ded*, p. 13.

51 See Neumann, *The Great Mother*, for a wide array of illustrations.

52 Norman O. Brown, in a response to Herbert Marcuse in his *Negations* (London: Allen Lane 1968).

53 Kaul, *Lal Ded*, p. 26.

III

Perspectives on Violence

10

Righteous Violence and Non-Violence
An Inseparable Dyad of Hindu Tradition

MADHU KHANNA

Modernity and violence have a special relationship. Communal riots, murder and rape are common urban phenomena. Almost all the major cities in India are besieged by a new kind of violence based on ethnic class, caste structure and community, largely precipitated by an erosion of the moral and secular order. Such forms of violence are looked upon as an aberration stemming from a personal or collective psychosis. Yet, throughout history, violence has persisted. Most of the world's religions began with fire and the sword, animal sacrifices, conversions and periodic massacres. But the modes of conflict resolution in a traditional society such as India's were self-contained and guided by a number of approaches: the notion of duty (*dharma*) or adherence to the religious ideology of tolerance; assiduously following the ethics of non-violence (*ahimsā*); complying with the norms of peaceful co-existence; or resorting to the revelatory means of the spirit. Violence was accepted as an instinctive feature of the human condition and as a natural expression of the nature of cosmic reality.

Underlying Indian thought, myths, legends, metaphors, symbols and icons, there exist a great many paradigms of violence. A large corpus of myths from the *Vedas* down to the *Purānas* repeatedly demonstrate the ambivalence inherent in the personification of the deities and their narratives. The mythological landscapes weave their narrative around stark and gory wars between gods and demons. Such descriptions are often found in the context of saviour myths that proclaim the triumph of good over evil, order over chaos, life over death, and light over darkness and the dismal forces of existence. In some legends, violence is structurally embedded in the story line; in others, all forms of violence get justified for upholding the ideal of sacrifice or *dharma* for the sake of righteousness and enlightenment.

This chapter explores some representations of violence in Hindu tradition that have found justification in the sacred codes. The chapter is divided into three sections. The first part is a brief excursus on some images and representations of violence in Hindu sources and the in-built strategies of conflict resolution. The second part explores the wrathful energy of the feminine principle in the personification of the goddess Durgā. The archetypal image of Durgā is a model of feminine violence *par excellence* and her images have been used as an instrument both to empower and to suppress women. This section attempts to present a brief outline of the social reality of the mythical model.

In the cognitive frame of the Indian imagination, the categories of violence and non-violence feature with equal intensity. They represent a complementarity rather than irresolvable binary oppositions. This reflection raises the fundamental question regarding the all-pervasiveness of the ideology of non-violence in Hindu tradition. Thus, the discussion in the third part of this chapter takes one back to the consideration of the notion of *ahimsā*.

I

Images of Violence

Acts of violence are either implicit or hinted at in several myths related to creation. Stella Kramrisch in the opening statement of her book *The Presence of Śiva* makes an illuminating observation: 'Creation is an act of violence that infringes upon the uncreated Wholeness that is the beginning of things.'[1] An ancient myth from the *Rig Veda* (Ch. 10: verse 61) mirrors this statement. In the dawn of the world, when night and morning lie in darkness, two figures appear: one of the father and the other of a virgin girl, his daughter. The father is visualized as an antelope. While the father lusts after the daughter, Agni (Raudra Brahman, *Rig Veda*, Ch. 1: verse 71), who is the divine hunter, inter-venes in this primal sexual act of creation and boldly shoots an arrow at the antelope. The antelope is Prajāpati; he sheds his seed. The seed falls on the earth and comes to life as his progeny. In this early myth from the *Rig Veda*, creation is not described as a benevolent, immaculate act, but as a wild, fierce event – an act of violence.

In another early description of primeval violence, the universe is portrayed as a colossal *Purusha*,[2] the cosmic being whose macrocosmic body contains the world. The bounds of this anthropomorphized being constitute the regions of earthly and cosmic creation. The universe is created and put in order through the dismemberment of the primeval male who is the victim of the Vedic sacrifice. The imagery of dismemberment is linked to the creation of explicit elements. Thus,

> the moon was born from his mind; from his eyes the sun was born ... from his navel the middle realm of his space arose; from his head the sky evolved; from his two feet came the earth, and the quarters of the sky from his ear. Thus they set the world in order. (*Rig Veda* Mandala 10, Section 90, Part 1, vs. 4–13, 14)

In later history, the image of the sacrificial myth of creation is vividly portrayed in the origin of the sacred holy centres[3] of the goddess (*śakta pīthas*) found all over India. In this celebrated myth, Śiva slung the corpse of his wife, Satī/Pāravatī on his shoulders and danced a wild and destructive dance. Visnu intervened and pleaded with him to stop the dance lest the world be destroyed. But Śiva was inconsolable; he continued his dance of grief. Thereupon, Visnu spun his discus and dismembered Satī's body limb after limb. Wherever in India each part of the body fell, those places became known as the holy places of the goddess.

In this late version of the story it is the goddess's body which is dismembered by Visnu for the creation of sacred centres dedicated to her, in a manner similar to the earlier dismemberment myth of the cosmic man. In all the three myths cited, violence is inherent in the imagery of creation.

Ritual and Sacrificial Violence

Ritual sacrifice was one of the main foundations of Vedic religion. According to Vedic injunction, sacrifice is an essential instrument of salvation. Sacrificial ceremonies formed an essential part of the Vedic way of life. Animal sacrifice (*paśu-badha*) was a fundamental element of ancient Vedic ritual. The most important feature of animal sacrifice in the Vedas is that by the time of the *Brāhmanas* a whole nomenclature of ritual had been formalized in which sacrificial violence and its ritual inversions were included side by side. Ritual violence was accepted as a part of the Vedic sacrifices, so much so that one may be able to reconstruct 'a ritual theory of violence'. However, in a later period this form of violence was treated as a 'ritual mistake', and several formulae were inducted into the rite to 'neutralize and cancel out' this mistake.[4] The ritual strategy adopted by Vedic seers is to repair the injury done to a victim by a series of symbolic ritual actions which would include the following: purification of the sacrificial animal; sacrificial killing; symbolic revitalization of the stake; dissection of the animal; symbolically reuniting the parts of the body; infusing them with life; and, the animal having been made whole, the priest's offering it to the gods.[5] What is essential to note here is that the violent form of sacrifice was gradually replaced by several symbolic, non-violent acts.

Sacrificial violence is also linked to the motif of personal sacrifice and devotion. This image is vividly depicted in the mythology of the Tantric goddess, Chinnamastā, the decapitated goddess, who cuts off her own head in order to feed and nourish her devotees. Her myth elaborates the context in which she assumes her headless form and gives her own blood to her devotees:

One day Parvati went to bathe in the Mandakini River ... with the attendants, Jaya and Vijaya. After bathing, the great goddess's colour became black because she was sexually aroused. After some time, her two attendants asked her, 'Give us some food. We are hungry.' She replied, 'I shall give you food but please wait.' After a while, again they asked her. She replied, 'Please wait, I am thinking about some matters.' Waiting a while, they implored her, 'You are the mother of the universe. A child asks everything from her mother. The mother gives her children not only food but also covering for the body. So that is why we are praying to you for food. You are known for your mercy; please give us food.' Hearing this, the consort of Shiva told them that she would give anything when they reached home. But again her two attendants, Dakini and Varnini, begged her, 'We are overpowered with hunger, O Mother of the Universe. Give us food so we may be satisfied, O Merciful One, Bestower of Boons and Fulfiller of desires.'

Hearing this true statement, the merciful goddess smiled and severed her head with her fingernails. As soon as she severed her head, her head fell on the palm of her left hand. Three bloodstreams emerged from her throat, the left and right fell respectively into the mouths of her flanking attendants and the centre fell into her mouth. After performing this, all were satisfied and later returned home. [As a result of this act] Parvati became known as Chinnamasta.[6]

Chinnamastā embodies the liminal quality which renders her ambiguous. She is alive, yet she is decapitated. The purpose of her decapitation is to feed her attendants and herself. Two bloodstreams gush forth from her neck and enter the mouths of her two attendants, while the central bloodstream swiftly returns into the mouth of her severed head which she holds on her left palm. In this image the goddess unites both violence and mercy. Chinnamastā is the embodiment of the sacrificial process whereby the world is eternally renewed.

Sacrificial violence is also a popular theme in religious devotion, and appears over and over again in the lives of saints and prophets who die for a beatific vision. It is recorded that when the saint Ramakrishna sought the 'vision' of goddess Kālī he could not eat, sleep or even blink. He could barely breathe. So great was his desire to unite with the goddess that he used to roll on the ground crying for Kālī. On one such day, tormented and frustrated by his unsuccessful attempts, Ramakrishna reached out for the sacrificial sword hanging on the temple wall. He picked it up and was about to decapitate himself before Kālī, when the goddess intervened and gave him a vision. This was the culmination of Ramakrishna's mystical life.[7]

It is interesting to observe that a violent setting can be an occasion for a discourse on enlightenment. In the *Bhagavad Gītā*, for example, the battlefield is an arena for resolving moral dilemmas, holding a philosophical discourse on the meaning of life, reflecting upon the perennial riddles of the mystery of creation, and inculcating an enhanced awareness of the true nature of the self.

The *Bhagavad Gītā*, an episode in the Indian epic, the *Mahābhārata*, is set on the battlefield of Kurukshetra. The opening chapters of this celebrated text describe a reflective conversation between Arjuna, the warrior prince of the Pandava clan, with Krishna, the supreme god and the agent of the divine voice, who articulates the truth and teaches what is appropriate for the occasion. Upon seeing his own kinsmen as his adversaries on the battlefield, Arjuna is overcome with grief. He throws down his arms and wants to withdraw from the battle. In a long discourse on what is right action and non-action, Krishna makes it clear that Arjuna's pacifist attitude is ineffective. According to the warrior tradition, it is his duty to kill. For a warrior, it is ennobling to fight.

What the conversation does is to convince Arjuna that ultimately the sages and warriors reach the same goal. It is the *dharma* of a warrior to 'take the sword' and not to 'shave his head'; therefore, Krishna urges him to engage in a righteous battle. In the same discourse, Krishna enlightens Arjuna that the violence inflicted on his kinsmen is 'logically' unreal. In this view, there is no violent agency nor any victim of violence that persists through time. The bloody wars are fought in the virtual ('*māyic*') world of appearances. The violence that is being meted out in is an act of deception, an illusion that the mind creates through attachment to the world. The soul (*ātman*), or the real self, is incorruptible and inviolable; 'it cannot be wounded by weapons', burned by fire, or wetted by water. As Krishna impels Arjuna from one ontological space to another, he convinces him that the battleground is, indeed, a *dharma-ksetra*, a space for enlightenment and liberation.[8]

Utpāta and *Anrta*: Nature's Violence

There is considerable speculation in Hindu thought on the violence caused by physical forces, or violence inflicted upon nature. These ideas emerge in the context of the notion of the divinity of the earth. The ancient notion of ecology was essentially a sacred model rooted in the spirituality of the earth. The earth is looked upon as the supreme, loving, life-sustaining mother of all beings. She is beautiful, fertile, nurturing and generous. As a person's entire existence depends upon her, man is of earth, part of earth. Hence, the earth was divinized as a goddess.

The entire earth, it is held, is sustained by a harmonious cosmic principle. In the Vedic code, this principle is known as *rta* or cosmic order. *Rta* is the universal cosmic flow, the self-regulating principle of harmony, order and balance. This single principle of order permeates the natural world and is born afresh in each *rītu*, season. *Rta* maintains the energy flow and pulse of the natural world. The opposite manifestation of *rta* is *anrta*, disorder, disharmony and chaos. These two mutually dependent principles form two sides of a single process.[9]

Tradition makes a distinction between *utpāta*[10] and *anrta*. Natural disasters in the form of floods, earthquakes, storms and volcanoes are a manifestation of *utpāta*. They are governed by natural laws. But when humans violate and exploit nature, as a commodity for trading, they are said to go against the natural order. They instigate disorder, chaos, falsehood (*anrta*). Several myths record the painful cry of mother earth, who constantly appeals to the gods for succour and pleads for help as she can no longer bear the sins and evil deeds of men. This is man-made violence, which corrupts the very bowels of the mother earth.

II

The Wrathful Energy of the Goddess

The epithet of a heroic warrior queen who vanquishes the might of the demons at the time of a critical cosmic crisis is the *locus classicus* of a large bulk of narrative of the goddess. The goddess, Durgā, is a formidable representation. Though serene and calm in her motherly manifestation she is depicted in her Mahiśāsurmardinī form as riding a lion, holding several weapons of destruction and piercing a trident into the chest of the demon Mahisha, who is shown emerging in human form from his buffalo body. At her feet lies the head of the slain Mahisha, stained with blood. The lower half of this image captures the moment of extreme violence that was necessary to repair the imbalance caused by the demons, who were out to undo the world. In the *Devīmahatmaya*,[11] although she is depicted as the supreme, cosmic energy, she is also the embodiment of militant energy of the cosmos, which she resorts to in times of crisis. Her wild and untamed power comes to the fore when the situation demands that she rise to the occasion to quell the anti-divine force to repair the imbalance caused by the demons. It is interesting to observe that apart from the nurturing qualities of motherhood, her militant role is exalted. She is described as 'the slayer of Mahisha', 'the destroyer of Cāmundā', 'the killer of Madhu and Kaitabha', 'one who holds all the weapons' (of destruction), 'slayer of all the demons'.[12]

Durgā's battle with the demons is narrated in three episodes, in which each confrontation is more fierce than the previous one. In the last episode, Durgā in her fury transforms into the icon of the fierce goddess Kālī, who wages a violent war of blood and death with an army of demons. Kālī's fanged mouth, bloodthirsty lolling tongue, emaciated body, locks of grisly hair and blood-smeared sword typify her as a warrior queen. She is now face to face with the forces of evil which only deathly violence can subdue.

The climax of the battle takes place when the goddess ropes the buffalo demon, Mahisha, in her noose. The demon escapes and emerges from his buffalo body in the shape of a lion. She confronts the lion form and beheads him. The demon then stands before her in a human form, armed with a sword. The goddess decapitates him. The demon, through his magic power, escapes and assumes the form of a wild elephant; he reaches out to her with his trunk and drags her towards him. The goddess severs his trunk. Now the enraged goddess, taking a break, lifts a chalice full of invigorating wine to her lips, while the demon uproots mountains with his horns. She then leaps into the air and descends upon her antagonist. She dashes him to the earth and pierces a trident through his neck. Once again the demon rises to abandon his buffalo body, swiftly emerging from its mouth in the shape of a human. He is half inside the buffalo and half outside. Then, at once, the goddess beheads him. He dies and his body loosely yields to the ground.

This gory mythological episode expresses the multiple personality of the demon, Mahisha, who is gradually divested of his many 'egos' by Durgā/Kālī's relentless fury. His ability to transmute and advance a new threat in diverse guises depicts the split image as the root of human violence. In contrast, the goddess's doubly violent role has been interpreted as a demonstration of the 'masculinized mother', a frenzied, almost psychotic state when she throws her femininity to the winds and reverses her gender role.[13] While the elemental powers of wrath, fury, anger and destruction are considered demonic or even dangerous in the Judaeo-Christian tradition,[14] the Hindu perception does not split these two aspects but views them as part of an integral totality of the divine feminine. The energy of the goddess is a seamless continuum of conscious force, which, when aroused, flows forth as violence or benign beneficence. The forces of opposition between militant masculinity and acquiescent femininity which Carmel Berkson speaks of are not so sharply defined. The emphasis of the Hindu views is precisely to highlight the interplay of the opposite categories reflected in the ambivalent personality of Durgā, who both destroys and heals. Wendy O'Flaherty has eloquently discussed 'the paradox of the evil god and good demon' – a view which upsets the neat East/West categorization of the moral contrast between the gods and demons.[15] And A. L. Coomarswamy illuminates the more complex assessment that is required:

> Although distinct and opposite in operation, [gods and demons] are in essence consubstantial, their distinction being a matter not of essence but of orientation, revolution, or transformation.... The Titan is potentially an Angel, the Angel still by nature a Titan.[16]

By the same logic, contrasting traits can be part of a single personification of the deity.

Women, Violence and the Social Reality of Mythical Models

I must now reverse the current of my discussion and address the question of the social reality of mythical models of violence. I shall comment briefly on this theme by raising the question of how women become agents of violence, either in the private space of their homes or in public spaces outside their homes. Cinema has become an influential signifier of women's social reality. In the post-independence era, we have witnessed a few films that portray the woman/goddess representations in a variety of contexts. I shall explore the first representation through the portrayal of Nita, who is the central character in the film *Megha–Dhaka Tara* (or 'Cloud-Capped Star') directed by one of India's outstanding film directors, Ritwik Ghatak. Ghatak's award-winning film portrays the protagonist as a character possessing the qualities of a goddess.[17]

In this film, Ghatak depicts the life struggle of a working woman. Though her character may be framed by the image of the goddess,

Nita is exploited by all the members of her family – a weak father, a clever and conniving mother, a selfish and self-centred sister and an idealistic brother, who is a musician. Sanat, the male friend with whom she is in love, betrays her and marries her sister. Her isolation is complete when all her siblings become established and go their separate ways. Helpless and lonely, she contracts tuberculosis. While his daughter is engulfed in a fit of depression, her father, too, turns against her, forcing her to leave the house. This is the critical moment in Nita's destruction. She is trapped in human conflict while perpetuating the image of the mother goddess, who gives in endlessly to all demands upon her, until she finally dies.

Ghatak sensitively shows the connection between the goddess and her symbols through the portrayal of Nita's character and the events that engulf her life. Throughout the film, Nita's own desires are sacrificed for the family, however unreasonable and harmful this is to herself. Her story is one of a woman who voluntarily inflicts violence on herself. While trying hard to live up to an image which her psyche cannot support, she gives in to self-destruction. There are countless women who inflict painful wounds on themselves, and tear their lives apart because they emulate, like Nita, an unattainable ideal.

A similar portrayal of the woman comes through in the protagonist of Satyajit Ray's film, *Devi*.[18] Set in late-nineteenth-century Bengal, the story takes us to the *zamidar* household of Kalikinkar Roy, an old widower who is a great devotee of Kālī. He has two sons and two daughters-in-law. His younger daughter-in-law Dayamoyee is beautiful and takes good care of him. He dreams one night that Dayamoyee is an incarnation of the goddess, his patron deity. The next day he deifies her and reveals her to the community as a beneficent deity in human form who can alleviate their sufferings by performing miracles, as goddesses are said to do. Her husband, Umaprasad, protests and persuades her to run away as she is suffering from religious delusion. She refuses to see reason. The story then takes a turn. One day Dayamoyee is compelled to try to save her dying nephew. The child dies in her lap and her sister-in-law accuses her of witchery. The father-in-law returns to his temple deity. Powerless and confused about her real identity, Dayamoyee becomes a casualty of her father-in-law's religious delusion. In the last scene she is shown running into the light of a sparse meadow.

The protagonists of both films are victims of an autocratic patriarchal family hierarchy. In the case of Nita, she is expected to be the silent caretaker of her family and bears her conflict silently. In the case of Dayamoyee, she is the spiritual buffer of her father-in-law's fantasies. She comes across as a woman who is alien to herself, and so suffers from a deep psychological disorder that brings about her tragic end.

The Durgā legend lives universally in the Indian imagination. The myth has many institutional and popular applications. It is found in calendar art, popular cinema, scholarly writing, popular songs and folk tales. Today, All India Radio takes pride in broadcasting the myth and the annual Durgā celebrations. Pathak and Sengupta[19] have deconstructed the hidden agenda of the patriarchal politics that underlies this image. While 'women's aggressive potential is recognized … the controlling creative force that empowers her and sets the agenda is unequivocally the privilege of the males who prescribe particular contexts in which it is allowed articulation'. 'The image of militancy', they conclude, 'is merely a textual representation.' According to this analysis, the image and the reality are far apart. In recent years, the politics of Hindutva expressed by the right-wing ruling Bhartiya Janta Party (BJP) and regional parties such as Shiva Sena has attempted to construct the image of woman as a 'clever balance of tradition and change'. While these political parties exalt the woman's role as wife and mother, they encourage women to reclaim public spaces and play a militant role at the same time. In this game, women become the most aggressive participants. Women are systematically mobilized into social and communal violence, either as active promoters or as passive victims.

This image of the goddess as a warrior challenges the stereotypical image of women in Hindu society. While there are few examples of warrior women in real life, Kathryn Hansen has drawn our attention to a unique female paradigm of Indian womenhood called *Virangana,* the woman who manifests the qualities of heroism.[20] In her work, Hansen shows that *Virangana* is a valiant figure who distinguishes herself by her exceptional skills in warfare, a domain reserved for men. She demonstrates her martial skills in combat, at the risk of her own life. Unlike the passive, husband-obeying, chaste and loyal heroines in the epics, *Virangana* is a leader among men and women, or a general in war. She assumes male attire and adorns herself with symbols of male status, such as a sword and a horse to ride on. She is devoted to the protection of people and is willing to sacrifice her own life for theirs.

Hansen further cites a number of historical figures, especially queens in various regions of India and lesser known folk heroines in the image of the bandit queen, Phoolan Devi,[21] for example, who are worthy of being celebrated. 'These women combine direct assumption of power with exemplary virtues,' she states. Hansen puts together an impressive list of such women. I shall simply quote a few examples here to demonstrate the outstanding contributions these women have made. One of them was Razia Sultan, the first woman of the Sultanate to accede to the throne of Delhi. Trained by her father in affairs of state, she is said to have discarded her female attire and worn a tunic and a cap like a man. She is known to have waged a war against several rebellious Turkish nobles. Then there was Rani Durgavati, who ruled among the Gonds, a tribal community living in Madhya Pradesh, and fought against Akbar's imperial army. Tarabai, a Rajput queen, wife of Prithviraj, is a legendary figure in Rajasthan who waged a war to recapture the region of Thoda from the Afghans. The most famous warrior queen, however, is Lakshmi Bai, Rani of Jhansi in North India. This legendary heroine was a freedom fighter in the War of Independence against the British in 1857. It is said that she fought with two swords. Her miraculous feats are preserved in Subhadra Kumari Chauhan's poem: *Khub lare mardani who to jhansi wali Rani.*

What is noteworthy is that all these warrior queens enjoy sovereign power, play male roles and resort to bloody warfare. These human warrior queens appropriate the mythical presence of Durgā and Kālī on the social plane. They fight the restrictions imposed on them by the patriarchal set-up and prove their latent feminine power through a masculine image.

III

Non-violence, Gandhi and Woman Power

In the foregoing discussion, we have considered confrontation and violent aggression as valid modes of conflict resolution. But this gives only partial insight into the Hindu view of violence. While the tradition validates violent aggression as a strategy of conflict resolution, it equally rejects all forms of violence. In the Hindu world view, power is also linked with the human virtues of self-surrender, endurance, tolerance and self-abnegation, which are generally regarded as passive. Thus, self-assertion, masterly aggressiveness and active violence are replaced by the practice of non-violence.

The ideology of non-violence[22] has is roots in ancient times. In 500 BC, a kind of an ideological revolution took place, overthrowing the obsessive magico-ritualistic practice of animal sacrifice. The overbearing ritualism of the Vedas gradually gave way to the fine values of compassion and non-injury (*ahimsā*) to all beings. These values were held in high esteem by the contemplative Brahmanic ascetics and by the heterodox communities. They then became a central guiding principle of the Jaina teaching, and were later adopted by the Buddhists as well. Both these traditions emphasized the importance of non-violence and advocated that *ahimsā* be adhered to in mind, thought and action in the quest for perfection. When the ideology of non-violence was accepted by emperor Ashoka (273–232 BC), he also instituted it as a state policy. Thus the ideal of *ahimsā* took firm root and was eventually to become an immutable principle accepted by most of the philosophies and religions in India. Despite modernity's advocacy of aggression, often with the implication that the first duty is to kill, the universally accepted moral code in India remains *ahimsā*.

In modern India, the notion of *ahimsā* was reinterpreted by Mohandas Gandhi (1869–1948)[23] who used it as a weapon of political freedom. Gandhi's approach to conflict resolution was through *satyagraha* ('holding firmly to truth') and he used non-violence as a litmus test for ascertaining truth. The pursuance of *ahimsā* was to be practised along with a host of virtues such as chastity, the absence of possessions, self-control and self-purity – qualities traditionally described as feminine. Gandhi's life was a model of how these feminine virtues could be cultivated by recognizing the hidden woman in himself.

In our age, Gandhi has been described as having 'invented tradition' among other achievements – a tradition of innovative acceptance of femininity and a deep-rooted respect for women. The recognition of the value of the feminine in him was a part of his psychological chemistry. The feminine virtues, such as self-surrender, power of endurance, courage, serenity in sorrow, intuition, passive forbearance and self-abnegation seemed to him a paradigm of existence and a moral guide. His views on feminine qualities and the values that they embodied formed a seedbed of ideas that nurtured his political philosophy and social activism. On the other hand, his explicit feminine identifications formed the basis of his personal philosophy, which was used as a powerful instrument to combat the rigours of *bhramacharya*. N. K. Bose, in his book *My Days with Gandhi*, refers to the feminization of Gandhi's personality through the adoption of the maternal role of a nurturer – 'it was by becoming a woman that he [Gandhi] tried to circumvent one of the most powerful and disturbing elements which belong to our biological existence'.[24] Gandhi felt that by inculcating the feminine in himself, he would ultimately release a 'passive' force that would prove a perfect foil to the conventional strengths of malehood, rooted in aggression.

This feminine empathy found its expression in his boundless internal capacity spontaneously to assume a maternal role. His natural instinct for maternal capacity came to the fore when he embraced all opportunities to practise this skill, acting as a mid-wife during the birth of his fourth son and caring for his sick wife and babies whenever they were ill. It was widely recognized that he served as a mother to his 'orphaned' grand-niece, Manu, who, overwhelmed by his mothering, described these experiences in her book, *Bapu – My Mother*.[25] Clearly, these experiences prove that nurturance was not only 'a feminine characteristic'. From his childhood he found his mother more appealing to him than his father. 'If you notice any purity in me,' he said to a friend in 1932, 'I have inherited it from my mother, and not my father.'[26] She appeared in his imagination as an elevated figure, a person with superlative excellences, an embodiment of feminine virtues.

'Woman is the incarnation of *ahimsā*, *ahimsā* means infinite love': *ahimsā* or non-violence is an expression not only of the potency of man but also of the potency of women.[27] This capacity of passive selfless personhood was transformed into an effective political weapon through non-violent resistance. Women, clearly, were the finest vehicles to propagate this ideal. Gandhi was able to inspire women, as living incarnations of this abstract ideal, to participate in *satyagraha*. Women, for him, were ideally suited to his kind of social mobilization and public activity. These instances prove that Gandhi had an ingrained aversion to 'male sadism'. In more senses than one, it was the feminine in Gandhi that constituted the archetypal Gandhian personality. Recognition of femininity led him not only to transform his baser virtues but also to liberate what was an imprisoned India.

Gandhi's non-violence philosophy inspired many women to join him in his struggle for freedom. Beyond the borders of India, a momentous battle is now being fought by Aung San Suu Kyi, in Myanmar, against one of the most militant military dictatorships. Though the daughter of a military hero, Aung San Suu Kyi has denounced the violent militarist path of her father and is instead following the political philosophy of Gandhi. In the words of Madhu Kishwar,[28]

> like Gandhi she aspires for spiritual truth. Her essential political strategy is based on *satyagraha*, truth, non-violence and self-responsibility. Her struggle is defined as the revolution of the spirit. She has extended the vision that if women translate womanly qualities into the political domain, rather than masculinise themselves in order to prove themselves equal to men, their entry into public life can act as a purifying force.

Aung San Suu Kyi's message transcends geographical boundaries and speaks of the ideals of women's freedom and dignity purely by following the feminine virtues of non-violence, natural to women. Both Gandhi's and Aung San Suu Kyi's lives are exemplary models of how violence may be met by women of today.

Conclusion

In this brief overview, two distinct mindsets on the approach to violence have emerged. On the ontological plane, violence is visualized as being inevitable for the purpose of creation (as exemplified in the myths of creation), and in its restoration from evil forces (as represented in the myth of Durgā and Kālī). Sacrificial violence is embodied in the goddess, Chinnamastā, who represents a continuous state of self-destruction and self-renewal. From this *mythos* of violence, thus, there emerges a well-defined ethos of aggression. All the myths that have been referred to earlier are justified for righteous ends. They function as paradigms of a positive use of power. Violence originates when there is malfunctioning in the harmonic structure of reality. The unbounded ferocity of the divine arises out of love and protection. It is not to be seen as an expression of a primal split in the divine psyche. Running parallel to this view is the other mindset which rejects outright all forms of violence and embraces the profound philosophy and practice of non-violence. Thus, the categories of righteous violence and non-violence form an inseparable dyad of Hindu tradition and have had a profound influence in shaping the concept of the divine feminine as well as the social reality of women. Both the categories can mobilize social action in favour of women today.

Notes and References

1 Stella Kramrisch, *The Presence of Śiva* (Princeton: Princeton University Press, 1981), Chapter I, discusses the myth extensively and contextualizes its symbolic meaning.

2 For the meaning and significance of *Purusha*, see W. N. Brown, 'The Creation Myth in the Vedas', *Journal of the American Oriental Society*, 62 (1942): 85–98; Jeanine Miller, *The Vision of Cosmic Order in the Vedas* (London: Routledge and Kegan Paul, 1985), pp. 82, 61ff., 248ff.

3 For the myth of the origin of holy places of the goddess, see D. C. Sircar, *The Śākta Pīthas* (Delhi: Motilal Banarsidass, 1973).

4 This has been convincingly argued by J. C. Heesterman, 'Non-Violence and Sacrifice', in *Indologica Taurinensia*, Vol. 12 (Torino: Edizoni Jollygrafica, 1984), pp. 118–27.

5 The mantra for revitalization of the body of the victim runs thus: 'In every limb is Indra's out-breath seated. In every limb is Indra's in-breath settled. God Tvashtar, let thine ample forms be blended that what wears different shapes may be one-fashioned [= made whole].' *Yajur Veda*, Ch. 6: verse 20, cited in Naama Drury, *The Sacrificial Ritual in the Śatapatha Brāhmana* (Delhi: Motilal Banarsidass, 1981), p. 30.

6 The legend of the origin of Chinnamastā is from the *Prānatoshanī Tantra*. (Calcutta: Basmati Sahitya Mandir, 1928), p. 378, cited by Elisabeth Anne Benard, *Chinnamastā, The Aweful Buddhist and Hindu Tantric Goddess*, Buddhist Tradition Series, Vol. 22 (New Delhi: Motilal Banarsidass, 1994), p. 7; cf. David Kinsley, *Tantric Visions of the Divine Feminine* (Berkeley: University of California Press, 1977), pp. 147ff.

7 See David Kinsley, *Hindu Goddesses: Vision of the Divine Feminine in the Hindu Religious Tradition* (New Delhi: Motilal Banarsidass, 1987), p. 145.

8 *The Bhagavad Gītā*, trans. and ed. Franklin Edgerton (Massachusetts: Harvard University Press, 1975), Chapters I and II, pp. 23–5; Antonio T. de Nicolas, *Avatāra: the Humanization of Philosophy Through the Bhagavad Gītā* (Nicolas Hayes: 1976).

9 For a fine discussion on the concept of *rta*, see Miller, *The Vision of Cosmic Order*, especially pp. 38–43, 273–81.

10 The notion of *utpāta* is discussed by Bhise, *'Utpāta'*, in V. N. Jha (ed.), *Proceedings of the National Seminar on Environmental Awareness Reflected in Sanskrit Literature* (Pune: Centre of Advanced Study in Sanskrit, 1991), pp. 212–15.

11 [*Devīmahatmaya*]. *The Glorification of the Great Goddess*, trans. and ed. Vasudev S. Agrawala (Varanasi: All India Kashi Trust, 1963).

12 *Śrīdurgāstotra*, verses 10–11, cited in *Śrīdurgāsaptaśatī*, Chapter 3 (Gorakhapur: Gita Press, 1969).

13 The relationship of the goddess and Mahisha has been interpreted by Carmel Berkson, *The Divine and Demoniac. Mahisah's Heroic Struggle with Durgā* (Delhi: Oxford University Press, 1995), pp.18ff.

14 Elinor Gadon, 'Revisioning the Female Demon, Lilith, and Her Indian Sisters: Those Other Goddesses', private communication, 1998.

15 Wendy Doniger O'Flaherty, *The Origins of Evil in Hindu Mythology* (New Delhi: Motilal Banarasidass, 1976), p. 59, chapters 5 and 7.

16 A. K. Coomarswamy, 'Angels and Titans, an Essay on Vedic Ontology', *Journal of the American Oriental Society*, 55, 5 (1935): 373–413, cited by O'Flaherty, *The Origins of Evil*, p. 59.

17 The protagonist of the film is brilliantly analysed in Ira Bhaskar, 'Mother Goddess Ascendant: Ghatak's Megha Dhaka Tara', in Kamala Bhasin and Bina Agarwal (eds.), *Women and Media Analysis, Alternatives and Action* (Rome and New Delhi: ISIS International and Pacific and Asian Women's Forum, 1984), pp. 44–7.

18 For an interpretation of Satyajit Ray's film *Devi* (1960), see Geeta Kapur, 'Mythical Material in Indian Cinema', *Journal of Arts and Ideas*, 14–15 (1987), pp. 79ff.

19 Zakia Pathak and Saswati Sengupta, 'Resisting Woman', in Tanika Sarkar and Urvashi Butalia (eds.), *Women and the Hindu Right* (New Delhi: Kālī for Women, 1996), pp. 270–98; Paola Bacchetta, 'All Our Goddesses Are Armed', in Kamala Bhasin, Ritu Menon and Nighat Said Khan (eds.), *Against All Odds, Essays on Women, Religion and Development from India and Pakistan* (New Delhi: ISIS International and Kālī for Women, 1994); 'Women Bear the Brunt of Post-Riot Trauma', *The Pioneer*, 23 December 1992.

20 My description here is a paraphrase of Kathryn Hansen, '*Virangana* (North Indian History Myth and Popular Culture)' *Economic and Political Weekly* (Sameeksha Foundation Publication), 23, 18 (30 April 1988), pp. 25–33.

21 See *Time* Magazine, 14 February 1983.

22 On the practice of non-violence in the South Asian context, see Christopher Key Chapple, *Non-violence to Animals, Earth and Self in Asian Traditions* (Albany: State University of New York Press, 1993).

23 See M. K. Gandhi, *Autobiography*, translated by Mahadev Desai (Washington DC: Public Affairs Press, 1948), p. 168.

24 N. K. Bose, *My Days with Gandhi* (Ahemdabad: Bose Press, 1953), p. 199.

25 Manuben Gandhi, *Bapu – My Mother* (Ahemdabad: Navjivan Publishing House, 1955), p. 3.

26 V. G. Desai, *The Diary of Mahadev Desai* (Ahemdabad: Navjivan Publishing

House, 1953), Vol. 1, p. 52.

27 For Gandhi's views on women, see Pushpa Joshi, *Gandhi on Women* (Ahemdabad: Navjivan Publishing House and CDWS, 1988); Madhu Kishwar, *Gandhi and Women* (New Delhi: Manushi Prakashan, 1986); Shane Ryland, 'The Theory and Impact of Gandhi's Feminism', *Journal of South Asian Literature*, 3, 4 (1977); Barbara Suthard, 'The Feminism of Mahatma Gandhi', *Gandhi Marg*, 31 (October 1971); M. K. Gandhi, *Women's Role in Society*, compiled by R. K. Prabhu (Ahemdabad: Navjivan Publishing House, 1959).

28 Madhu Kishwar, 'Of Warmongers and Peace Seekers', *Manushi*, 112: 24–32.

11

Theological Reflections
on Violence against Women
(A Catholic Perspective)

SR MARY JOHN MANANZAN OSB

Violence against women is one of the most blatant manifestations of patriarchy, cutting across class, race, creed and nationality. Many sociological, anthropological and psychological treatises have been written about it. But authorities in the Catholic Church, except for a few, have been silent about this, even after they have written pastoral letters on ecology, the unjust economic order, racism and other issues. The Church of Canada is the rare exception and I refer extensively in this chapter to the Pastoral Letter of the Canadian Bishops entitled: *A Heritage of Violence: a Pastoral Reflection on Conjugal Violence.*[1] My own contribution attempts to see how the phenomenon of violence against women has been present in the life of the Church, how the Church has handled it so far, and what possible alternative actions can be taken.

Violence in the Bible: Texts of Terror

There are four Bible stories about women that I have always taken in my stride every time I have read them. These are the stories of Hagar, Tamar, the daughter of Jepthah and a nameless concubine. In her book *Texts of Terror,*[2] however, Phyllis Trible uses the literary critical method and a feminist perspective to retell these stories. Amazingly, the horror of these texts is revealed.

There is the story of Hagar, who suffered what could be considered psychological and emotional violence as the repudiated and abused maid of Sarah. There is Tamar, the sister of Absalom, who is lusted after, raped and repudiated by her own half-brother, Amnon. This causes a war of revenge that leads to the rape and enslavement of six hundred more women. Then there is the gruesome tale of the nameless concubine who was gang-raped and brutally cut into pieces by her 'master'. Last, there is the sacrifice of the daughter of Jepthah, who had to die in her youth to fulfil the vow of her father. These horrible stories could only reflect a highly patriarchal world.

The Hebrew world considered the wife to be the exclusive property of her husband: no different, sometimes, from his material possessions. A woman was treated as a perpetual 'minor under the guardianship of her father, her brother, her husband, or her husband's brother' (Deuteronomy 25: 5–6). There was no place for her except in domestic duties and she acquired social status solely through her sexual functions as wife and mother, not through her personal worth or basic dignity as a human being. Denied access to any kind of learning, even of the Torah, women were not allowed to speak, even to their husbands, in public. Their testimony was not admissible in a court of law and they had no say whatsoever in political decision making. In the Temple, women could not enter the court of the Israelite and even less so the sanctuary where sacrifices were offered.[3]

No wonder women's fate in such a society was often tragic. Stripped of all autonomy, they were objects of lust, contempt and violence; as shown by our stories, they were subject to abandonment, rape, mutilation and death. The New Testament, in the teachings of Christ and in the respectful and humane way Jesus treated women, gave a glimpse of the change that might have been. However his disciples, and eventually the Churches that the apostles established, did not absorb this aspect of the teachings of Christ. If they ever did, this was soon forgotten in the re-patriarchalization of the early Church in order to accommodate the patriarchal values of the Roman Empire.

Misogynistic Writings in Church History

The writings and teachings of the fathers of the Church had a very important role to play in the formation of normative principles and attitudes of the new Church. These supposedly holy and intelligent men had a particularly low opinion of women and, unfortunately, their misogynistic attitude became the foundation of the way women would be thought of and treated in the course of the centuries. Some examples of their misogynism are:

St Paul: 'Wives should submit to their husbands in everything' (Ephesians 5, 24).

Tertullian: 'You are the Devil's gateway. You are the unsealer of that forbidden tree. You are the first deserter of the Divine Law. You are she who persuaded him whom the Devil was not valiant enough to attack. You destroyed so easily God's image – man. On account of your dessert, that is death, even the Son of God had to die' (Tertullian, *De Cultu Feminarum*, I, 1).

Augustine: 'We are men, you are women, we are the head, you are the members, we are masters, you are slaves.'[4]

Jerome: 'As long as woman is for birth and children, she is different from man as body is from soul. But when she wishes to serve Christ more than the world, then she will cease to be a woman and will be called man' (Commentary to the Epistle to the Ephesians, III, 5).

The later doctors of the Church were no better. The active force in the male, Thomas Aquinas writes, 'tends to the production of perfect likeness in the masculine sex, while the production of woman comes from defect in the active force or from some material indisposition, or from some external influence' (*Summa Theologica*, Q. 92, art. 1). Woman is therefore a misbegotten male. She is also less rational than the male, because the latter, as a foetus, has to wait for at least fifty days.

One can give countless examples. The point is that there is a long and continuous history of misogyny in the Church. It accounts for the tenacious internalization in both men and women of the inferiority and subordination of women. It has also contributed to other stereotyped ideas about women, including their susceptibility to victimization.

The Inquisition and Violence Against Women

It is not only the misogynistic writings in the history of the Church that are so reprehensible. There are also documented acts of violence against women during the Inquisition. Women mystics, healers or women who did not quite fit the categories allotted to them were persecuted, hunted and even burned at the stake.

In 1484, *Malleus Maleficarum* classified all the supposedly foul activities of these 'witches'. The most modest estimate was about two million women killed, after being tortured, between the twelfth and seventeenth centuries, including Joan of Arc. Women who gave birth without screaming might be regarded as 'not saved' by the pangs of childbirth that were supposed to be the retribution for the sin of Eve in 'tempting' Adam. It could be interpreted that childbirth was aided by the devil, which would make woman a likely candidate for witchhunt.

Canon Law itself justified wife beating:

> In the Middle Ages, the Church as well as the state gave husbands the legal right to inflict corporal punishment. There were laws that specified in which cases of bad conduct women could be severely beaten with a whip or a stick, and in which cases moderate chastisement was in order. Some within the Church went so far as to demand that this be done with dignity![5]

Religious Education and Violence against Women

One can establish a direct connection between the traditional religious education of women and their victimization. Women have always been taught to be submissive, docile, patient, long-suffering, self-sacrificing. These are all characteristics of a victim consciousness. Thus, religious education is a conditioning of women to become victims of violence.

In Philippine history, many books written for the formation of young girls were translated into the native languages and dialects. Such books contained admonitions to the virtues listed above with horror stories to illustrate the punishment of those who did not conform to the model the friars had set up. Ironically one of the virtues the friars taught the *mujer indigena* was chastity or virginity, which did not belong to the values of the pre-Spanish society. The irony lies in the fact that while teaching this virtue, many of them were at the same time robbing our women of that very virtue. The documents on the Inquisition in the Philippines stored in the *Archivo General de Nacion* illustrate the solicitations done by friars. These solicitations are not a thing of the past. They are happening even today. I am sure many of us have concrete examples.

There is also an excessive emphasis on virginity which is oppressive to women. In fact, many prostitutes I interviewed say that aside from the economic need, the thing that finally pushed them into prostitution was loss of virginity through incest or date rape.

The whole theology of marriage in mainstream teaching is based on subservience to men, enjoined in the wedding ceremony: 'Husband love your wife, wife obey your husband.' Many women are conditioned just to keep quiet in order 'to preserve peace' in their marriage. Battered women find it difficult to end a marriage because of the injunction that a woman should 'preserve the marriage at all costs for the sake of the children', etcetera. The Social Affairs Committee of the Assembly of Quebec Bishops points out the danger of such a discourse:

> A certain discourse within the Church sacrifices persons for the sake of the conjugal bond when it seeks to maintain the conjugal union 'for better or for worse', by exhorting women to forgive endlessly and often unconditionally, and forever to make peace in the name of a mystical ideal which is very difficult to attain.[6]

Church teachings on contraception control women's reproductive rights. Many Catholic women are pushed to the wall because they are not only forbidden to abort but are also forbidden effective means of fertility control. Many just have to suffer the adverse consequences of frequent pregnancies.

Theological imperatives

Violence against women has been studied from many viewpoints: psychological, anthropological, sociological and the rest. But there has been no documentation of the conditioning of women's consciousness throughout the centuries. The Church should make a public confession of guilt and repentance for ecclesiastical misogyny and for the violence done to women during the Inquisition.

Pastoral consequences

Pastoral theology, above all the others, needs to concern itself with this appalling victimization of women and children. The statement by the Canadian Conference of Catholic Bishops lists some harmful pastoral approaches to violence against women.

The first of these is 'being uninformed'. Even when surrounded by reports of violence, ministers do not seem to understand the complex dynamics of domestic violence and are not prepared to discern signs of abuse among the people they are counselling.

The second is 'premature reconciliation'. Religious counsellors are so concerned about the preservation of the marriage that they hardly register the very real pain and suffering of the victim, and the danger to her. The problem is not really resolved, so there are many cases of repeated and continuous wife battering.

The third is 'silence'. The bishops write:

> The abused woman is often very isolated, [and the] Church may be the one place she is still able to go. If she never hears a homily on this topic, her sense of isolation may be increased or she may not feel free to approach the pastor or a member of the pastoral team. (p. 2)

The last harmful approach is 'misuse of Scripture'. The Bible has been used throughout the centuries to rationalize and justify the oppression of women, but the Canadian bishops categorically say that 'the misuse of scripture to justify the domination of women is unacceptable'.

Helpful approaches are:

- taking the woman or the incest victim seriously when she discloses abuse;
- avoiding sentimental clichés;
- following up after initial contact;
- acquiring the ability to detect abuse and becoming informed of the available community resources;
- being ready to deal with the profound spiritual questions that arise concerning the woman's relationship with God, especially in the case of the incest victim who understandably recoils at being told to relate to God as Father;
- creating a parish atmosphere where clergy and laity can discuss the question of violence against women and children openly and sensitively. (p. 3)

To prevent violence against women and children, parishes should have catechetical programmes and marriage preparation programmes that teach equality of persons. The parishioners should be exhorted to support social policies and programmes that address the problem. Theologians and other scholars should be enjoined to reflect and write more on the root causes of violence against women and children. More women should study theology and become teachers or seminarians so that they can give education in gender equality and on the dynamics of domestic violence.

Towards a Spirituality of Life

Violence against women is an orientation towards death and destruction. Women should develop a spirituality for life. For me, this means: a spirituality of self-affirmation, a spirituality of empowerment and a spirituality of inner freedom.

A spirituality of self-affirmation is the recognition by women of their worth and dignity. They are made in the image and likeness of God, just as men are. They are temples of the Holy Spirit. If women are so regarded by themselves and by men and society, how can there be incest, rape and wife battering? Women must learn to affirm themselves and to make others see their worth. This is against all their previous conditioning that they are mere sex objects, or that they have no role in public life. They must get rid of all false humility, of victim consciousness, of determining their worth only in relation to men. They have to learn to be autonomous subjects. They have to decide according to what they think is right and not conform to laws and regulations for the sake of convention.

A spirituality of empowerment is the discovery of the power within us. Violence against women is a matter of power. It is the imposition of the powerful against the powerless. Women must realize that they are not helpless or weak. They have an inexhaustible source of inner strength. Even in their victimization, female survivors feel this unquenchable urge to survive, and they must utilize this to the fullest. This should give them the courage to struggle against injustice, discrimination, exploitation and oppression. They have to empower one another so as to have the strength to confront patriarchal power. Mutual empowerment is a must for women. It is the hope of transforming unjust enmities, career rivalries and other forces that divide them.

A spirituality of inner freedom means freedom from fear, from idols and from bitterness and resentment. The psychological basis for this is self-knowledge and self-acceptance. As long as we do not know and accept ourselves, we will never be free of our inner slaveries – the strongest shackles of the spirit. Freedom from fear does not mean not feeling fear. It is the ability to discriminate between unfounded fear and substantiated fear, because one is committed to a cause bigger than oneself. Idols are either negative or positive. Negative idols are those that exert fatalistic pressure on us so that we are paralysed. Positive idols are those on whom we have either an emotional or intellectual dependence, and therefore also cripple the development of our subjective autonomy. We have to demythologize the power these idols have over us. The more we recognize our own worth and dignity, the less power they have over us. Finally, even if we have the right to feel bitter and resentful because of negative experiences, we have to exorcise ourselves of this poisoning of our spirit. It is only then that we can be creative and productive.

There are many things that we cannot change or control in our lives. But we still have the power to see how these will affect our lives. This reminds me of the Zen *koan* about Chinese calligraphers. Painting in the West means to pin down the paper so one can draw freely. The Chinese calligrapher follows the movement of the paper. The paper cannot be controlled, but the artist can still create a beautiful work of art in relation to its movement. This is the artistry of life. This is the spirituality of life.

This spirituality, I believe, is also a healing spirituality. As women learn to appreciate themselves and to delve into their inner resources of strength and survival, their wounds also get healed. And then they become 'wounded healers'. They can then also help other women who suffered similar fates as they did, so that their most negative experiences become positive; they can heal others best where they were wounded themselves the most.

Notes and References

1 Pastoral Letter of Canadian Bishops, *A Heritage of Violence: a Pastoral Reflection on Conjugal Violence* (Quebec: The Social Affairs Committee of the Assembly of Quebec Bishops, 1989).
2 Phyllis Trible, *Texts of Terror: Literary Feminist Readings of Biblical Narratives* (Minneapolis: Fortress Press, 1984).
3 Pastoral Letter of Canadian Bishops, *A Heritage of Violence*, pp. 28–9.
4 Quoted in Julia Kelly, 'Women in Sixteenth-Century Spain', *Revue Hispanique*, 70: 500.
5 Pastoral Letter of Canadian Bishops, *A Heritage of Violence*, p. 31.
6 *Ibid.*, p. 40.

12

Violence and the Feminine in Islam
A Case Study of the Zikris

DURRE S. AHMED

In recent years, the issue of violence against women in the name of Islam has gained considerable attention. The treatment of women by the Taliban and the controversies around female circumcision in many African countries are just two examples of how religion is used to justify brutality against women: the spectrum of violence ranges from wife beating and child marriage to denial of divorce and property. None of these are sanctioned by Islam. But they occur in many societies which are overwhelmingly Muslim; where a convenient conflation of customary practices with Islam ensures that the patriarchal *status quo* is not only maintained but strengthened.

Religiously inspired violence inevitably has covert socio-economic and political agendas and the Pakistani context is no exception. Frequently, victims have little legal support within the system, while the perpetrators – individually or as a group – gain in economic or political terms. But one must be careful not to reduce *all* such human actions only to the socio-economic, since this type of reductionism forecloses the logic(s) of religion itself. I will, therefore, not simply be adding to the litany of woes pertaining to violence, women and Islam, since they are by now well known and amply documented.[1] What interests me is the self-evident fact that in their teachings and doctrine, religions are not inherently violent, nor do they encourage violence against women. Sidestepping the hair-splitting debates of theologians – or even stepping right into their middle – the fact is that the basic issue is really about how any religion is *interpreted*. This is primarily a psychological and cultural process, having to do with language and image and our cognitive capacities *vis-à-vis* these essentially symbolic systems. For psychologists like Carl Jung, these interpretive mechanisms are rendered even more complex through their interaction with other symbolic systems of individual and collective memory and thereby fall into the realm of the imagination.

The sociologist Daniel Bell anticipates that the 'cultural wars' of the twenty-first century will be fought over gender and interpretation.[2] Locating itself within such an emergent discourse *vis-à-vis* women and religion, this chapter attempts to explore and understand the psychology of violence against women in Islam. Here violence is understood not in the literal sense of physical assault, but as having more to do with what woman – as idea and image – represents symbolically, and how (in the theological context) this idea/symbol is interpreted by the orthodox Pakistani Muslim psyche.

Theoretical Framework

Given the recent emphasis in some feminist circles on the feminine in different religions, the question is frequently posed, are there 'macho' religions and 'feminine' religions? That is, what is the psychology of different religions with reference to gender? One level of the response can be related to the discipline of psychology itself which, one must remember, originally meant a '*logos* of the soul'. A review of the history of psychology from the perspective of archetypal theory shows that the earliest conceptions of the human psyche were based on a recognition of its diversity as exemplified in numerous mythic pantheons in which, by and large, the powers of gods and goddesses were widely dispersed. Over the millennia this gendered diversity was steadily overwhelmed by the mythic heroes.[3]

In terms of post-Jungian analytical psychology, this 'ascent of the hero' means that modern norms of mental health essentially reflect the psyche of particularly young males and their ideals: overvaluation of will power, action, rationality, mastery and control over the body and the material world. Such a phallagocentric attitude is incapable of dealing with paradox, metaphor and ambiguity, even though metaphysical truth is primarily poetic and symbolic. Anything that does not fit into or runs counter to these literal and material ideals is considered 'pathological' and has to be cured in accordance with masculine heroic 'norms'. Thus, along with a range of less-than-macho gods (for example, Dionysius) the more feminine dimensions of the psyche have been pathologized. This is why, as noted in Chapter 4, the first diseases to be 'discovered' by modern psychology were hysteria (wandering uterus) and then schizophrenia (multiplicity of personality). And this, perhaps, is also why a cure for the latter is as distant as ever; and why in our world there are more women than men who continue to receive more drugs as treatment for 'mental' problems.[4]

In this framework, the feminine is not simply the image of a goddess; rather it is a constellation of qualities. Life is both male and female. 'Masculine' and 'feminine', like the terms *yin* and *yang*, are primarily psycho–symbolic concepts. They represent broad *attitudes* towards life, events, situations. For example, masculinity may refer to a certain type of reasoning and rationality, one that is linear and works analytically by breaking down ideas into their various components. 'Feminine' may refer to a different intellectual attitude, one that is receptive, contemplative, synthesizing rather then analysing, more metaphorical and poetic, more inner-oriented rather than externally focused exclusively on quantifiable facts. Neither is better, neither is worse; both are necessary for balanced functioning.

If the first level of the answer to the question whether there are 'macho' religions and more feminine ones had to do with the history of psychology and its macho bias, the second level concerns the history of religions. As stated earlier, the original psycho-religious paradigm of mythologies suggests diversity and paradox as crucial to conceptions of the divine and human. Emerging from a feminine bedrock, all religions, including Islam, reflect this 'mix' of feminine and masculine. As in psychology, religions, too, have been hypermasculinized – even though the religious *experience* in all religions requires a 'feminine' (receptive) consciousness. As Ong has observed, 'In relation to God ... we are all, men and women alike, basically feminine. Macho insights reveal nothing of God.'[5] Yet, in our conceptions of self and of the Divine (or of the transpersonal, of nature, etcetera) we have constructed an unbalanced, one-dimensional, phallogocentric and hypermasculine ideal. This is the psychology of fundamentalism, secular- liberal or religious.

Based on the above framework, this chapter will discuss how, when a given religious expression emphasizes the feminine, it evokes violence in those in whose self-image and notions of divinity the feminine has been relegated to the realms of the unconscious, where it continues to exist as the unknown Other. The response is then to exterminate and marginalize that which is seen as utterly alien, but which is in fact always a part of oneself and a larger whole.

These ideas will be illustrated through a case study of the Zikris, a small Islamic sect in Pakistan. Despite a sporadic history of persecution, until the 1980s the Zikris were relatively unknown in Pakistan, peacefully absorbed into and accepted by the Muslims of an overwhelmingly Muslim state. Following their success in getting another small sect – the Ahmadiyyah – declared heretics in terms of the constitution, and hence 'non-Muslim', the orthodox ulema began a similar campaign against the Zikris. By the late 1980s they were being actively and violently persecuted.

The larger population is periodically incited to violence against the Zikris through the pamphlet press. Zikri graves and shrines have been desecrated and Zikri women have been kidnapped and forced into marriage. Courts have been known to reject Zikri witnesses because the judge considered them non-Muslim. The violence against them reached a climax in 1993 when, in an attempt to prevent the community from gathering for an annual ritual, four rockets and other weapons were fired at their place of meeting.[6] Though at present reigned in by the authorities, covert hostility and intimidation remains.

The Zikris: Historical Background

The Zikris are a small peace-loving sect, founded about 500 years ago in Djawnpur (Jaunpur) in the Indian province of Gujerat.[7] An established centre of religious learning, Djawnpur was the birthplace of Sayyid Muhammad (1443–1505), the founder of the sect. By all accounts a precocious and spiritually gifted child, Sayyid Muhammad was given the title of *Asad al 'Ulama* at a young age, in recognition of his knowledge of the Quran and Islamic theology. His stature continued to grow and by the time he was forty and an established teacher and scholar, he set out to perform the pilgrimage of Haj. Arriving in Mecca in 1495, while circumambulating the Kaaba, he announced that he was the promised Mahdi.[8] Ignored by the Meccan ulema, he returned to India where he won many adherents and made many more enemies, particularly among the ulema. Moving from place to place in an effort to escape harassment, he died in Farah, Khurasan, where his shrine in still visited by his followers.

The spiritual mantle of the founder was taken up by various *khalifas*, the first being his son Sayyid Mahmud. By this time the Mahdawis, as the sect came to be named, had established a number of centres called *dai'ra* (circles), and had considerable popularity among the masses. This grassroots support was perceived as a threat to the state and led to accusations of heresy and persecution. Sayyid Mahmud was incarcerated and died in prison. Although some prominent personalities joined the sect, its antagonists gained momentum, particularly when many ulema of Gujerat declared that it was permissible to kill a Mahdawi on grounds of heresy. By 1576, the movement had virtually collapsed, its followers dispersed. Nevertheless, it is thought to have had between three to five hundred thousand adherents. There are small communities in Iran and the Gulf, and in India pockets of the sect exist in Hyderabad, Mysore and Gujerat. Similar small groups live in Pakistan, mostly in Sind and Baluchistan, where they are called Zikris.

Despite the withering of the community under persecution and in the absence of able leadership, the history of the Mahdawis has continued, seeming to fluctuate between periods in which they faced intense disfavour and periods of absorption and acceptance by the larger Muslim community. In its heyday it 'fired the Indian Muslim community with a new zeal and religious fervour',[9] counting among its adherents two of the 'jewels' in Akbar's court, the emperor Humayun's son and other prominent personalities.[10] Similarly, while the majority of ulema hardened in their view of the Mahdawi heresy, there were some well-respected ones who, despite being severe critics of the founder, continued to regard him as a great saint and did not doubt his piety, scholarship and sincerity.[11]

The dynamics of religious persecution inevitably include a strong element of politics and economics, and the history of Mahdawi persecution is no exception. Many Mahdawi beliefs regarding distribution of wealth were in collision with various state structures. During the eighteenth century, a major movement of persecution was inspired against Mahdawis settled in Mehran, Baluchistan. Ostensibly a drive against heresy, all accounts indicate the essentially expansionist motives of Mir Nasir Khan of Kalat. His series of persecutory campaigns destroyed most Mahdawi records and texts.[12]

A closer look at the regional (and national) state politics clearly indicates that the motives of those behind the violence in recent years have less to do with religion and more to do with the fact that the Zikris support liberal and secular politics.[13] By necessity, minorities tend to be supportive of their members. While the Zikris can hardly be considered affluent, over the centuries their economic philosophy rendered them a threat to the *status quo*. They abhor accumulation of wealth and do not believe in personal property. The emphasis is on an egalitarian, almost rigidly Marxist distribution of wealth. While the community as a whole remains impoverished, these 'progressive' ideas have had their impact on other related social structures, particularly regarding Zikri women. Despite the extremely conservative cultural context of Baluchistan, they are not subject to the strictures imposed on Baluch women either through custom or religious orthodoxy.

This inherent 'liberal socialism', along with the fact that they are a religious minority, makes the Zikris a regional political force, since they continue to vote for those with a secular point of view. Once this core of opposition is identified by the religious extremist-politician, theology is used to erode it.

The obvious stick with which to beat the Zikris is the question of the Mahdi, a problematic and contentious area within Islam. The promised coming of the Mahdi has continued as a motif, particularly during the past five hundred years, across the Muslim world, from North Africa to South Asia. Over the centuries, there have been numerous messianic movements, some of which have disappeared while others continue to coexist in an enormously varied 'house of Islam'. However, when one studies the polemical writings on the Zikris, the question of Muhammad Ahmed Jaunpuri's claim to being the Mahdi is not paramount. That is, the issue of whether or not the Zikris are Muslims has less to do with their belief in the claims of the founder and more to do with their (perceived) practices.

Zikri Doctrine

The question of whether or not any belief system, large or small, can in fact be reduced to a set of clear-cut doctrines remains highly

problematic. Reflecting the diversity of humanity, the enormous variations among and within religions are self-evident. To impose a monolithic order of 'doctrine' is to falsify the multiple realities of human
belief and fall into reductionism, which is one dimension of fundamentalism. The Zikris are no exception to this sort of reductionism.
Whereas there are a number of interviews and accounts of their rituals,
the material in fact presents a spectrum of beliefs. As with any other
domain of human activity, it all depends on who is providing the
information to whom, and the extent of a person's commitment to,
and knowledge of, the subject. I have not come across any detailed
information by a Zikri author but, for our purposes, this is not an issue.
To the extent that there is a broad consensus within available sources
about key elements of Zikri doctrine and ritual, there is enough
material to show how the Zikris are *imagined*. More importantly, it can
illustrate the psychodynamics at work not only in the rituals themselves
but also in the psyches of those who *interpret* these rituals differently
from the Zikris.[14]

Apart from its central tenet of Sayyid Mohammad being the Mahdi,
Zikri doctrine encompasses a range of beliefs which remain confusing
to the outsider. This is partly because most of the Zikri historical
records, along with the original writings of the founder, were
destroyed – a great many, as I have mentioned, in the war with Mir
Nasir Khan. The absence of primary sources is further compounded by
the fact that non-Zikris are not permitted to participate in, or observe,
the key rituals of the community and there is thus very little reliable
anthropological or descriptive information. Within this restrictive frame
there have been a few attempts to document Zikri belief. Despite
claims to objectivity, most modern studies remain grounded in mainstream Islamic Sunni orthodoxy and firmly reject the Zikris' claim to
being Muslim.[15] Keeping these provisos in mind, what follows is a
summary of the main elements of Zikri doctrine and rituals.

Theological

1 The mission of the Prophet Muhammad was to preach the Quran
   but in his time its content was literal. It was up to the founder, to
   whom Zikris refer as Syed Mahdi, to elucidate the Quran since he
   was *Sahib-i-Taweel* (Master of Interpretation).

2   The Muslim *Kalima* is recited as 'No God but God and Muhammad Mahdi is his messenger'.

3   There is great emphasis on *Zikr* as a form of worship, particularly recitation of the names of Allah. The word literally means 'remembrance' and, while not obligatory, is a widespread Islamic practice usually involving the recitation of the names of Allah or other sacred phrases. It is difficult to say if the *Zikr* is a complete substitute for the Islamic *salat* (liturgical prayer) since many postural elements of the *salat* are included in *Zikr* as practised by the Zikris. Whereas in mainstream Islam the *salat* is usually performed five times a day, the *Zikr* is done six times.

4   The fast of the month of Ramadan is replaced by seven days of fasting each month.

Sociopolitical

1   The Zikris place great emphasis on *Sawiyat* which they interpret as the equal distribution of wealth and material possessions. Each community constitutes a *da'ira* or circle, and all wealth is collectively owned. The Zikri view of society is egalitarian and denounces personal property in favour of equality among members of the community.

2   There is an emphasis on mutual help and a disregard for ethnic origin.

3   Contrary to the practice of many orthodox Muslims, Zikri women participate in the community's public and socio-religious life.

It is interesting to note that the *Encyclopaedia of Islam* does not mention anything peculiarly non-Islamic about Zikri doctrine. In tracing the history of the movement, the key doctrinal issue concerns the question of Sayyid Muhammad's claim to being the Mahdi. As mentioned earlier, to the extent that this question is itself a recurring motif in the history of Islam, it is not unusual. Beyond the historical events of five hundred years, the only doctrinal aspect that is noted is that of *sawiyat* or abolition of private property, and the emphasis on community life is seen as 'the cardinal point of the teachings of Sayyid Mohammad'. This is far removed from the present hair-splitting attempts to 'define' the Zikris through the details of their beliefs and beyond questions of Mahdism.

Detractors have tried to make all manner of tenuous connections as 'proof' that the Zikris have made a travesty of certain central rites of Islam such as the *salat* and the Haj. This does not seem to be the case. Indeed, one can argue that, on the face of it, these rituals either have nothing to do with Islam, and are essentially cultural in nature, or else are part of the widespread Sufi phenomenon which is more free-wheeling than rigidly orthodox, but which nevertheless remains, like the Zikris, anchored in Islam.

Placed in its wider social and historical context, the Zikris are one instance in an enormous spectrum of Sufi movements and sects occurring not only within the subcontinent but in various forms across the entire Islamic world. Accordingly, none of the sect's main doctrinal elements is exclusive to the Zikris. The Alawis, for example, in North Africa, Central Asia and Turkey, also do not place great emphasis on the ritual prayer or *salat*. The practice of *salat* itself is varied in its postural details in the Islamic world. It is particularly marked in the differences between the Shias and Sunnis and their many sub-sects. The main points raised by the orthodoxy regarding the Zikri 'heresy' are either insufficient or disputed by the Zikris themselves. Thus the present violence evoked by the sect seems to have deeper psychological roots; it is possible that we will find evidence of these in Zikri rituals.

Zikri Rituals

Zikr

A widespread practice in Islam, *Zikr* consists of recitation of the names (attributes) of Allah, passages/phrases from the Quran and the first and fundamental part of the Muslim creed 'No god but God'. The Zikris perform it six times a day and this again is not unusual in Islam. Debate continues as to how many times a day the liturgical prayer is mandatory and views range from two, three or five, to recommendations of seven.[16] The timings of the *Zikr* are roughly similar to those of the liturgical prayer. As stated earlier, the *Zikr* does include some postural elements of what is, in any case, a spectrum of *salat* positions.

Zikr can be both *jali* (aloud) and *khafi* (silent), and this pattern too is similar to the Islamic prayer, in which certain passages can be recited out loud while others are not. Similarly, as in the liturgical prayer, certain parts of *Zikr* are done, or can be done, individually, whereas other parts are collective. This motif, of incorporating collective/public and private/individual elements, is a *leitmotif* of Islamic ritual. However, Zikri prayer ritual departs from orthodox Sunni Islam in certain ways. While many of their places of worship are built like mosques, they are called *zikranas* or *zikrkhanas*, much in the same way that Ismaili 'mosques' are *jamatkhanas* and Shia call theirs *imambargahs*. The issue of direction, of facing the Kaaba in Mecca, is not paramount. Instead of the straight rows of worshippers facing Mecca, people form a circle. After going through different stages of *zikr/salat,* the worshippers prostrate themselves within the circle and hence face each other and not Mecca. However, similar practices are reportedly common to the Alawis in Turkey.[17] The Ismailis too, are not particular about facing Mecca.

Fasting

There are conflicting reports about whether Zikris observe the month of Ramadan. A week of fasts before the festival of Eid-ul-Azha is observed, which is not the case with most Sunni Muslims.

Annual Ziarat

The most important rite for Zikris, and the one cited most frequently as 'evidence' of their being non-Muslim, is their annual gathering on the 27th of Ramadan. Most devout Muslims consider this an auspicious day and night and it is thought to be a time of great blessing. Vigils of prayer are kept and the Quran recited round the clock. While their detractors insist that this ritual is a substitute for Haj, the Zikris insist that it is a *ziarat,* that is, a pilgrimage to a holy shrine. Again, this is an exceedingly common practice among Muslims. People go for *Ziarat* to the graves of innumerable saints, or to places of significance to a community, as for example, visiting the Kerbala.

The Zikri pilgrimage centres around a mountain in Turbat, Baluchistan, which they refer to as Koh-i-Murad (Mountain of Murad), named after a major Zikri leader/saint. However, the word *murad* also means desire/wish and the orthodoxy insists that actually the ritual of the mountain constitutes a form of idolatory. Every year between twenty and thirty thousand Zikris gather on the 27th of Ramadan at the base of Koh-i-Murad. After performing *Zikr* in a circle, they start to climb the mountain barefoot. Men and women are not segregated. En route, they purportedly kiss/touch a stone which has the *Kalima* inscribed on it. Whereas the Zikris see this simply as an act of devotion, others see it as confirmation of a sham Haj, in as much as one minor aspect of Haj is to kiss, touch or acknowledge with reverence the famous black stone embedded in the wall of the Kaaba. However, the black stone does not have the *Kalima* inscribed on it. Another aspect of the ritual ascent is the drinking from a well-spring which the Zikris call Zamzam, namesake of the spring near Mecca, held sacred by Muslims. This, of course, is fuel to the fire for anti-Zikris.

Chogan

Once the pilgrims reach the top they proceed to form a circle. Some say it is marked by stones. In either case, the pilgrims form a circle around a modest hut-like dwelling. Inside the hut, there is a woman who must have a strong and beautiful voice. She sings and recites ancient Baluch verses and the pilgrims respond in chorus and dance around the hut in a circle, clapping and singing rhythmically. The dance steps are traditional Baluch.

There are reports that some participants see visions; one can surmise that the experience is not too different from other similar collective rites of Sufic worship, particularly those involving music and a strong rhythm. Such experiences are found in most mysticisms and they are particularly common in many types of Sufic Islam. The subcontinent has innumerable shrines where musical celebrations leading to trance are a routine affair. In a similar vein, Zikri poetry and song commemorate the love, power and miracles of their founder and other spiritual leaders.

Despite the fact that, as a whole, the annual *Ziarat* has very little in common with the Haj, the ritual has evoked a violent response from the orthodoxy and it is being gradually stifled through intimidation. All manner of weapons and violence are used to prevent the community from gathering for this rite.

Kishti

Kishti is another Zikri ritual, held on any Friday night falling on the fourteenth or fifteenth of each month, on the night of the full moon. It is also enacted during the first ten days of the month of the Haj and the day after the Eid-ul-Azha. *Kishti* is also enacted for events such as birth, marriage or circumcision. Once again, the participants form a circle, typical also of many Baluch dances. No drums are used. One or more women – they must have strong and melodious voices – stand in the middle and sing the praise of the Mahdi. The men circle around and function as a sort of chorus. Singers change from song to song. Many of the verses are like refrains. For example, when the woman singer asks, '*Hadia?*' (Who is the leader on the right path?) the men answer, '*Gul Mahdia!*' (Our flower, the Mahdi).

The non-segregated nature of *Kishti, Chogan* and the *Ziarat,* not to mention the literally central importance given to women, are once again a fuel to anti-Zikri sentiment. All manner of crude rumours abound regarding these rituals, highlighting the licentious and libidinous. Even though the most conservative of scholars admit there is no basis to these rumours, the popular perception of Zikri 'immoral' practices remains.

Zikri Rituals and Archetypes

There are a number of archetypal elements evident in Zikri rituals such as the ascent to the mountain, the kissing of the stone, and the circle. While all are significant, here I will focus only on the recurring theme of the circle.

The pivotal archetype in Zikri ritual pertains to the circle: the sect literally refers to itself as 'people of the circle' and community settlements are referred to as *dairas* (circles). The significance of the circle is central to the main rituals of *Kishti, Chogan* and the *Ziarat* to Koh-i-Murad. In all instances a woman or a group of women are at the centre of the ritual circle.

The circle as archetype

Drawing on extensive cross-cultural material, Jung showed how the circle is a universally occurring and powerful symbol, a representation of the idea of the Divine.[18] The circle represents totality, having no beginning or end, hence the saying 'God is a circle whose circumference is nowhere and centre everywhere.' Almost every culture uses the circle as a depiction of cosmological order and perfection. The motif of the mandala, Sanskrit for 'magic circle', forms the basis of most classical religious architecture. It also forms the ground plan for many cities. Typically, mandalas involve the circle and the square but the main emphasis is always the centre. An Indian creation myth relates how Brahma stood at the centre of a huge lotus and turned his eyes north, south, east and west. The spiritual geometry of this spatial orientation is exemplified in the mandalas of Tibetan Lamaism and in the geometric design of *Yantras*. The *Shri Yantra* mandala is composed of nine interlinking triangles enclosed in a circle which, in turn, is circumscribed by a lotus and square. It is considered as 'form in expansion' and thus a symbol of creation. A common *Yantra* motif is two interpenetrating triangles set in opposite directions. It is the symbol of the union of Śiva and Śakti, the male and female principle, expressing the union of opposites. This union is not just male and female, but of opposing yet equally important cosmic forces; of time and eternity, of the personal ego dissolving in non-ego and, thus, of the soul with God. Like the mandala, what is being represented is the notion of wholeness and totality.

The abstract circle also appears in European Christian art. The splendid rose windows of cathedrals are one example. The halo around the holy family and other saints is another. Numerous other examples from a range of cultures led Jung to believe that to the extent that the mandala motif is ubiquitous, it was an archetype of what he termed the Self. The Self is the totality of the psyche of which the ego, according to Jung, is only a small part. The goal of Jungian analysis, indeed of human life, is to realize the Self, which, as suggested earlier, is the experience of the union of the opposites and the ensuing state of wholeness and balance between them. Speaking of the picture entitled *The Circle* by the famous Zen priest Sangai, another Zen master wrote: 'In the Zen sect, the circle represents enlightenment. It symbolizes human perfection.'[19]

The circular form as a psychological projection is thus linked to the ideas of wholeness, eternity and cosmic harmony. This is reflected in most forms of magic when the practitioners draw a circle, creating a hermetically sealed arena. To quote a Native American chief, 'when we pitch camp, it is in a circle, when the eagle builds a nest, it's in a circle, the horizon is a circle'.[20] The idea of the healing power of the circle is similarly evident in Navajo healing ceremonies in which the patient is brought into the apotropaic circle which consists of mandala-like sand paintings.[21]

The centre and the circle

The notion of the centre is inseparable form the idea of the circle. We speak of 'centring' our life and self. The act of meditating on the mandalas of Tibetan Buddhism is an attempt to move eventually to the centre, which represents stillness and eternity as opposed to time and motion represented by the circumference. The circle contains both these dimensions. The existence of this form and its variants across history and cultures suggests that it is a reflection of human spiritual potential. Through the contemplation of its form we try to evoke this power and presence in our life. The centre thus becomes that point of dissolution of ego consciousness as it merges into a larger unity which Jung termed the Self. T. S Eliot speaks of the 'still point of the turning world', simultaneous motion and stasis, the hub where the movement of time and the stillness of eternity are together. Circular movement represents that which brings into being, that is, which activates and animates, all the forces involved in life; and circular motion sweeps them along together, these forces which otherwise would act against each other. Almost all representations of time reflect circular motion. It is one basic meaning of the symbol of *Yin/Yang*, the sigmoid line in the middle of the circle implying the idea of rotation. The Hindu swastika has a similar dimension of movement.[22]

Movement from the circumference to the centre is equivalent to moving from outer to inner, from multiplicity to unity, from space to void, from time to eternity. In all symbols expressive of the mystic centre, the idea is that God resides at that point. Different religious cosmologies depict God at the centre, surrounded by concentric circles spreading outwards. Among the Chinese, the Infinite Being is frequently depicted as a point of light with concentric symbols spreading outwards from it. In the *Shri Yantra* mandala of the Hindus, the centre itself is not actually portrayed but has to be supplied mentally by the contemplator. A great many ritual acts have the sole purpose of finding out the spiritual 'centre' of a locality which then becomes the site, either in it-self, or by virtue of the temple built upon it, of an 'image of the world'.

One can now begin to see how many of these ideas pertaining to the religious symbolism of the mandala – and particularly to the circle and the centre – are powerfully present in the rituals of the Zikris. More significantly, in almost all instances, the centre is represented by woman. Before amplifying this feminine centre, it is necessary to place the Zikris into their larger spiritual context of Sufism, which, in turn, must first be understood in the general context of mysticism.

Prophets and Mystics

In tracing a history of religion and the shift from matriarchy to patri-archy, Amaury de Reincourt draws a distinction between prophetism and mysticism. As he suggests, the etymology of the word 'mysticism' betrays its feminine affinity, derived as it is from the ancient Greek mystery cults which in turn can be traced to the worship of the great Mother Goddess.[23] Mysticism draws its energy from feeling, its aim being complete relatedness and union, 'the oneness of Being'. In *The Varieties of Religious Experience,* William James refers to this emotional element of mysticism as a 'downward transcendence', exemplified by the symbol of a child in relation to the mother, seeking the 'security of the infantile state and the prenatal shape of the embryo enclosed in the mother's womb'.[24] The mystic quest, in this instance, is dissolution in the Absolute, and many symbols typical of 'nature mysticism' – ocean, sea, air, trees, water – are quintessentially 'feminine, both mythologi-cally and psychologically'.[25]

The contrast between prophetism and mysticism is again evident in the origin of the word prophet, which comes from the Hebrew *nabi,* announcer of the future. The idea of the *nabi* or prophet is in stark contrast to foretelling by oracular divination carried out earlier almost exclusively by women.

> Hebrew prophetism arose in antagonism to Baalism and fertility cults in general, that is, against female oriented, goddess worshipping cults, to teach a highly ethical, history oriented monotheism [...] the emphasis was on morality rather than ritual magic, that same morality that man set up as an artificial substitute for the female emphasis on closeness to nature, indeed in *opposition* to nature.[26]

Whereas prophetism and patriarchy developed in tandem, the ancient bedrock of matriarchy lived on in the mysticisms of especially those religions which developed along strongly prophetic lines. While immensely varied, mysticism as a whole remains a great spiritual current running under almost all the major religions.

> The feminine nature of mysticism is obvious: the surrender to nature or to God, the passive attitude waiting for the spiritual blessing and uplift to ecstasy, essentially quietist, contemplative and resigned ... an expression of femininity as expressed through the feminine side of all human beings.
>
> The 'prophetic' aspect of religion, on the other hand is uncompromisingly masculine: a self assertive will to live, active, aggressive, ethical, believing in God-given revelation rather than individual ecstasy and seeing the handwork of the Almighty as revealed through the historical process rather than the more poetic, spatial display of nature, through time rather than space.[27]

Differentiating these two broad types of religious expression is not to suggest the superiority of one over the other. Indeed, even with sternly prophetic religions such as Judaism and Islam, for example, there are numerous combinations of these dimensions. For our purpose, they are different archetypes, *styles* of relationship with the Divine which, like the mythic pantheon, are actually much more nuanced than would appear under the broad and general category of, for example, the archetype of Great Mother (matriarchal/mysticism) and the Hero or Wise Old Man (patriarchal/prophetic). But these nuances can only be articulated in detail once the basis of the broad gender distinctions is established. What is important at this stage, then, is to see how, like its psychological counterpart, when masculine orthodoxy is forcefully confronted by feminine mysticism, it can frequently prove dangerous for the latter, which is dubbed 'heretic'. The most vivid example in the West is Joan of Arc, doubly damned not only for her convictions but also because she was a woman. And while she may not have a literal counterpart in Islam, the history of Islam has had more than its share of male mystics who met a violent end at the hands of orthodoxy.

Sufism

As a feminine expression of the religious impulse, mysticism has long been powerfully present in Islam in the form of Sufism, and the Zikris are just one drop in this ocean. Jung referred to Sufism as Islam's 'secret backbone', and de Reincourt has outlined how 'the frustrated anima of Islam' emerged as a reaction to Islam's 'uncompromising monotheism':

> The massive theological superstructure that Muslims elaborated during the first three or four centuries following Muhammad's death was a replica of the Christian one; but it never satisfied the Muslim soul: sternly ethical and dryly philosophical, it made no appeal to sentiment, emotion or intuition. So it was that mysticism soon appeared within the confines of Islam in the guise of Sufism, to enlist the enthusiastic support of the masses, not expressed directly in the increasingly repressed Muslim women but in the feminine emotionalism of Islamic mysticism.... In the end, Sufism defeated and routed the ulemas....[28]

The triumph of Sufism was not without violence, and mystics such as Hallaj and Suharwardy are legendary in Islam because of the terrible violence that was directed at them. Sufism is itself a vast and nebulous area with a great range of styles and expressions. Within its enormous rubric, one dimension emphasizes the ecstatic above all. Music, dance and poetry play a major role in ecstatic Sufism all over the Muslim world. From across Africa and the Middle East to Central Asia, South Asia and Indonesia there are a myriad shrines where this expression of ecstatic abandonment has a central place. Pakistan is no exception. This abandon is, again, just one end of a spectrum in Sufism: the other end is the extremely sophisticated metaphysics of Sufis such as the Andalusian Ibn'Arabi and the Persian poet and philosopher Jalaluddin Rumi. (Both, incidentally, were accused of heresy and threatened by orthodoxy.) Corbin sums up their vision:

> [I]t follows that a mystic obtains the highest theophanic vision in contemplating the Image of Feminine Being, because it is in the Image of the Creative Feminine that contemplation can apprehend the highest manifestation of God .... [T]he spirituality of our Islamic mystics is led esoterically to the apparition of the Eternal Womanly as an Image of the Godhead ... because in her it contemplates the secret of the compassionate God, whose creative act is a liberation of beings.... [T]he Feminine is not opposed to the Masculine ... but encompasses and combines the two aspects, receptive and active, whereas the Masculine possesses only one of the two .... This intuition is clearly expressed by Rumi: Woman is beam of the Divine

Light/she is not the being whom sensual desire takes as its object/she is Creator, it should be said/she is not creature.[29]

One can note here that dance was very much part of Rumi's spiritual expression and the whirling dervishes of Turkey originated with him. Their dance is a beautiful and complex elaboration of cosmic concepts, a spiritual geometry, symbolic of an inner journey and the union of opposites within it. Among these, within the Islamic idiom, is the Quranic geometry of the 'straight path', on one hand, and its preoccupation with circularity on the other, both within a constantly moving three-dimensional universe.[30] In short, one is back to the idea of the centre and the circle – and to the Zikris with their emphasis on circularity, and woman at the centre.

The Zikris and Violence

Seen in this context of a free-wheeling ecstatic Sufism, it is evident that the Zikris represent an overwhelmingly – and at times almost literally – feminine spirituality. To begin with, the economic stance of sharing of wealth is essentially a feminine one, the emphasis being on community and relatedness rather than on a macho, 'cut-throat' competitiveness, which glorifies individualism. The acknowledgement and regard for the feminine is also evident in the egalitarian ideas of gender, in which women are not forced to veil themselves and they actively and freely participate in all areas of community social and religious life. This is all the more remarkable in the geographical and cultural context of an overwhelmingly tribal society and its customs.

Most significant is the role of women in Zikri rituals. While remaining anchored in an essentially Sufist expression of poetry, music and dance, the key rituals are almost literal enactments of the insights of Ibn'Arabi, Rumi and numerous other Islamic mystics and philosophers who gave central importance to the idea of the Divine Feminine.[31]

Reference has already been made to the profound metaphysical concepts encapsulated symbolically in the idea of the circle and the centre. It is a form containing a range of dialectics expressing totality and union of various opposites: motion and stillness, time and eternity, ego and self, male and female, the finite and infinite. In sum, the circle and its centre reflect the idea of wholeness, completeness and perfection, which is why almost every culture uses it as a depiction of cosmic order. In all instances, the centre is synonymous with whatever it is that each culture calls God or the goal of the human spiritual quest. As stated earlier, the ubiquitous existence of this symbol suggests that it is a reflection of human spiritual potential: through its contemplation, especially of the centre – imaged or imagined – we attempt to evoke the power of what it represents and hence its presence in our lives.

The key Zikri rituals of *Chogan* and *Kishti* place a woman or women at the centre of a circle (or circles) formed by males. In *The Power of Myth* Joseph Campbell tells how the African Bushmen have a ritual which is uncannily similar to those of the Zikri:

> The Bushmen live in a desert world. It's a very hard life, a life of great, great tension. The male and female sexes are, in a disciplined way, separate. Only in the dance do the two come together. And they come together this way: the women sit in a circle in a little group and beat their thighs, setting a pace for the men dancing around them. The women are the center around which the men dance. And they control the dance and what goes on with the men through their own singing and beating of the thighs.[32]

Slave, Master (Mistress)

The sacred geometry of woman-as-centre and male-as-circumference is, according to Campbell, a symbolic enactment of a basic truth: *Woman is life and man is the servant of life.*[33] The theme of servanthood, in fact of being God's slave, is very powerful in Islam, adumbrated at the outset in the nuances present in the word 'Islam' itself, including the idea of surrender. Campbell's words, that woman is life and man its servant, provide an insight into the psychology of Muslim masculinism as it relates to the power of the feminine. The Zikri rituals confront Pakistan's orthodoxy with a literal enactment of this basic truth. The ulema's hypermasculinized (hence violent) and Cyclopean vision can only recoil in horror at the notion of a feminine centre, which, if 'seen' consciously, must in fact be surrendered to and served. But, forgotten over the centuries – veiled into oblivion, textually mutilated, excised and banished from the ulema's psyche – She (re)appears as utterly unknown, alien; and She evokes, as the unknown often does, fear in the beholder.

The Taliban embody literally this fear-full alienation from the feminine. The vast majority were raised as war orphans in all-male seminaries with little or no experience of any type of female presence – neither mother nor grandmother, neither sister nor aunt, no one.

> These boys were from a generation who had never seen their country at peace .... They had no memories of their tribes, their elders, their neighbours .... They were literally the orphans of the war. Their simple belief in a messianic, puritan Islam which had been drummed into them by simple village mullahs was the only prop they could hold on to and which gave their lives some meaning ....
>
> Moreover, they had willingly gathered under the all-male brotherhood that the Taliban leaders were set on creating, because they knew of nothing else. Many in fact were orphans who had grown up without women – mothers, sisters or cousins .... They had simply never known the company of women .... They felt threatened by that half of the human race which they had never known and it was much easier to lock that half away, especially if it was ordained by the mullahs who invoked primitive Islamic injunctions, which had no basis in Islamic law.[34]

A product of mass violence itself, once this type of unnatural mutation occurs on a vast scale – as it did during the Cold War years and into the present – large-scale violence becomes inevitable, making the alien-nation which is Afghanistan: an extremely violent and macho vision of self and God, utterly devoid of those quintessentially feminine qualities such as mercy, graciousness, compassion, beauty and wisdom (Sophia). Unable to comprehend the meaning of that which has become wholly Other, the masculine psyche's impulse is to obliterate it. Given the life–servant relationship, it is either that or surrender-servanthood. By definition, the macho hero does not surrender and can respond only through violence to that which, in any case, it no longer recognizes.

Conclusion

Given their intertwined roots, modern psychology and religion have 'developed' along similar lines. In the former, modern heroic consciousness refuses to accept our inner psychological diversity and aims to overcome it through willpower, a lopsided idea of reason and violent 'treatments' such as electric shocks and mind-numbing drugs.

To paraphrase Jung, the goddesses have become diseases. Thus, psychopathology is a secular name for heresy.

Many religions, including Islam, have followed a similar trajectory. As prophetic religions overshadowed the goddesses and advanced patriarchy, the mystical and feminine dimensions surfaced and continue to live among vast numbers of people, although not recognized by the official 'malestream'. Despite disapproval and persecution by the orthodoxy, Sufism remains the 'hidden backbone' of popular Islam. Opposed to this is the 'official' version(s), saturating places such as Afghanistan and Pakistan with a theological machismo alternately expressed by the military and the mullah,[35] and sometimes by both as in the case of the dictator Zia-ul-Haq and the Taliban. In such overarchingly masculine psychological environments, theological paranoia perceives heretics at every corner and insists they be punished for deviating from the overwhelmingly masculine 'norm'. Thus, the more feminine a religious perspective – in idea, image, content and interpretation – the greater the chance of its being labelled as heresy, followed by violent attempts to marginalize, stifle and obliterate it.

The case of the Zikris telescopes the notion of the Divine Feminine centre to which Muslims must surrender as its servants. Unable to discern the psycho-spiritual implications of the symbolic woman-at-the-centre of Zikri rituals, orthodoxy sees it as wholly Other. Of course, in the process of violently attacking the symbol, justifications for other agendas such as economic and political gain are also reinforced. To the extent that women *embody* these symbolic truths, violence directed at women in the name of Islam flows from these psychodynamics.

Notes and References

1 *Pakistan Country Report on Violence against Women: the Legal System and Institutional Responses* (UNICEF Regional Office for South Asia, 1997). See also: *Crime or Custom? Violence Against Women in Pakistan*, Report by Human Rights Watch (1999).

2 Daniel Bell, 'The Cultural Wars: American Intellectual Life 1965–1992', *Wilson Quarterly* (Summer 1992).

3 See James Hillman, *Archetypal Psychology: a Brief Account* (Dallas: Spring Publications, 1990, 4th edition); see also Durre S. Ahmed, 'Women, Psychology and Religion' p. 70 above.

4   Muriel Nellis, *The Female Fix* (New York: Penguin, 1981); see also S. Matteo, 'The Risk of Multiple Addictions: Guidelines for Assessing a Woman's Alcohol and Drug Use', *Western Journal of Medicine*, 149 (1988): 742.

5   Walter J. Ong, *Fighting for Life: Contest, Sexuality and Consciousness* (Ithaca: Cornell University Press, 1981), p. 77.

6   Azhar Munir, *Zikris in the Light of History and Their Religious Beliefs* (Lahore: Izharsons, 1998); Dr Tahoor Khan, 'Why the Pressure on the Zikris?' Human Rights Commission of Pakistan newsletter (January 1995), pp. 33–9.

7   Basic information primarily from *Encyclopaedia of Islam* (new edition) (Leiden: E. J. Brill, 1996), see 'al'D'jawnpuri' (pp. 499–501) and 'Mahdawi' (p. 1230).

8   The Mahdi, or 'rightly guided one', is the name of the restorer of religion and justice who, according to a widely held Muslim belief, will appear before the end of the world to rule the earth. For details of these extremely complex debates, derived primarily from *hadith* literature and with differing ramifications for Shia and Sunni, see 'al-Mahdi' in *Encyclopaedia of Islam*, pp. 1230–44.

9   *Encyclopaedia of Islam*, p.500

10   Ahmed Salim, 'The Chalk Circle', *Weekend Post* (Lahore), 17 July 1992.

11   *Encyclopaedia of Islam*, p. 500.

12   Inayatullah Baloch, 'Islam, the State and Identity: the Zikris of Balochistan', in Paul Titus (ed.), *Marginality and Modernity: Ethnicity and Change in Post-Colonial Balochistan* (Karachi: Oxford University Press, 1996).

13   *Ibid.*; see also Munir, *Zikris in the Light of History*.

14   See bibliography in Baloch, 'Islam, the State and Identity'.

15   The most recent and detailed descriptions of Zikri rituals appeared in the early 1990s in the religious magazine *Sirat-al-Mustakim* (The Straight Path), printed in Birmingham, UK. Written under the pseudonym of 'Dr Abu Mauz Tariq, PhD', the series of articles offers an interesting study of how the Zikris are viewed by Sunni scholars. There is a wealth of detail about Zikri places of religious significance in Baluchistan and an attempt to contextualize them *vis-à-vis* the question of the Mahdi. The series is titled 'Mahdism and the Zikri sect'. While the author has tried to be objective in his account, he concludes that they are heretics and 'not Muslims'. However, he does not prescribe the usual severe punishment and suggests that the sect – among quite a few others – should be 're-educated' in Islamic doctrine. Studies such as these do not attempt to place their subject in its wider context (e.g., of Sufism in Islam) but focus on the Sunni dimension of Mahdism, even though the Zikris are arguably closer to many aspects of Shia belief. In this sense, the Zikris are to the Shias what another 'heretical' sect, the Ahmadis, are to the Sunnis.

16   See *Awaz* (quarterly, Lahore), 8 (July–September 1999); Khawaja Ahmaduddin, *Aquamat e-Salat aur Quran*, p. 20.

17   For a recent cross-disciplinary study of an Alawi community in Turkey and their ritual dances, see Fahriye Dincer's work on the Alawi *Samah*: Fahriye Dincer, *Alevi Semahs in Historical Perspective* (Istanbul: Dogazici University, 1999). Many of the 'heretical' elements would be familiar and acceptable to the Zikris, including music and dance and the full participation of women.

18 Carl Jung, *Man and His Symbols* (New York: Doubleday, 1964), pp. 212–29.

19 *Ibid.*, p. 213.

20 See Joseph Campbell, *The Power of Myth* (New York: Doubleday, 1988), p. 214.

21 Jung, *Man and His Symbols*, p. 217.

22 J. E. Cirlot, *A Dictionary of Symbols* (New York: Philosophical Library, 1988, 2nd edition).

23 Amaury de Reincourt, *Woman and Power in History* (Delhi: Sterling Publishers, 1989) (London: Honeyglen Publishing, 1983).

24 William James, *The Varieties of Religious Experience* (New York: Anchor Books, 1958).

25 Amaury de Reincourt, *Woman and Power*, p. 199.

26 *Ibid.*

27 *Ibid.*

28 *Ibid.*, pp. 197–203.

29 Henry Corbin, *Creative Imagination in the Sufism of Ibn'Arabi* (Princeton: Princeton University Press, 1987), pp. 159–60. As Winters points out, 'Sufism is an integral part of Islam, not an esoteric sect; but it is a multifaceted phenom-enon, and what applies to one Sufi order or Shaykh may not apply to others': Michael Winters, 'Islamic Attitudes towards the Human Body', in Jane Marie Law (ed.), *Religious Reflections on the Human Body* (Bloomington: Indiana University Press, 1995), p. 41.

30 For details see Earnest McLain, *Meditations through the Quran* (Maine: Nicholson-Hays, 1981).

31 See Corbin, *Creative Imagination*.

32 Campbell, *The Power of Myth*, pp. 86–7.

33 *Ibid.*

34 Ahmed Rashid, *Taliban: Islam, Oil and the New Great Game in Central Asia* (London: I. B. Tauris, 2000), pp. 32–3. For the record, the observation about the absence of women was first made in Suroosh Irfani's article, 'Taliban: the Islamic Challenge', *Dawn*, 12 October 1997.

35 See Durre Ahmed, *Masculinity, Rationality and Religion: a Feminist Perspective* (Lahore: ASR, 2001, 2nd edition).

Index

Brownmiller, Susan 6
Buddha, attains Enlightenment 93; misrepresenta-
 tion of 96-8; ordination of women by 95;
 women accorded equality by 95-8
Buddhaghosa 97
Buddhism, *Abhidhamma Pitakas* doctrine of 94;
 Abhinna powers 94; *ahimsā* and 199; American
 24; Buddha Jayanti day 145; *dhamma* doctrine
 94; *dhutanga* precepts 94; diversity within 24;
 feminine characteristics of 84; *Garudhammas*
 rules 95; hero myth in 77; in Kashmir religious
 convergence 174-5; Kashmiri saints 172; as
 living tradition in the South 24; lotus symbol in
 84; Madhobi Ma and 145; *Mahayana* school of
 99; monks' order in 92-101; and mother love
 151; *Mutya* traditions of Philippines 113; nuns'
 order in 91-101; Rishi movement and 166;
 śakta teaching and 141; *sotapatti* 93; in Sri
 Lanka 91-100; *Sutta* doctrine 94; Tantras and
 137; *Tantrayana* school 100; *Theravada* school
 91-2, 98-9; and 'Universal Sovereign Catholic
 Church' 122; *Vinaya* rules of 13, 93-9; and
 women 12-13, 70, 95-8
Bulalakaw 111
Bulleh Shah 158
bulong (internal whisper) 119-20
Bushmen people 231

cakras 47-8
Cambodia 101n
Campbell, Joseph 73, 231
Canada 205
Canadian Conference of Catholic Bishops 209-10
Candramali 100
carnival 18
Casirer, Ernst 73
caste 36, 44, 46, 52, 54, 144-7, 187; *see also* class
Cebuano language 112
Chaitanya 146
chaos theory 84
Chaplin, Charlie 15-16
Chauhan, Subhadra Kumari 198
China 83, 85, 96, 99-100, 113, 212, 226
Chinnamastā 50, 190-1, 201
Chirawa 142-4
Chowdhary, Sasadhara 138
Christ, Carol 6
Christianity, Catholic Church 14, 60-8, 77, 116,
 118, 122-4, 130, 205-12; Christmas festival
 145; diversity within 24; feminine characteristics of 84; fundamentalism in 20, 23, 116; and
 hero myth 77; Jesus 60, 130-1, 174, 180, 206;
 Jungianism and 87n; in Kashmir religious convergence 174-5; as living tradition in the South
 24; Madhobi Ma and 145; Mary figure in 84;
 and other religions 113-4; Protestant Church
 77; and 'Universal Sovereign Catholic Church'
 122; women under 206-7
circle/centre symbol 217, 220, 224-7, 230-1, 233;
 mandala 225-7

circumcision 213, 224
Ciriddhi 94
Ciudad Mistica de Dios (CMDD) 129-34
class 22, 38, 187, 205; *see also* caste
Coburn, Thomas 38
Cold War 232
colonialism 10, 20, 22-3, 79-80
communism 81
consciousness, diverse styles of 72-6; either/or
 163; feminization of 83-4, 87n, 178, 215;
 Filipino 103-4, 108, 110-11; Freudian view of
 71-2; heroic 76-82, 232; individualized cosmic
 109-10, 114; journey of, see *pamamaybay*;
 Jungian view of 72-6; Kashmiri 170; monotheistic and polytheistic 80-86, 173; of a people
 103-4, 108, 110-11; religious 124-7, 136, 177-
 8, 215; symbolic 75; transcendental 113-114,
 144, 148-52; universal 140; of a victim 61,
 207-11
contraception 209
Cooey, Paula 83, 169
Coomarswamy, A. L. 195
Corbin, Henry 32n, 73, 76, 176-7, 229
Cosmic Mother 104, 110
cosmos 37-47, 50, 55, 73, 107-10, 114-15, 120,
 137-8, 141, 146-7, 149-50, 187-9, 192-3, 225-
 6, 230
Council of Trent (1563) 63
creative arts 10, 19
Cullavaga 95-9
cults 117, 123, 227
culture, archetypal perspective of 74, 176; and
 circle symbolism 226; diversity of 24, 36, 155;
 feminine and masculine 83; feminized 84;
 Freudian view of 79-80; gender wars and 214;
 Hebrew 174; Kashmiri 173-4; mother archetype in 179-80; patriarchal 60, 82; in Philippines
 104; pluralism of 36; and politics 164-5; and
 power 22; and religion 3, 23-4, 165, 173, 213-
 14; in South East Asia 113
Cuyo Island 105
Cuyonin language 113

Dabba Mallaputta 98
dairas (circles) 217, 220, 224-7, 230-1, 233
Dakini 190
Daly, Mary 6
dance 125-7, 157, 229-31
Darwinism 79
Daśamāhavidyās 141
Dasi 94
Dasiya 94
Datta 94
Daughters of Charity 63
Davao City 107, 120
Dayamoyee 196-7
death 74, 76-7, 83, 85, 148, 177, 179-80, 187, 194,
 210
Delhi 139
Demeter 179